Justine Tal

The Story of *Jazz*

FORECAAST

(Forum for European Contributions
to African American Studies)

Volume 7

LIT

Justine Tally

The Story of *Jazz*

Toni Morrison's Dialogic Imagination

LIT

Grafik der Umschlagseite: Gerhard Kiegerl

Gedruckt auf alterungsbeständigem Werkdruckpapier entsprechend
ANSI Z3948   DIN ISO 9706

Die Deutsche Bibliothek – CIP-Einheitsaufnahme

Tally, Justine:
The Story of *Jazz* : Toni Morrison's Dialogic Imagination / Justine Tally. –
Hamburg : LIT, 2001
   (FORECAAST ; 7.)
   ISBN 3-8258-5364-0

© LIT VERLAG Münster – Hamburg – London
   Grindelberg 15a 20144 Hamburg Tel. 040 - 44 64 46 Fax 040 - 44 14 22

Distributed in North America by:

Transaction Publishers
New Brunswick (U.S.A.) and London (U.K.)

Transaction Publishers
Rutgers University
35 Berrue Circle
Piscataway, NJ 08854

Tel.: (732) 445 - 2280
Fax: (732) 445 - 3138
for orders (U. S. only):
toll free (888) 999 - 6778

For Luci,
with thanks for a bit of serendipity.

For Ronnie,
With thanks for
all your help :)
ustine

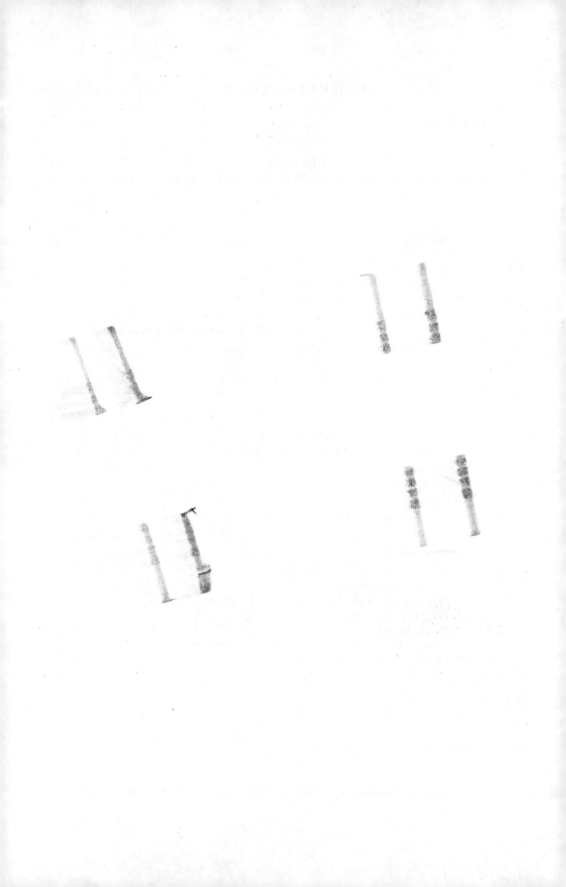

TABLE OF CONTENTS

ACKNOWLEDGMENTS

The research necessary for the present project was funded by a grant from the Autonomous Government of the Canary Islands (Spain) and was carried out for the most part at the State University of New York, Albany, during the summer months of 1999. Faculty and staff of the Africana Studies Department at SUNY were as welcoming as they were supportive, especially the department secretary, Ronnie Saunders, who was most helpful, as was the very efficient staff of the University Library. Our stay there was not only professionally fruitful but wonderfully rewarding on the personal level as well.

It would be difficult to recall the many conversations with colleagues from different parts of the world with whom I discussed the theoretical approach developed in this book, but I do want to particularly thank Pavel Jedrzejko, whose observation on Morrison's use of theory in her fiction sparked the dramatic insight that neatly concluded this work.

My thanks once again to Maria Diedrich for her encouragement, suggestions, corrections and general support in evaluating the original manuscript, and to Patrick Miller for taking the time in the middle of overwhelming "hectivity" to read and critique the revisions. Because I was so very pleased with the cover design of *Paradise Reconsidered*, I again requested the artistic abilities of Gerhard Kiegerl, who combined his skill with unfailing patience as he endeavored to draw my ideas into a delightful illustration – a good trick since we don't speak the same language!

And, of course, my heartfelt appreciation for my colleague and partner, Walter Hölbling, whose undying devotion and patience combined with sharp critical appraisal has been instrumental in the development of this project from its conception and gestation – consistently playing both sounding board and devil's advocate – right down through corrections and formatting, and without whom this work might never have seen the light of day. I hope you know just how important you are to me.

And to my kids, who once again demonstrated that in the midst of CHAOS, good things can happen.

La Laguna, February 2001

ABBREVIATIONS

Texts by Toni Morrison:

B	*Beloved*
J	*Jazz*
P	*Paradise*
TBE	*The Bluest Eye*
PD	*Playing in the Dark*

Texts by Raymond Chandler:

FML	*Farewell, My Lovely*
HW	*High Window*
LL	*Lady in the Lake*

Internet resources:

For information taken from various websites I have adopted a "shorthand" of listing and enumerating the different webpages under "Webliography." Reference to the different pages within the text are cited simply as "W," with the numerical referent as indication to which webpage is being cited.

[...] in "being" (être) we should read: the other (autre).

Mikhail Bakhtin

PART ONE

HISTORY, MEMORY, AND STORY:

TEXTS AND THEORETICAL CONTEXTS

The Premise

I. INTRODUCTION

After the immediate and overwhelming success of Toni Morrison's excruciatingly lyrical novel of slavery and its aftermath, *Beloved* (1988), the publication of *Jazz* (1992), her sixth fictional work and second in the projected trilogy, sent reviewers and critics scurrying to discover its ties to the former novel. The enigmatic central character of *Jazz*, Wild, is often seen as the reappearance of Beloved, who is consistently associated with the water and the wind and who, pregnant, flees the house at 124 in Ohio at the end of the novel:

> By and by all trace is gone, and what is forgotten is not only the footprints but the water too and what it is down there. The rest is weather. Not the breath of the disremembered and unaccounted for, but wind in the eaves, or spring ice thawing too quickly. Just weather. Certainly no clamor for a kiss.　　　　　　　　　　　(*B*, 275)

According to Sara A. Aguiar, the time-frame is feasible; this is roughly the same year the wild, naked black woman surfaces (this time in the rain) to give birth to Joe. "Judging the date in *Jazz*, Joe Trace is born at the same time that Beloved's baby would have been; he is in his early fifties in 1926 when his story is told. Moreover, given the proximity of Ohio and Virginia, it is also possible that, following her banishment, Beloved may have fled to the fictional Vesper County in Virginia where Golden Gray discovers her" (12). Textually as well there are indications of a "smooth transition" from one novel to the other: Wild is associated with the redwings and her "breathing" is the only noise from her that Joe ever hears. Aguiar also points out that Wild "'haunts' a cane field, attracted, presumably, by the 'sugared air.' These images of infantile mannerisms, a potentially supernatural existence, pregnancy, fluidity, and hunger for 'sweetness' are also associated with Beloved" (11). The second paragraph of *Jazz* reiterates another of the images of the paragraph quoted above: "The snow she [Violet] ran through was so windswept she left no footprints in it, so for a time nobody knew exactly where on Lenox Avenue she lived" (*J*, 4). Moreover, the "trace" that is gone at the end of *Beloved* becomes the name Joe gives himself, based on the information that he receives from his adoptive mother in answer to his query about his biological parents: "'[...] O honey, they disappeared without a trace. The way I heard it I understood her to mean the "trace" they disappeared without was me'" (*J*, 124).

Though in this same passage Joe speculates about his mother's return, and indeed the

1

search for some kind of confirmation of his birth-mother propels much of the story, he only demonstrates a minor interest in knowing his father, mentioning it only once: "She be back. She coming for me. My Daddy too." The lack of critical attention to this (admittedly minor) point is interesting. Andrea O'Reilly states that "Interestingly, Joe does not wonder who his biological father may be, nor does the text speculate on the identity of the father" (375). But if we understand, as do Elizabeth House and Gurleen Grewal, the character of Beloved as a real young woman made of flesh and blood, and not a ghost, then it is reasonable to infer that it is her seduction of Paul D that has left her pregnant. This would also "make sense" textually in that both Paul D and Joe Trace are described as men whose relationship with women is exceptional:

> Not even trying, he had become the kind of man who could walk into a house and make the women cry. Because with him, in his presence, they could. There was something blessed in his manner. Women saw him and wanted to weep – to tell him that their chest hurt and their knees did too. Strong women and wise saw him and told him the things they only told each other: that way past the Change of Life, desire in them had suddenly become enormous, greedy, more savage than when they were fifteen, and that it embarrassed them and made them sad; that secretly they longed to die – to be quit of it – that sleep was more precious to them than any waking day. Young girls sidled up to him to confess or describe how well-dressed the visitations were that had followed them straight from their dreams. Therefore, although he did not understand why this was so, he was not surprised when Denver dripped tears into the stove fire. Nor, fifteen minutes later, after telling him about her stolen milk, her mother wept as well. (*B*, 17)

> They laughed, tapped the tablecloth with their fingertips and began to tease, berate and adore him all at once. They told him how tall men like him made them feel, complained about his lateness and insolence, asked him what else he had in his case besides whatever it was that made Sheila so excited. They wondered why he never rang their doorbells, or climbed four flights of double-flight stairs to deliver anything to them.
> (*J*, 70)

> Besides, they liked his voice. It had a pitch, a note they heard only when they visited stubborn old folks who would not budge from their front yards and overworked fields to come to the City. [...] So they looked right at him and told him any way they could how ridiculous he was, and how delicious and how terrible.
> (*J*, 71)

Even Alice Manfred puzzles over the incongruity of such a well-like man murdering her niece:

> A man store owners and landlords liked because he set the children's toys in a neat row when they left them scattered on the sidewalk. Who the children liked because he never minded them. And liked among men because he never cheated in a game, egged a stupid fight on, or carried tales, and he left their women alone. Liked among the women because he made them feel like women [...] (*J*, 75-76)

If the reader wants to read the novels "realistically" rather than "metaphorically," therefore, there are enough plausible references to indicate that Joe is Paul D's son.

The search for textual clues that would link the stories of the novels which Morrison had previously declared a trilogy[1] comes unraveled, however, when this type of analysis is applied to the third novel in the trilogy, *Paradise* (1998). Typical responses to the latest Morrison novel echo Jill Matus:

> If *Beloved, Jazz* and *Paradise* form a trilogy, as Morrison once envisioned, it is a very loose one. There is no obvious overlap of character or setting; nor can the strong historical focus of these novels be said to distinguish them markedly from Morrison's other work.   (Matus, 155)

In *Paradise* one finds no clear links among characters nor venue, and, although the history of the founding fathers of Haven reaches back into the Reconstruction period as well, there are no ostensible characteristics that so easily define the relationship among the three.

Even the initial reaction to *Jazz* upon publication was one of consternation, prompting critics like Karen Carmean to complain that the "novel itself has the tentative quality of a self-consciously written middle volume of a trilogy [... which] doesn't seem to have any other critical flash points beyond those arising from questions about the narrator's identification and the narrator's cool sound [...] progressing toward - what?"; or that "the narrator tells us what happened to but never seems to transmute the events into any meaning" (Howard, 8). Some critics took a wait-and-see attitude, appearing to rely on *Paradise* to illuminate the "meaning" of *Jazz*.

Over the years since *Jazz* made its appearance in the literary world in 1992, both before and after the publication of *Paradise*, more and more serious critics have tried to elucidate the text using a variety of sophisticated hermeneutic tools to great effect. Derek Alwes employs a theory of identity politics to substantiate the idea of freedom of choice as a central motif in the text. Desire is a central theme for Karin Luisa Badt, who uses a feminist approach arguing that the "literal or figurative maternal presence [...] dominates each of the characters" (567) and that "it is the mother's body which bears culture and history" (575). Elizabeth M. Cannon reiterates the theme of desire but uses psychoanalytic feminism to argue that this desire in the female characters is for subjectivity: "First, women must recognize each other as subjects, and, second, the new subjectivity must be cemented through action" (243). Andrea O'Reilly states that "*Jazz* is [...] a story about the wounding and healing of unmothered children," and that the "absence of foundation marks a fundamental Lacanian lack, or a selfhood without core or center" (368).

In a different vein entirely, Deborah H. Barnes borrows a standard paradigm U-curve from social psychology to argue that the migrant experience, south to north, rural to urban, is a fundamental theme in *Jazz*. In her analysis, Morrison "proffers a unique depiction of migration that interrogates the destructive and distorting effects of physical and emotional dislocation on culturally mobile blacks" (285). Kristeva's theory of abjection is instrumental for Angela Burton in substantiating hybridity and mixed origins as the meaning of the novel, particularly illustrated

---

[1] Morrison has indicated that her original intention was to publish everything under the name *Beloved* but that she was obliged by her publishers to break up the story.

in the character of Golden Gray: "Gray's hybridity and quest for not only a myth of origins but also a current myth of identity [...] are all paralleled in the national body politic of black America" (189). Madhu Dubey resorts to vernacular theories of black women's fiction to highlight what she believes to be contradictions between Morrison's "authorial pronouncements on migration, oral tradition, and black fiction," and her "fictional practice in *Jazz*" (292): "*Jazz* [...] italicizes its narrator's failure to assume the voice of Southern oral tradition [and] forces a recognition of the fact that novelistic communication is inevitably mediated by the material object of the book [...]" (309).[2]

Influenced by recent studies of Holocaust victims, Gurleen Greewal draws on psychoanalytical means to further her thesis that it is traumatic memory that propels the characters, not only in *Jazz*, but in all of Morrison's novels. Richard Hardack does a brilliant reading of the text as a play on double-consciousness and goes so far as to say that "for Morrison, the Harlem Renaissance occupies the crucial juncture where the transcendental nature of the American Renaissance is transformed into a transcendental City" (460). Michael Nowlin uses semiotic theory to discuss Morrison's concerns with racial identity and the racialist discourse surrounding double-consciousness, stating that "Morrison's ambivalence toward that authority is a critical theme of *Jazz* and finds expression through the voice of that novel's equivocal narrator" (152). Roland Walter also states that "the dialectical structure of [the text] is based upon the consciousness of duality," of being an African American woman, and "the tensions between different ways of perceiving values and reality and the friction caused by the interaction between (*sic*) generation, class, race and sex" (55), but then spends much of his piece speaking rather of a dialogue between the author and the reader. Carolyn M. Jones uses Jacques Derrida's concerns with the "trace" to discuss the concepts of "tracks" and "cracks" which are so predominant in the text, while Philip Page appropriates Derrida's theory of "erasure" and "trace" to "question the usual assumptions about the privilege of presence, self and signified" (56).

The narrator and the narration is the subject of much attention (and speculation), and create so much ambiguousness that Katherine J. Mayberry is even led to remark that "Morrison's novels do not seem entirely easy with the narrative medium – more particularly, with the implications inherent in the relationship between subject and narrated objects" (297-298), while Edna O'Brien accuses the author of being "bedazzled by her own virtuosity" and therefore unable to translate the experience of *Jazz* into "our very own experience" (51). Certain critics like Vincent A. O'Keefe take their critical cue from the epigraph of *Jazz*, a quotation from the largely gnostic scriptures that compile the *Nag Hammadi Library*, to read *Jazz* as an alternative to Western rationalism via a gnostic view of life and spirituality. The argument, however, is pushed quite to the limit: "The narrator's inclusion of the characters' actual voices in this exchange emphasizes the jazz-like orality of their gnosis" (339). For his part, Herbert William Rice understands the epigraph as a contradiction of "much of what we see in the novel" (134).

Nested within far too many of these critical approaches are often found irreconcilable contradictions. In the first place, the title of the novel itself has led many, many critics to explore what they denominate as a "jazz aesthetic" as the basis for a complete semantic, syntactic and

---

[2] I will argue specifically against this thesis below.

structural understanding of the novel (Birch; Burton; Eckard; Gates,"*Jazz*"; Jones; Leonard; Lewis; Manzanas; Matus; H.W. Rice; Rodrigues), but these analyses have been thoroughly and convincingly trounced by Alan Munton, who meticulously explains the actual concepts of jazz and their lack of correspondence in written prose. There *is*, in fact, a corollary between Morrison's writing and jazz as music which the author herself has acknowledged: "the need to perfect technique in order to make literature, or music, *seem 'natural' and unforced* when it is in truth *the result of application and rehearsal*" (Munton, 246; emphasis added).[3] Morrison's jazz critics are misled, Munton fears, by a "crude spontaneism attributed to jazz music by those who do not understand that what they are listening to is controlled self-expression determined by musical rules" (246).

While most other approaches are indeed interesting and useful, they can only account for certain aspects of the novel, and often the critics themselves acknowledge their limitations. Badt, for example, locates culture and history in the mother's body, but she also qualifies this application in Morrison's novels:

> The ambivalence about maternal power and the uneasiness about what radical Afro-American politics entails explain the reason that, in many of Morrison's novels, those characters who signify the mother and evoke the desire for her meet with a depressing end. After the boundaries of the community and the self have been upset and reorganized, the characters who have inspired this revolution are exorcised: Pecola, Sula, Beloved, and Dorcas are all banished in some way or other (death, disgrace, rejection) from their communities.   (Badt, 575)

In O'Reilly's reading of the search for the semiotic, she quotes Clarssa Pinkola Estes definition of the "Wild Woman":

> The Wild Woman, Estes explains, is the "female soul [...] She is the source of the feminine [...] She is the Life/Death/Life force. She is the incubator. She is intuition [...] She encourages humans to remain multilingual: fluent in the languages of dreams, passions, and poetry. She whispers from night dreams [...] She is the source, the light, the night, the dark, and daybreak. She is the smell of good mud [...] The birds which tell us secrets belong to her."   (Qtd. in O'Reilly, 378, Note 5)

The suggestion that Wild embodies this source and, at the same time, the semiotic runs into trouble in that Wild, as character, has refused even to acknowledge, much less mother her son. A positive image of the feminine is conjoined with a negative character or, if she is not defined enough to be considered negative, at least it is her absence of mothering that is so influential as to drive Joe to murder. Although Estes refers to the "Innate Instinctual Self," Joe complains that even the lowliest animal knows to suckle its own; Wild does not even respond to instinct: "Too brain-blasted to do what the meanest sow managed: nurse what she birthed" [*J*, 179].

On the other hand, Elizabeth Cannon qualifies her own discussion of female subjectivity

---

[3] "I rewrite a lot, over and over again, so that it looks like I never did. I try to make it look like I never touched it, and that takes a lot of time and a lot of sweat" (Morrison, "Site"; 200).

by wondering "whether Morrison is speaking only of a black female desire or is theorizing a more universal concept of female desire seen in a new light because of the African-American context of jazz and the Harlem of the 1920s" (245). In any case these feminist readings can only account, and partially so, for the female characters in the book, even to the point of ignoring the problematic narrator.

Burton's reading of *Jazz* as a text about hybridity, on the one hand, burdens the minor figure of Hunters Hunter with enormous import –

> [The] traces of Lestory's radical act of procreation [... are] structured genealogically and chronologically [...] as the point of origin for all subsequent narratives of identity in *Jazz*.
> The geographic dissemination of Lestory's descendants to cities in the north mirrors the dissemination of jazz music.   (Burton, 180)

– and, on the other, provides only a limited vision of the novel's relevance:

> [T]he novel's improvisational narrator positions readers of *Jazz* in such a way that they are forced to consider, alongside those of racist characters and unreliable narrator, their own conceptions and prejudices in relation to contemporary conceptions of the hybrid African-American identity. Behind this strategy is an attempt to reintegrate the mixed-race figure into the cultural corpus of black America, for reasons of ethnic pragmatism not hegemonic assimilation.   (Burton, 188)

The affirmation that "rather than return to Baltimore, Gray remains with Wild on the margins of Vienna" (Burton,187), or that "[...] Golden Grey becomes in a sense Joe's (absent) stepfather through his union with Wild" (Page, 58), or that Wild and Golden Gray "go away together" (Rodrigues, 261) is imposing an interpretation that is at best tenuous. Joe simply finds the clothes Golden Gray was described by the narrator as wearing on the day he encountered Wild in what Joe supposes is the cave where Wild (whom he supposes to be his mother) lives. Reading a subsequent relationship between Golden Gray and Wild not only pushes the credulity of the reader, it serves little or no purpose in an exegesis of the novel.

Hardack's reading of the novel as an exploration of double-timing and double-consciousness leads him to the conclusion that "Morrison reverses the polarity of human predictability, of the involuntary, in a manner not convincing, since the weight of the book is devoted to staging its inevitability." He rather lamely exonerates the author from inconsistency by adding that she "allows herself along with her narrator to be changeable, complicated, and unpredictable" (467). O'Keefe's gnostic interpretation also runs into contradiction in the value of gnosis itself as viable alternative. How does one invest the narrator with a knowledge that challenges "orthodox" Western epistemology, only to have the narrator herself acknowledge her own unreliability? And if "Morrison's narrator is 'taking on the big city' of conventional readers by frustrating their impulse to detect 'all there is to know' about her story" (343), could we not therefore read other post-modern texts as gnostic?

For Jones the structure of *Jazz* is at times a jazz (musical) structure (quoting Morrison to that effect), but at others it is a Greek tragic structure (492); Lewis, who looks at the function of jazz in the novel, suspects that "Toni Morrison, with all her great talent, simply does not know how to bring closure to her narratives"(272), and Mayberry worries about the problem of "white feminist critics working with texts by African American women writers [.. their] appropriation by white feminists and African American men" (306), which "brings white critics uncomfortably close to a reinscription of oppression" (307).

Not one of these interpretations is comprehensive; they all leave gaps or concentrate on individual aspects of the novel at the expense of others which are equally important. Although almost all of these articles have a valuable contribution to make to the interpretation of what is perhaps Morrison's most difficult text to date, even when they are limited to certain aspects or troubled by contradiction, none of these critical approaches even attempts to envision the place of *Jazz* within the trilogy. What I would like to propose in the present study is a theory of *Jazz* that will encompass not only the varying interpretations expressed above, but will resolve many of the contradictions that these critics have posed, as well as link this novel to both *Beloved* and *Paradise*. To do so I wish to apply the ideas of discourse and the novel as elaborated by Mikhail M. Bakhtin, whose theories have also received an enormous amount of attention in fields beyond literary criticism within the last twenty years, particularly since the publication of four of his most important essays in *The Dialogic Imagination* as translated and edited by Michael Holquist (1981).

The Hypothesis

II. HISTORY, MEMORY AND STORY

I have argued elsewhere ("Reality") that, taken as a whole, the trilogy encompasses a wide cross-section of African American life. All three books reach back to the 1870s for their historical grounding, though *Beloved* focuses on the 1870s, *Jazz* on the 1920s, and *Paradise* on the 1970s, covering one hundred years of the history of black people in the United States. All three have major wars as their immediate prior reference: the Civil War, World War I, and the undeclared Viet Nam War; and all three take place during major eras of historical import for African Americans: post-Reconstruction, the Great Migration South to North and the Harlem Renaissance, and the final phase of the Civil Rights Movement. The different settings for the main action of the stories also cover the different aspects of black experience: *Beloved* is set in a rural environment, *Jazz* in the City, and *Paradise* in a small mid-western town. It seems obvious that Morrison envisioned the three novels as a comprehensive examination of black experience in the United States.

Yet it is perhaps the major underlying themes of these novels that most securely bind them as a trilogy. In *Paradise Reconsidered* (1999) I have argued that *Beloved*, *Jazz* and *Paradise* are *all* deeply concerned with the relationship of memory, storytelling, and history but that the focus of each novel changes, respectively. Even before the publication of *Paradise* in 1998, it was clear to me that *Jazz* was overwhelmingly concerned with the process of storytelling and its influence on both history and memory,[4] one of the major clues being Morrison's wordplay with a minor, but influential character, Hunter's Hunter, the missing father whom Golden Gray, son of Vera Gray, sets out to find. Golden Gray is not even completely sure of the name of the man he is looking for:

> A man he assumes is named Henry LesTroy, although from the way True Belles pronounced it, it could be something else. [...] Henry Lestory or LesTroy or something like that, but who cares what the nigger's name is.   (*J*, 148)

On page 149 his name again appears as "Henry LesTroy" in the first paragraph, but again the

---

[4] I presented this hypothesis at the annual AAAS Conference in Vienna in November of 1995; publication was delayed until 1999 (cf. Tally, "Specter").

confusion in the third: "Might you be related to Lestory? Henry Les Troy or whatever his name is?" On page 157 the name reverts to Henry Lestroy, this time without capitalizing the "T," yet in the following chapter the Hunter's name is settled definitively as "Lestory":

> When Henry Lestory, the man so expert in the woods he'd become a hunter's hunter (and when spoken of and to, that is what they called him), got back and saw the buggy and the beautiful horse tied near his stall, he was instantly alarmed.   (*J*, 168)

> "You ain't said where they at. Where you come from."
> "Baltimore. My name is Golden Gray."
> "Can't say it don't suit."
> "Suit you if it was Golden Lestory?"   (*J*, 172)

This playing with Hunter's name is more than just linguistic confusion; clearly Morrison is giving a strong sign that it must be interpreted.

Angela Burton uses this name play to substantiate her claim that Lestory is a character of major import in the novel ("Allusions encoded in Henry Lestroy's name index his status as the seminal and originating figure in all subsequent personal histories told in *Jazz*."), though she links "story" with the legendary Storyville, a red-light district in New Orleans, allegedly "the specific area in which jazz music was first developed" (179). Carolyn M. Jones also notes the discrepancy in naming but does not develop the idea further: "The episode of Golden Gray, the Wild, and Henry 'Le-story' or 'Les Troy' – either the story or the Troy, the destruction – is the pivotal, even mythical, center and the most consciously narrated part of *Jazz*" (487). However, and as I intend to demonstrate in subsequent chapters, the "conscious narration" of *Jazz* is manifest throughout the novel and not just in this specific section. The process of storytelling is foregrounded conscientiously, as Morrison experiments with the ways and means that stories are told.

The importance of storytelling in the relationship mentioned above is further emphasized in the names of the two boys that the Hunter's Hunter trains. Joe, the main male protagonist and possibly (probably) the baby Wild would not nurture, gives himself the surname "Trace": As Joe tells it, when he asked the woman who took him in and brought him up about his real parents, she "gave me the sweetest smile, but sad someway, and told me, O honey, they disappeared without a trace. The way I heard it I understood her to mean the 'trace' they disappeared without was me" (*J*, 124). This emphasis on "trace" has led some critics to explore Jacques Derrida's theory of "trace," on the one hand, as the place "where the relationship with the 'other' – specifically, the transcendent 'other' – is marked" (Jones, 482) and, on the other, as the designation of "the play or oscillation between a present, a thing-as-it-is, and an absence, an other (Page, 56). Andrea O'Reilly recalls that "[Julia] Kristeva defines the semiotic as a trace," identifying it with Wild, whose "home is presented as a pre-Oedipal maternal space" (374). For the purposes of this analysis, however, I wish to note that "trace" is also Stephen Greenblatt's term for historical event, though David Johnson plays with the term when he complains about the fact that new historicist critics do not question

> the status, ontological or epistemological, of the event (History, semiotic event, trace). None of them asks how a text inscribes an event, how events are encoded in texts, in the

first place. For example, is the event linguistically determined? If so, why do so many of the new historicists refer with a *trace* of contempt to what they call more formalist practices? If the event is not linguistic, what is it? And how do we locate it in texts constituted by signs? (Johnson, 94-95)

I will return to this idea of the "trace" as historical *and* linguistic event in discussing Bakhtin's theory of discourse, but for the present I simply wish to establish the presence of "history" in Joe's name.

Although certain critical attention has been paid both to Henry Lestory and to Joe Trace, no one has mentioned the function of Joe's adopted brother and best friend, and the other youth that Hunter's Hunter has trained. Victory never actually appears as a character *except* in Joe's account of his youth, either in his own words or through the narrator's pseudo-diegesis (see below). That is, Victory only assumes form within the memory of the main characters. Moreover, almost every time he is mentioned, he is specifically related to memory:

> She was good at it and bragged so much Victory practiced every chance he got. I remember his shadow darting in the dirt in front of me. (*J*, 124)

> Victory might remember. He was more than Joe's chosen brother, he was his best friend, and they hunted through and worked in most of Vesper County. Not even a sheriff's map would show the walnut tree Joe fell out of, but Victory would remember it. (*J*, 173)

> They were cleaning up after eating some of what they'd caught. Joe believed later it was fowl, but it could have been something with fur. Victory would remember. (*J*, 175)

> In 1926, far away from all those places, Joe thought maybe it was Wordsworth Hunter moved near to, and if he could ask him, Victory would remember exactly (assuming he was alive and prison had not rattled him) because Victory remembered everything and could keep things clear in his mind. (*J*, 180)

When Joe sets out to "hunt" for Dorcas, "he can practically feel Victory at his side" (*J*, 180).

This relationship is clear on the literal/textual level, for Hunter's Hunter trains Joe and Victory to track and hunt, and teaches them invaluable lessons which become important for both the origins and the denouement of the novel:

> "I taught both you all never kill the tender and nothing female if you can help it. Didn't think I had to teach you about people. Now, learn this: she ain't prey. You got to know the difference." (*J*, 175)

> Never. Never hurt the young: nest eggs, roe, fledglings, fry [...] (*J*, 181)

On the metaphorical level as well, Le*story* informs both history and memory, and the refusal to heed his teaching engenders disaster:

Le*story*

(History) Joe   Victory (Memory)

      Morrison's concern with stories and storytelling has been a constant in her novels and in the trilogy assumes even greater importance. Beloved is obsessed with Sethe's stories ("Tell me your diamonds"). Denver only wants to hear the ones which tell of her almost miraculous birth, though when she asks her mother about the circumstances of her going to jail, she goes deaf rather than assimilate that story. The final pages of *Beloved* repeatedly insist that "It was not a story to pass on" (*B*, 274-275), echoed on page 167 of *Jazz*: "Wild was not a story [...]" Stories and tales, both explicit and inferred, figure prominently in the text, as both the narrator and the characters themselves try to make sense of events and their lives in general. But the outstanding concern of the novel is not just the stories that are told, but the examination of *how* these (in fact, *all*) stories are told. It is indeed the whole process of storytelling that becomes part and parcel of the significance of the novel.

The Motive

III. STORYTELLING AND THEORIES OF *HOMO NARRANS*

The work of cultural materialists and new historicists makes it clear that literary works are cultural manifestations of the age in which they have been written. Although a writer may be writing ostensibly about the past, she is inevitably addressing her contemporaries and voicing concerns about her own era. According to Bakhtin/Medvedev,[5]

> Literature is one of the independent parts of the surrounding ideological reality, occupying a special place in it in the form of definite, organized philological works which have their own specific structures. The literary structure, like every ideological structure, refracts the generating socioeconomic reality, and does so in its own way. But, at the same time, in its "content," literature reflects and refracts the reflections and refractions of other ideological spheres (ethics, epistemology, political doctrines, religion, etc.). That is, in its "content" literature reflects the whole of the ideological horizon of which it is itself a part.   (Bakhtin/Medvedev, 1928; in Morris, 128)

In writing a novel that deals with storytelling, Morrison echoes many contemporary thinkers from a surprisingly wide range of fields which are *a priori* not usually so closely related. Nevertheless, at the end of the twentieth century, an era which has seen no end to destruction and genocide on a massive scale, many intellectuals are now turning against the rationalist, scientific, "objective" forms of discourse, touted since the Enlightenment, in which "progress" and "technology" have seemingly left humankind morally bankrupt. Bakhtin had earlier elaborated on these preoccupations which have only increased as the century moved to its close,[6] criticizing

---

[5] As I am in no way qualified to enter the debate as to the precise authorship of the several texts published by Medvedev and Voloshinov but attributed by some to Bakhtin, for the present project I will follow the convention advocated by Todorov of citing both names. Todorov reasons that the ideas espoused by Medvedev and Voloshinov were certainly present in their discussions with Bakhtin, but that even if they are not the sole or even the primary authors of the theories in question, the high price they later paid for their publication warrants their mention at the very least. For discussion supporting Bakhtin's authorship, see Holquist & Clark (and Sprinkler's review) and Lodge; for contrary views see Todorov and Morris.

[6] "Bakhtin was well acquainted with both the breadth of early twentieth-century European intellectual culture and the sense of crisis which pervaded it. He would have known that European achievement in the arts, in philosophy and science, in law and government, was impressive in a technical sense and a complete failure in a moral

what he considered to be the

> legacy of European "rationalism," which understands truth monologically, that is, it understands truth as the sort of thing that can be best represented by impersonal propositions. By contrast, it is possible to conceive of truth as something that can only be represented by a conversation, as something that by its very nature demands many voices and points of view. (Morson, 266)

Contemporary critics across the board are now, in effect, urging the adoption of a new paradigm which understands that the discourse of "science" has erected a false god; their growing concern with moral questions leads them to re-evaluate the methods via which we discover "truth," and chief among these is a return to narrative as a fundamental activity of the human race. In an age in which primates are being taught to "speak" via computers (see Dreifus), it may well be that what distinguishes humans from other species of life is their capacity, indeed their penchant for telling stories. There is a "growing belief that narrative represents a universal medium of human consciousness – in Hayden White's terms, a 'metacode' that allows for the transcultural transmission of 'messages about a shared reality'"(Lucaites & Condit, 90). Morrison has always been certain of the importance of stories and therefore the novel. As early as 1977, she is on the record as saying,

> People crave narration. Magazines only sell because they have stories in them, not because somebody wants to read those ads! Aside from the little game shows, television is all narrative. People want to hear a story. They love it! That's the way they learn things. That's the way human beings organize their human knowledge – fairy tales, myths. All narration. And that's why the novel is so important! [...] People want to hear a story. (In Bakerman, 35)

Under the scrutiny of certain critics, our "human knowledge," the "truths we hold to be self-evident" are demonstrated to be simply based on stories we all accept as communal. Research in such diverse fields as information science (Bennet & Edelman), law (Baron), economics (Rose), history (White), feminist studies (Lanser), and even the "pure" sciences (McGee & Nelson) demonstrates that first there is ideology, followed by narration which reinforces, substantiates and perpetuates the ideology.

Dominated peoples have traditionally borne the brunt of such ideologically-based science. Black critics have been instrumental in revealing the contradictions and fallacies inherent in what was often solipsistic discourse. As Morrison herself has remarked,

> The Age of Enlightenment was also the Age of Scientific Racism. David Hume, Immanuel Kant and Thomas Jefferson, to mention only a few, had documented their

---

sense, having led inexorably to a horrific war and an apparently endless series of social crises and conflicts. Bakhtin did not, however, turn to either sociological or political analysis, but to philosophy, for an explanation of this failure. In fact, he went even further: he argued that it was the forgetting of philosophy, its displacement by the methods of natural science, which lay at the bottom of the crisis to begin with" (Hirschkop, 584).

conclusions that blacks were incapable of intelligence. [...] Jefferson said in "Notes on the State of Virginia," "Never yet could I find that a black had uttered a thought above the level of plain narration, never see even an elementary trait of painting or sculpture" – [...] Hegel, in 1813, had said that Africans had no "history" and couldn't write in modern languages. Kant disregarded a perceptive observation by a black man by saying, "this fellow was quite black from head to foot, a clear proof that what he said was stupid."   (Morrison,"Memory"; 189-190)

Such considerations have led leading theorists of communication to posit a narrative paradigm – "a dialectical synthesis of two traditional strands in the history of rhetoric: the argumentative, persuasive theme and the literary, aesthetic theme" (Fisher, 2). This narrative paradigm supposes *homo narrans* — that humans are storytellers by nature — and as such it competes with a "rational world paradigm." "The theory explains the appearance of a group consciousness, with its implied shared emotions, motives, and meanings, not in terms of individual daydreams and scripts but rather in terms of socially shared narrations or fantasies" (Bormann, 135 & 128).[7] Ernest G. Bormann finds that "a single dramatic case (fantasy theme) has greater impact on attitudes and commitment than base-rate statistics or other abstract, generalized statements" (132). Clearly the function of narrative in modern world has been sorely devalued and underestimated. Thus, McGee and Nelson argue that "what we need is to dispel the dichotomy: to understand and improve the place of narrative in rationality and of reasoning in storytelling" (145-146).

> From the perspective of the rational world paradigm, myths are untrue and to tell stories is to recount falsehood. From this perspective, too, fantasy is something that is unreal and untrue. Yet, for those using the narrative paradigm, the stories of myths or fantasy themes are central.   (Bormann, 136)

Yet this dichotomy was not always functional. In "The Narrative Paradigm: In the Beginning," Walter R. Fisher traces the development of the divide created among the original meanings of "*logos*," which in the beginning meant "story, reason, rationale, conception, discourse and/or thought" (74). He states that at issue in the story of *logos* and *mythos* is "which form of discourse – philosophy (technical discourse), rhetoric, or poetic – ensures the discovery and validation of truth, knowledge, and reality, and thereby deserves to be the legislator of human decision making and action" (76). In his review he follows the progressive devaluation of rhetorical and poetic discourse through the centuries (citing Plato, Aristotle, Bacon, Descartes, John Locke, Thomas Sprat, among other) as the "rational" form of discourse took precedence

---

[7] Within this general theory, Ernest G. Bormann has elaborated a "symbolic convergence theory of communication" with a three part structure: "The first part deals with the discovery and arrangement of recurring communicative forms and patterns that indicate the evolution and presence of a shared group consciousness. The second part consists of a description of the dynamic tendencies [...] that explain why group consciousnesses arise, continue, decline, and disappear and the effects such groups' consciousnesses have in terms of meanings, motives, and communication within the group. The basic communicative process is the dynamic of people sharing group fantasies. The third part consists of the factors that explain why people share the fantasies they do when they do" (129).

over the poetic. Not that there were not advocates of the contrary. Aristophanes insisted that "the standard of excellence in poetry was not only 'skill in the art,' but also 'wise counsel for the state'"; Longinus celebrated the qualitites of communication that appeared in "any genre"; for Boccaccio the truth could be "allegorical"; and Sir Philip Sidney alleged that "no learning is so good as that which teacheth and mooveth to verture; and that none can both teach and move thereto so much as Poetry" (in Fisher, 79-80). Even so, according to Fisher, "by the end of the nineteenth century, proponents of poetics could not, or did not, challenge science's claim on the domain of the physical sphere of life" (81), the consequences of which we have witnessed particularly in this century.

> One cannot blame all the ills of the world on this historic struggle. Yet, it is safe to say that it has contributed to the contemporary condition by repressing the realization of a holistic sense of self, by subverting the formulation of a humane concept of rationality and a sane praxis, by rendering personal and public decision making and action subservient to "experts" in knowledge, truth, and reality, and by elevation one class of persons and their discourse over others. (Fisher, 87)

This concern with authoritative discourse that privileges certain groups and disempowers others is echoed time and again across the board. McGee and Nelson state that "if narratives are forms or mirrors for cultural commitments, then they may privilege oppressive patterns of judgment" (149) and that "it is such an epistemology of storytelling that a community requires in order to reintroduce morality effectively into public discourse" (153). Baron notes that in the realm of justice and the law, "the system is positively tilted" to such a degree that it is "not likely to be reformed any time soon. And this tilt contradicts the premise of neutrality" (Baron, 70). Lanser recalls "the lesson formulated by Bakhtin: that in narrative there is no single voice, that in far subtler situations than this one, voice impinges upon voice, yielding a structure in which discourses of and for the other constitute the discourses of self" (349).[8] And Rose believes that the storyteller, "by structuring the audience's experience and imagination, helps to turn her audience into a moral community" (55).

Far from a feature of secondary importance in contemporary society, storytelling is currently recognized as a powerful influence in the cohesion of communities and in the development of individual psyches.[9] Intellectuals in fields from communications theory to economics, from law to narratology, from "pure" science to political science are therefore strongly advocating an understanding of narration as a basic building-block in the structuring of our lives and as a creative force for shaping a better future. For as Holquist states, "Narrative as it organizes most information, whether in scientific tracts or literary texts, seems to give itself as a writing about life" (1989, "Body-Talk,"33).

---

[8] She finds the "polyphony" "more pronounced and more consequential in women's narratives and in the narratives of other dominated peoples" (Lanser, 350).

[9] Even the relatively new science of chronobiology, "the study of rhythm and its governance in essential life operations, is making it increasingly clear that the human body is drenched in time, and that in order to systematize its heterogenous chronologies the body, too, resorts to storytelling" (Holquist, 1989, "Body-Talk"; 8).

That Morrison should devote a novel to the process of storytelling is at once coherent with much contemporary philosophy of communication and very much rooted in her own concerns. It is not just that as a novelist she "tells stories"; it is at once homage to a cultural background whose values have been communicated for thousands of years through an oral tradition and a firm belief that these stories are vital for the preservation of her tradition as well as a force for positive changes in pervasive attitudes that have been pernicious for her people.

Morrison has argued that the breakdown in the traditional black community, the dispersal of families during the great migration north (the time-frame for *Jazz*) meant that the stories so necessary for the cultural cohesion of African Americans were no longer being effectively transmitted (in Evans, 340). She believes, therefore, that it is the black novel that has come to take the place of the communal storytelling and she continually strives to achieve that oral quality of narration that characterizes her people, a people in love with language, a people who treat language "like the same intricate, malleable toy designed for their play" (*J*, 33). That this has been very much on her mind, particularly at the time she was working on *Jazz*, is everywhere evident in her other work. In her introduction to *Birth of a Nation'hood* (1997), "The Official Story: Dead Man Golfing," she describes her anger at the narrative that developed around the figure of O.J. Simpson – a narrative so authoritative and relentless in its interpretation of the "facts" that it left no room for others that might question or contradict it. Her introduction to *Race-ing Justice, En-gendering Power* (1993), "Friday on the Potomac," also lashes out at Clarence Thomas's appropriation of a narrative of black life to defend himself from accusations by Anita Hill, while at the same time denying his heritage and the benefits he had reaped from the sacrifices of others, embracing a conservative narrative which degraded and denied his own sister.

On the occasion of her acceptance of the Nobel Prize for Literature in 1993, Morrison's speech entitled "The Dancing Mind" actually uses a story to speak of the importance of literature and language. In it there is an old blind woman of reputed wisdom who lives on the edge of a town. Certain children, in an attempt to taunt her in her blindness, ask her if the bird which they are holding in their hands is alive or dead. The old woman is quiet for a long time, but then answers, "I don't know if the bird you hold is dead or alive, but what I do know is that it is in your hands" (318). The author interprets the bird in this story as language and the old woman as a practiced writer, and finds one meaning in the possibilities presented to all of us in the way we use language. For Morrison, the old woman is very aware that a language may die, but a dead language

> is not only one no longer spoken or written, it is unyielding language, content to admire its own paralysis. Like statist language, censored and censoring. Ruthless in its policing duties, it has no desire or purpose other than to maintain the free range of its own narcotic narcissism, its own exclusivity and dominance. However, moribund, it is not without effect, for it actively thwarts the intellect, stalls conscience, suppresses human potential. [...]

> Oppressive language does more than represent violence; it is violence; does more than represent the limits of knowledge; it limits knowledge. Whether it is obscuring state

language or the faux language of mindless media; whether it is the proud but calcified language of the academy or the commodity-driven language of science; whether it is the malign language of law-without-ethics, or language designed for the estrangement of minorities, hiding its racist plunder in its literary cheek – it must be rejected, altered, and exposed. It is the language that drinks blood, laps vulnerabilities, tucks its fascist boots under crinolines of respectability and patriotism as it moves relentlessly toward the bottom line and the bottomed-out mind. Sexist language, racist language, theistic language – all are typical of the policing languages of mastery, and cannot, do not, permit new knowledge or encourage the mutual exchange of ideas.

(Morrison, "Dancing"; 319 & 320)

Writing stories, using language to create and sustain alternative visions, other realities, is the serious business of literature, particularly of what we lightly refer to as "minority literature," or what we might refer to in the definition of Giles Deleuze and Feliz Guattari as "minor literature": "that which a minority constructs out of a major language." [... I]t is "the glory" of minor literature "to be the revolutionary force for all literature" (qtd. in Grewal, 9). Gurleen Grewal adds that "minor literature [...] constructs a different discourse, whose burden is to challenge dominant ideologies and representations by claiming an alternative epistemological and ethical space" (19). "Fiction is not random," Morrison has stated (1988; 193) and "narrative is radical, creating us at the very moment it is being created" (1995; 323). Perhaps this emphasis on constructing stories that offer a different reality, or better, that offer multiple realities, is why certain critics of *Jazz* have read its epigraph as an indication of the Gnostic religious philosophy of many of the Coptic texts of *The Nag Hammadi Library* within which "Thunder, Perfect Mind" was discovered.

The Clue

IV. *THE NAG HAMMADI LIBRARY* AND THE RIDDLE OF THE "THUNDER"

> I am the name of the sound
>   and the sound of the name.
> I am the sign of the letter
>   and the designation of the division.

The epigraph Morrison has chosen for *Jazz* comes from an enigmatic tractate entitled "Thunder, Perfect Mind," one of thirteen codices containing 52 texts written on papyrus, found in a cave in the mountain range of Djebel-AlTarif in the Upper Nile area, close to the modern town of Nag Hammadi in Egypt, in 1945.[10] The manuscripts were discovered in a large, three feet high jar by an Arabic fellahin, Mohammed Ali es-Samman, a nomad who obviously had no understanding of the find he had made. Apparently, and by his own account, his wife actually burned two large codices and some pages of the manuscripts in the process of tea-making. Although it is believed that the original text was probably written in Greek, no manuscripts have survived with which to compare them, and given the frequent changes in style and editorial marks, they are apparently the work of many, or at least various scribes who may not actually have been Gnostics themselves (W, 13). Some complain that this successive reworking and rewriting have left the Nag Hammadi texts "completely incomprehensible" (W, 10). Why the texts were so carefully hidden remains unclear but it is certain that the circumstances around the time of the burial (probably about 367 CE) were "grim":

> St. Athanasius of Alexandria had issued forth an edict demanding that all heretical and pagan texts in the possession of the Church and her monasteries should be burnt, [and] anyone who resisted this order would be tried as an heretic. (W, 13)

---

[10] Although discovered in 1945, the "hostile climate" during Nasser's mandate in Egypt and the circumstances of nationalism meant that Egyptian authorities were highly jealous of allowing any of its history outside its borders (W, 13). The project of reconstruction and translation of the texts, therefore, was not completed and published until 1977 (Hedrick, 7).

That Gnosticism has traditionally been described as "heretical" was probably due to the fact that, up until the discovery of the *Nag Hammadi*, knowledge of this religious philosophy was largely derived from the

> polemical and sarcastic accounts of the early Christian heresologists and polemicists such as Justin Martyr, Irenaeus, and Epiphanius. These men, coming as they did from the narrow framework of conventional Christianity, were unable to understand any other form of spirituality except as a departure – a heresy [...] – from their own One True Faith.   (W, 12)

According to Charles W. Hedrick, because the Nag Hammadi Library contains several gnostic texts "that show no evidence of having been influence by Christianity (*The Apocalypse of Adam*, the *Paraphrase of Shem*, the *Three Steles of Seth*, and *Eugnostos*), it demonstrates beyond question that gnosticism was not simply a Christian heresy" (9). It is, however, the "heretical" – literally "free-thinking" – nature of Gnoticism that would jibe naturally with the philosophy underlying Morrison's exploration of language and storytelling as encompassed in a Bakhtinian theory of discourse (see below). Its undermining of the "straight-jacket conformity and heresy-hunting of the Christian Church" (W, 16) perfectly echoes the author's complaint against authoritarian, dogmatic language that excludes other voices. It is interesting to note that in Gnostic Christianity, the God of the Old Testament is depicted as an *evil* force, "a supernatural dictator who keeps the mind (= 'spirit') enslaved with dogma, and demands absolute belief," an "anti-Divine being" (W, 8 & 1).

Gnosticism itself was unusually syncretic, drawing on various and sundry philosophies abroad before and during the first centuries of the Christian Era. "It blended inspiration from biblical, Christian, Jewish apocalyptic, neoplatonic, and various mystery religion (*sic*) and astrological sources." Unlike the Neoplatonists and Hermeticism, however, the Gnostics had a "pessimistic view of the world":

> The visible cosmos was a creation of inferior and anti-spiritual powers, the Archons or "rulers." It is a place of ignorance and deficiency, controlled by heimarmene – fate, destiny – and ruled over by the evil archons. As such it is a prison in which the spirit or Divine Spark is trapped, in exile from its true home above. The goal of existence is to extract the sparks trapped in matter, so that they can return to their true spiritual home. [...] In contrast to exoteric religions, is it not blind faith in, or obedience to, a God, but spiritual Self-Knowledge, that confers salvation. Indeed, the Gnostics were very critical of exoteric religion, identifying the God of the Old Testament with the chief Archon.
> (W, 9)

The "self-knowledge" of the Gnostics, however, is not based on external teachings and revelations; "the essential knowledge comes from within." Even though the term "Gnosticism" is a modern denomination, it is essentially an accurate one in that it is "derived from the Greek gnosis, higher or spiritual or Intuitive or Divine Knowledge, as opposed to episteme, which is knowledge in the more mundane sense" (W, 12).

Indeed, the cosmology of the Gnostics seems to include a "dig" at the ancient Greek philosophers. In the Gnostic account of the fall and creation of the world, it is the willfulness of a lower "Aeon," who tries to emulate the power of the Forefather, that creates the world. As a result, she produces "not a genuine creation but an 'abortion,' which after a long series of transformations, became the Cosmos and the lower powers which rule it." That the Gnostics would name this lower, arrogant "Aeon" "Sophia" (wisdom) seems almost a contradiction, only understood in relation to the claims of the Platonistis, Aristotleans, Stoics, Epiccureans and others that "it was possible through reason alone (or 'wisdom' ...) to know the Absolute. The Hellenistic Gnostics, however, said that such perception can only come about through a higher, intuitive, knowing." The Crisis, or the Fall, is brought about not through sexuality, but through an "absence of sexuality; that is, through an absence of balanced polarity, in which only one aspect, rather than both, participates in the creation" (W, 6).

In this sense, and as O'Keefe argues, *Jazz* does interrogate the possibility of "knowing" anything at all about "the other." The narrator's opening line, "Sth, I know that woman" (*J*, 3) dissolves into her own admission of unreliability and the fact that "Something is missing there" (*J*, 228). In O'Keefe's interpretation, however, the novel "enacts agnosticism, another form of resistance to 'orthodox' Western epistemology, through the narrator's gradual realization of the impossibility of asserting any knowledge claims" (331). But it is also clear in the novel that by the end of the book the narrator's obsession with relating the lives of Joe and Violet dissolves into her own "gnosis," a concern for greater awareness of her "self." This is no less true of the main protagonists, who, through their stories recounted to themselves and others, also arrive at self-awareness: Joe and Violet come to terms with their "motherlessness" and its influence on their lives; Alice finally acknowledges her anger and sense of loss over having lost her husband first to another woman and then to death; even Felice, still a young teenager, returns time and again to listen to Violet and Joe, to learn about the discovery of the self:

> "'Now I want to be the woman my mother didn't stay around long enough to see. That one. The one she would have liked and the one I used to like before. [...] My grand-mother fed me stories about a little blond child. He was a boy, but I thought of him as a girl sometimes, as a brother, sometimes as a boyfriend. He lived inside my mind. Quiet as a mole. But I didn't know it till I got here. The two of us. Had to get rid of it.'
> [...]
> "'How did you get rid of her?'
> "'Killed her. Then I killed the me that killed her.'
> "'Who's left?'
> "'Me.'[11]   (*J*, 208-209)

Another interesting feature of Gnosticism as it might relate to *Jazz* is its characteristic conception of time:

> To put it very simplistically, one could say that there are two ways to consider

---

[11] O'Reilly (369) points out that this passage also echoes the final words of Sethe in *Beloved* in response to Paul D: "You your best thing, Sethe. You are." [...] "Me? Me?" (*B*, 273)

the temporal nature of the Cosmos: Cyclically, and Historically.

Cyclic time means, obviously, that the same patterns repeat themselves, and there is no absolute progress. Tribal peoples, living close to the rhythms of nature, see time as cyclic, as expressed for example the alternation of day and night and of the seasons.[12] [...]

A more complex historical position – advocated by Gnosticism for example – sees "history" as a catastrophic sequence of events, beginning with a "Fall" from an original Perfect State, and finishing in a yet to be consummated cosmic Restitution, whereby the original perfection will be re-established [...] As with exoteric Judaeo-Christian religion, the universe is seen as moving in a specific direction: towards the resolution of the original Fault.   (W, 3)

The narrator of *Jazz* seems to be caught in the cyclic reproduction of history, unable to believe that "her" characters could avoid what was for her the "inevitable:"

So I missed it altogether. I was sure one would kill the other. I waited for it so I could describe it. I was so sure it would happen. That the past was an abused record with no choice but to repeat itself at the crack and no power on earth could lift the arm that held the needle.   (J, 220)

I have argued elsewhere ("Specter") that *Jazz* in many ways is a metaphorical rewriting of Morrison's first novel *The Bluest Eye* (1970), a text which is structured cyclically (the seasonal sections of the book, the metaphorical use of seeds and flowers, etc.) and which moves inexorably toward the destruction of Pecola's self. In its conception of time as well, *Jazz* depicts characters who will elude the narrator and history and move toward "gnosis" and the possibility of greater understanding of the self and, hence, a better future. Gnosticism, however, is more "concerned with the beginning of things," as opposed to "Apocalyptic" tendencies that concern themselves more with the immanent end of the world. Like apocalyptic beliefs,

Gnosticism despaired of the world and its history. But whereas [the] apocalyptic regarded the world as ultimately under God's control, Gnosticism regarded the world as under the control of spiritual powers hostile to God. Gnosticism expected a savior who would come into the world and impart knowledge as a means of escaping from this lower world to the transcendent Divine or spiritual realm. It despaired of the flesh and believed that imprisoned within the body was a divine spark, the true Soul, that could be liberated by "knowledge."   (W, 7)

The question of the "savior" in Gnosticism poses another potentially important reference. In the most important sect of Gnosticism this "savior-figure" was Seth, the third son of Adam and Eve, regarded, unlike his brothers, to have "possessed the 'spirit' or 'seed' from above," and therefore to be the "father of all the Gnostics" (W, 2). Even though the term "Sethian Gnostics"

---

[12] The same applies to more urban civilisations as well: The Egyptians, Greeks, Indians, Chinese, and Mesoamericans, for example. With them, the agricultural and "pagan" cycles of nature are replaced by the celestial and at times fatalistic cycles revealed through Astrology.

is a modern one, "a number of Nag Hammadi texts do share a great deal in common as regards their cosmology and terminology [which] for the sake of convenience we can refer to [...] as 'Sethian'" (W, 14). According to John D. Turner,

> During the later first to second century C.E. Sethianism became gradually Christianised through contact with Christian baptismal groups, and identified Seth or Adam with their pre-existent Christ. Here then Seth and Adam are transformed from human to *supernatural beings.*   (Turner, 56)

Given Toni Morrison's exquisite care in the naming of her characters, it is not difficult to assume that her exploration of alternate "supernatural" realities in *Beloved* (Tally, "Reality") would lead her to name her central protagonist Sethe. Clearly yet another attraction of Gnosticism for the inspiration of Morrison's trilogy is "the beauty and evocative nature of its language, especially when describing the Absolute Reality" (W, 15). Moreover, and equally important for the present reading,

> The (apparently Sethian) Gnostic work *Trimorphic Protennoia* shows the concept of *Logos* as a revealer figure set in the context of a complex of divine emanations (apparently non-Christian despite the superficial and most likely secondary Christianization of the text): *Voice, Sound, Word.*   (MacRae, 91; emphasis added)

I must insist, however, that this intertextual reading in Gnosticism not divert attention from the actual selection of the epigraph from the *Nag Hammadi*. In the first place, the *Nag Hammadi* are said to be a "late (early 4th Century C.E.) and a degenerate expression" of Gnosticism (W, 12); in the second place, as cited above, the continual reworking and rewriting of the texts have made them exceedingly difficult to translate/interpret; and in the third place, and most importantly, the four lines that introduce *Jazz* are taken from "Thunder, Perfect Mind," a tractate that George MacRae finds "difficult to classify" in terms of religious tradition (in Hedrick, 296) and which is "unique in the Nag Hammadi collection and virtually unique as a distinct literary work in the context of literature from the Roman and Hellenistic periods" (qtd. in Layton; note 1, 38). "It presents no distinctively Jewish, Christian, or Gnostic themes, nor does it seem to presuppose a particular Gnostic myth [...]" (1977; 270). The fact that MacRae speaks of a "female revealer," coupled with the fact that the texts were discovered in the Upper Nile region, has lead some critics to speculate that the female voice of the narrator in *Jazz* could be Isis, the African goddess speaking.

Taking her cue from the previous speculation, Gurleen Grewal states that

> We can appreciate how Morrison absorbs this figure into the persona of her narrator, who is designated by the sound and name of jazz. Further, the unknown gnostic revelator's stance as a persecuted outsider (an Egyptian's relationship to the dominant Greco-Christian discourse?) allies her with the position of a female African American narrator of the 1920s. Consider these lines from "The Thunder, Perfect Mind":
>
> Why have you hated me in your counsels?

For I shall be silent among those who are silent,
    and I shall appear and speak.
Why then have you hated me, you Greeks?
    Because I am a barbarian among [the] barbarians?
For I am the wisdom [of the] Greeks
    and the knowledge of the barbarians.

The ancient one "who has been hated everywhere" and who declares, "I am peace, /and war has come because of me/ And I am an alien and a citizen" becomes a perfect correlative for the narrator of post-Civil War, post-Reconstruction mayhem.

(Grewal, 121)

Benton Layton, however, traces elements in "Thunder" which would link it to a presupposed "strong text," and makes a strong case for understanding this "strong text" as the *Gospel of Eve*. While it is impossible to reconstruct this original text, he speculates on its characteristics:

It is a riddle gospel, called *euaggelion*, in which the possibility of liberation is implied by monologues of the heavenly Eve or female spiritual principle. It uses the authoritative Isiac and/or Jewish Wisdom style, combined with the paradox of Greek riddle.[13]

(Layton, 49)

In his analysis of "Thunder" itself, Layton sets out five main features worthy of consideration:

(1) The text is a monologue, concerned not with plot, but with the building up of persona. [...]
(2) [...] the speaker's use of the formula ego eimi, "It is I who am [...]." [is a] hallmark of Isis propaganda [...]
(3) [...] what she predicates of herself [...] there is the outrageous pairing of the predicates so as to express a paradox, often phrased in balanced antithesis. Since paradox is utterly foreign to the content of Isis monologues, the strong disjunction between self-predicating (Isiac) rhetoric and paradoxical logic is the true exegetical crux of our text.
(4) Modern interpretation stresses the combination of *ego eimi* and paradox as the characteristic feature of this text [...][14]
(5) Finally, there is a fragmentary mythic framework, comprising a mere twelve verses [...] [which] summarizes a myth of the soul's descent into the body, its entrapment in a disastrous cycle of reincarnations [...] (Layton, 39-41)

---

[13] "It is set in Paradise atop a high mountain, where reference to thunder (bronte) is at home. It also contains a(?) riddle – some puns based ultimately on a Semitic language. [...] The speaker also lapses into the style of the gnostic diatribe[...]" (Layton, 49-50).

[14] "[...] yet, in fact, the same number of lines is given to quite different rhetorical mode, the philosophical sermon or gnostic distribe" (Layton 40).

Given the puzzling nature of the text and its syncretic fusions of different *genres*, Layton centers the underlying problem of its deciphering as a question:

> What was the normal locus of outrageous paradox in the ancient Mediterranean word? The very simplicity of the answer may explain why it has eluded earlier students of this text: it is the Greek riddle. (Layton, 42)

Morrison, then, has elected an epigraph that must be deciphered, and the importance of such a choice is fundamental for the interpretation of the text:

> A riddle is the occasion for rethinking the sense of what otherwise seems obviously impossible, a time for a shift in perspective, a search for a deeper meaning. Even when the solution has been revealed or recognized, the riddle itself must finally be reread – exegeted – to discover how the solution applies, how a seeming a paradox is not really a paradox. This invitation to exegesis is part of the riddle game. [...] But riddles have one thing that most gnostic texts do not – namely, a definite solution. (Layton, 44)

For his part, Layton hypothesizes that the solution to the riddle of "Thunder, Perfect Mind" is "Eve," an intertextual reference that would give meaning to certain allusions in *Jazz*:

> Well, he says, well no point in picking the apple if you don't want to see how it taste. How does it taste, Joe? (*J*, 40)

> I told you again that you were the reason Adam ate the apple and its core. That when he left Eden, he left a rich man. Not only did he have Eve, but he had the taste of the first apple in the world in his mouth for the rest of his life. The very first to know what it was like.[15] To bite it, bite it down. Hear the crunch and let the red peeling break his heart. "You looked at me then like you knew me, and I thought it really was Eden, [...] (*J*, 133)

> Your first time. And mine, in a manner of speaking. For which, and I will say it again, I would strut out the Garden, strut! as long as you held on to my hand, girl. (*J*, 134-135)

> "Then she opened them wide and said real loud: 'There's only one apple.' Sounded like 'apple.' 'Just one. Tell Joe.'" (*J*, 213)

Our concern here, however, is not so much with the resolution of the riddle of "Thunder, Perfect Mind" as with the simple nature of the riddle. According to Newbell N. Puckett in his seminal study, *Folk Beliefs of the Southern Negro*, published precisely in 1926, the year that the main action of *Jazz* takes place,

> Riddles are also favorites with the Negroes, especially around the country fireside on

---

[15] Also a reference to the fact that the Gnostics considered the Old Testament God an evil, jealous god who refused to share knowledge with humankind.

winter evenings, and, while I have located no direct African survivals, there are some
built according to the very common African plan of guessing the simile used, while
others approach the form, apparently more common to European peoples, of deciphering
the partial description. (Puckett, 52)

Puckett's research makes clear that riddles were not only common but much enjoyed among
African Americans at the time he was writing his book; he cites the following examples, among
others:

> Got an ear but does not hear?
> *Ans.* An ear of corn.
>
> A riddle, a riddle, as I suppose,
> A hundred eyes and never a nose.
> *Ans.* A sifter (sieve).
>
> What goes through the woods and never touches anything?
> *Ans*: Smoke. (Puckett, 53)

It makes sense, therefore, to look at the exact verses that Morrison has chosen from "Thunder,
Perfect Mind" and examine the paradox.

Many of Morrison's "jazz" critics have taken the epigraph to substantiate their claim that
jazz music is the basis for the text, or indeed, the identity of the narrator. This *might* work for the
phrases "I am the name of the sound and the sound of the name," but how does it resolve "I am
the sign of the letter and the designation of the division"? Herbert W. Rice complains that

> if we look at these lines closely, we find that Layton is correct: their logic unravels. If
> we apply the first two lines to the word jazz, they lead us nowhere. Jazz is the name of
> a certain kind of music, but it is also a sound in its own right, a word. The second line
> is even more puzzling. What is "the sign of the letter" if it is not the letter itself?
> Further, is "the designation of the division" once again the letter? Does such a phrase
> imply that we are somehow divided from true knowledge by words themselves? None
> of these questions can be answered. (H.W. Rice, 134)

Rice concludes that "these words of "omnipredication" from a female deity contradicts much of
what we see in the novel" (134).

I wish to propose an answer to the riddle which is, I believe, a more viable solution and
a more coherent resolution to the problems posed. If we read the answer to this riddle as
"language," and, by extension, "*logos*" in its wider meanings, coherent with the revelatory figure
as described by MacRae cited above, Morrison's epigraph makes perfect sense within the
parameters of the hypothesis set out in the present project: "I am the name of the sound and the
sound of the name" makes sense if the voice is language/*logos* itself. "I am the sign of the letter"
will fit (albeit, perhaps metaphorically) within a Saussurian conception of "signs" as "conveyors
of meaning" (Abrams, 280) and the sign as double-sided: signifier and signified. "And the

designation of the division" alludes to the power of language/*logos*/discourse to classify and structure reality, credibly extended to language that has stipulated a hierarchy of peoples into empowered and powerless. Layton's alternative translation of the last two phrases of the epigraph coupled with another that appears slightly later –

> It is I who am the meaning of text,
> And the manifestation of distinction; ...
> Behold, then, ... all the texts that have been completed.
> Thund.VI, 2:20, 33-21,12

– indicate that this interpretation is a viable one.

Let us return for a moment to the lines included by Gurleen Grewal to substantiate her claim that the revealer figure is a "persecuted outsider" and therefore an apt representative of the era for which she speaks in *Jazz*:

> For I shall be silent among those who are silent,
> and I shall appear and speak. ...

The "voice/sound/word" is not heard if not uttered, but reappears with speech.

> Because I am a barbarian among [the] barbarians?

As Morrison noted in her Nobel Acceptance speech, language (in the mouths of "barbarians") does not just represent violence, "it is violence."

> For I am the wisdom [of the] Greeks
> and the knowledge of the barbarians. ...

"Wisdom" here is contrasted with "knowledge" as the Greeks are contrasted with the "barbarians," but language is the source of both.

I do not mean to imply in any way that the entirety of "Thunder Perfect Mind" (or, "Thunder, Perfect Intellect," as Layton translates it) can be interpreted in this light. It is the words Morrison has *specifically* chosen from the text for her epigraph, however, that should most interest us and throw some light on the meaning(s) of her novel. As Layton points out,

> the riddle ... demands, first, a solution and, second, a reexegesis of the entire text as riddle to see how the solution applies. Riddles often speak with a mythic directness that demands the active application of the listener's intellect, in a way that sermons and aretalogies rarely do. (Layton, 44)

I want, therefore, to insist upon the relevance of looking at language and discourse as a vehicle for storytelling as a basis for the exegesis of *Jazz*. Far from a "distraction" causing us to "miss the obvious point,"[16] if we interpret the epigraph in the way suggested, there is, in fact, no

---

[16] John Leonard thinks that the epigraph, coupled with the fact that Morrison was spending "part of every week at Princeton [where she is now holds the Rober Goheen Professorship in the Humanities Council] with Elaine

contradiction between these words and Morrison's text.

A few other critics have mentioned or come close to mentioning this possibility, but have skirted the issue in favor of other interpretations. Although Jill Matus' main concern is with "history, trauma and replay" in *Jazz*, at one point she does state that " the book itself is conceived as a narrative performance, the narrator becoming indistinguishable from the story itself" (124), referring to John Leonard's observation that "the Voice is the book itself, this physical object, our metatext [...] a whimsy and a wickedness worthy of a Nabokov (49).[17] Matus qualifies her observation by emphasizing that

> the narrator is not always to be thought of in this way; in moments of "concert" and readerly participation, however, the fusion of parts of the narrative enterprise makes narrator and book the same.   (Matus, 124, Note 6)

Herbert W. Rice states in the conclusion of his chapter on *Jazz* that "still, there is a larger issue at work here: language itself," and notes also that "Morrison's Nobel Lecture underscores the centrality of her conception of language to her work" (140). He does not, however, in any way develop this idea. Henry Louis Gates, Jr., notes the importance of storytelling to the novel –

> But what is compelling here is not only the novel´s plot, but how the story is *told*. A disembodied narrator slips easily and guilelessly from third-person all-knowingness to first-person lyricism, without ever relaxing its grip upon our imagination. It is a sensitive, poetic narrator, in love with the language of fiction, enraptured with the finest and rarest of arts, the art of telling a good tale, reflecting, as it goes along, upon its responsibilities as a composer, and its obligation to the individual characters whose sole destiny is to make this composition come alive, to sing.   (Gates, 1993; 53-54)

– but basically employs this observation to further his argument that jazz is "the structuring principle for [the] entire novel" (52). And Gurleen Grewal states that "*Jazz* is self-conscious about the capacity of art to mediate in its time and space the desires of historic subjects" (136). More than just "self-conscious," however, the novel actually deals with the process of that mediation.

The critic who perhaps comes closest to the hypothesis of the present study is Trudier Harris in her heading to the section on Toni Morrison in the *The Heath Anthology of American Literature*:

> Intended to incorporate the rhythm of jazz musical structuring as its *raison d'etre*, the novel instead becomes a story about narrators, about how the voice that creates a story can change it at will, with no accountability or requirement for reliability to anyone but

---

Pagels, who wrote the book on The Gnostic Gospels" tends to obscure rather than clarify Morrison's theme (48).

[17] Hardack disagrees, however, saying that "[t] his narrator then is not just the book, as John Leonard notes in his review of *Jazz*, but the sweet and sharp tooth of double-consciousness itself; she hungers for and feeds off what she projects and constructs as the split-consciousness of her characters, waits for them to feel pain so she can appropriate it" (463). Lewis also questions Leonard's interpretation: " [...] it brings up the question can a book write itself? I think it is safer to say that the narrator tries to write her own story and discovers that she is the open book we are reading" (278).

itself. It can intrude where it will, directly contradict information it has just given the reader, and still claim that it has a story interesting enough to be told. The book received numerous reviews, most of them mixed, few critics seeing clearly what Morrison had tried to accomplish with the work. (Harris in Gates *et al*, 2875)

In the present analysis, however, I wish to look at the *raison d'etre* of *Jazz* not as an experiment with jazz musical forms, nor as a story about narrators, but as a story about the ways and means of storytelling itself and the language of the narrative process. This has always been, after all, a primary concern of the author herself. When asked by an interviewer what she thought was distinctive about her fiction, what made it good, Morrison readily replied:

> The language, only the language. The language must be careful and must appear effortless. It must not sweat. It must suggest and be provocative at the same time. It is the thing that black people love so much – the saying of words, holding them on the tongue, experimenting with them, playing with them. It's a love, a passion. Its function is like a preacher's: to make you stand up out of your seat, make you lose yourself and hear yourself. The worst of all possible things that could happen would be to lose that language. (Morrison in LeClair, 123)

The first step on the road to this analysis of discourse and narrative, however, should be a look at the use of narrative form, of *genre*, as a vehicle for that narration.

The Vehicle

V. *GENRE* AND STORYTELLING

Based on certain observations made by critics such as Trudier Harris and Linden Peach together with my own analysis, I have elsewhere postulated (*Paradise Reconsidered*) that Toni Morrison chooses a different popular genre on which to base each successive novel, only to subvert some of the specific genre's major premises. According to Harris, this "subversion" is taken from her folklore tradition: "[Morrison's] primary folkloristic technique is reversal, where outcomes consistently fall short of expectations" (1991; 12). Her first novel, *The Bluest Eye* (1970), takes its cue from the *memoire*; *Sula* (1973) from the fairy tale; *Song of Solomon* (1977) from the romance quest; *Tar Baby* (1981) from the fugitive story; *Beloved* (1987) from the ghost story; and *Paradise* (1998) from the western (Tally, *Paradise*; 58-68). With *Jazz* (1992), however, I confess to having made a mistake: the genre Morrison uses as her touchstone is not the tabloid as I originally argued. As my interest was from the very beginning in language and storytelling in *Jazz*, it seemed only logical to listen to Morrison's recording of her own work. It took only a few minutes to realize that in this case the "voice" of the narrator is very much an imitation of the hard-boiled detective, specifically of Philip Marlowe, popular creation of the man who is considered to be the best of this genre's authors, Raymond Chandler.[18]

Interestingly, two critics have alluded to the detective novel in writing their analyses of *Jazz*, but neither develops the possibility of the genre as a vehicle for Morrison's story. Eusebio Rodrigues at one point states that "[p]atiently we play detective, note the clues, make deductions about this narrator who tries to be self-effacing, never intrusive" (260), though, given the nature of the narrator, the latter evaluation is at best hard to accept. On the other hand, in his arguments for an a/gnostic reading of *Jazz*, Vincent O'Keefe calls on Catherine Belsey and William Spanos, who compare conventional realism to detective stories whose aim is to "dispel magic and mystery, to make everything explicit, accountable, subject to scientific analysis" (Belsey, 111; qtd. in O'Keefe, 332). Spanos proposes "the anti-detective story, the formal purpose of which is to evoke the impulse to 'detect' – to track down the secret cause – in order to violently frustrate this impulse by refusing to solve the crime" (40; qtd. in O'Keefe, 332-333), but O'Keefe feels that *Jazz* "does not fit neatly into Spanos's definition of anti-detective fiction" (333). Obviously he

---

[18] Sigelman and Jocoby state that Chandler is "widely regarded as the foremost writer of hard-boiled detective fiction" (12); Silet notes that Chandler was the first crime writer to be honored by the Library of America series (101).

is correct in this assertion in that the "crime" – the murder of Dorcas – is "solved" on the first two pages of the book (we know immediately that Joe is the perpetrator), but he misses the implications of Morrison's using the detective genre to tell another kind of story.

Moreover, Grewal (133) and O'Keefe emphasize the importance of tracking and trails while Page asserts that Hunter's Hunter, Lestory, is a synecdoche for the story of tracking (58), though they link these terms with game hunting and not with a detective, and certainly the repetition of the word "trace" could allude to clues. Jill Matus remarks that jazz itself "became a *symbol of crime,* feeble-mindedness, insanity and sex and was under constant attack by the press from the early 1920's on" (139; emphasis added). The similarities of Morrison's novel with crime fiction, however, has gone unnoticed.

In fact, using the detective novel as foundation text is a brilliant choice: a paradoxical epigraph in the form of a riddle gives way to a genre that develops a "puzzle-oriented story" (Gregory, 15). Willard Huntington Wright[19] even contends that "[t]he detective novel does not fall under the head of fiction in the ordinary sense, but belongs rather in the category of riddles; it is, in fact, a complicated and extended puzzle cast in fictional form" (in Haycraft; qtd. in Steele, 563). And a logical choice at that: the kernel of the plot for *Jazz* around which the story/stories whirl is indeed Joe's murder of Dorcas and Violet's attempt to desecrate her corpse. It is a shrewd choice as well,[20] for Morrison has often insisted on the need for an active participation on the part of the reader; indeed, this is one of the major attributes of a good storyteller: the reader/listener must work hard imaginatively to fill in the gaps. David Lodge writes that the meaning

> inheres in the hermeneutic process itself: the reader's activity in interpreting and making sense of the story, responding to the clues and cues provided by the text, constantly readjusting a provisional interpretation in the light of new knowledge, re-enacts the efforts of the characters to make sense of their own lives. (Lodge, 162)

(And, as I am of the opinion that the author can be wonderfully playful in her strategies, it may just well be a snare/challenge for "professional literary critics" as well.)

That Morrison should choose crime fiction as a starting point seems clear. But why the hard-boiled detective novel and not the classic detective story? Why Marlowe and not Coffin Ed Smith or Gravedigger Jones? Why Chandler and not Chester Himes? In order to understand these choices and then analyze Morrison's use and reversal of their rather stringent norms, we must look to the characteristics of the detective novel and its development from the classic or traditional mode to the tough-guy story.

The classic detective story is generally acknowledge to have begun with Edgar Allan Poe's "Murders in the Rue Morgue," and "stresses careful plotting and even more careful

---

[19] Wright was the author of the Philo Vance novels under the pseudonym of S.S. Van Dine.

[20] "[A]lthough the fictional detective is the most obvious example of a reader's insisting upon his own more symmetrical assertions about a less symmetrical case, he is not the only one. We can of course imagine all sorts of motives that might produce such behavior. Some of these would reflect – as does the example of the detective – an occupational necessity for this way of reading, as in certain forms of professional literary criticism. But the essential point here is that such assertive reading is a quite special kind of reading, and a logical response only to a quite special 'text'" (Guetti, 153).

attention to its own rules. [...] [W]e may be fooled by the author but we can never be lied to" (Gregory, 15-16). G.K. Chesterton's "How to Write a Detective Story" sets out five basic principles which could be very briefly summarized as clarity, simplicity, familiarity, common sense and artistic consistency, to which Gregory adds a belief in " the ultimate triumph of reason" (16).[21]

In the classic detective story, moreover (Christie, Doyle, Queen, etc.), crimes and their solutions are played out in an (often English) "upper-crust" milieu in which the environment does not greatly impinge upon the rationale for the unveiling of the murderer. Crime-solving is simply an intellectual game, "not only a purely intellectual mode of knowing events, but a puzzle in which the faculties of analysis are to be exercised" (Jameson, 644). In the 1920s and 1930s, however, and on the other side of the Atlantic, the detective genre was being radically altered, first in the dime-novel series entitled "Black Mask," edited by Joseph Shaw in its hey-day, and then in the work of the writers who transformed and popularized the so-called "hard-boiled detective" novel: Erle Stanley Gardner (creator of Perry Mason), Dashiell Hammet (famous for Sam Spade) and Raymond Chandler, whose legacy in Philip Marlowe has touched almost every writer of crime fiction thereafter, including Chester Himes (see Nolan, 408-416).

According to Gregory, the rules for the classic detective novel "can be almost completely rewritten to fit the hard-boiled story":

1. The aim of the story is not towards illumination at the end. The story is written "for the many preliminary moments" (Chandler).
2. The soul of hard-boiled detective fiction is very often complexity rather than simplicity. The world of corruption and evil is complex and pervasive.
3. The guilty party may be as familiar as the detective's client or as obscure as the chauffeur's landlady.
4 ... the artistic consistency of the story does not hinge on who did it.
5. Like the traditional detective story, "a tale has to be founded on truth," but what the hard-boiled writer sees as truth may be – and often is – entirely different from what the classical writer sees. (Gregory, 19-20)

In Gregory's view, what can be deduced from this "re-writing" of the classic rules is "hard-boiled fiction's lack of rules and its open-ended form":

Just as the hard-boiled detective disregards the rules, he also disavows the classical detective's faith in reason. Although he is not stupid, his primary talents are not mental, and he rarely demonstrates the analytical powers of a Hercule Poirot or a Sherlock Holmes. He finally figures out the crime by forcing his way through a problem whose boundaries are constantly shifting. The pattern is one of ever-increasing complexity; the simple murder at the beginning of the story is wholly absorbed by the

---

[21] "[E]very solution must come solely through the application of the detective's intellect; thus, one of the form's strictest prohibitions is that chance or luck must play no significant part in the solving of the crime. [...T]he good person's capacity for ratiocination and for placing the world in order is stronger than the bad one's capacity to disrupt. [...] This belief in the power of reason is correlated with the classical detective's belief in essential order: [...] the shared understanding between author and reader that the crime is an individual aberration and is not symptomatic of a whole society" (Gregory, 17).

> end into a larger scheme with unsettling implications about the nature of our world. The detective learns much more than the identity of the murderer. His knowledge is not so much a product of reason as it is the result of the detective's personal involvement with the case.   (Gregory, 20)

Ratiocination no longer plays a major role in this novel and the world is no longer an orderly place in which crime is an aberration. In hard-boiled fiction the "criminal act is the norm." Just as importantly, the genre is transformed in setting, in language and in "an ethical code that replaces a pre-war sense of objective propriety with a post-war relativism." It establishes itself as "an urban genre whose big city atmosphere pervades the work until the city itself becomes almost a character" (22). Indeed, Frederic Jameson even remarks that "the real content of these books is an almost scenic one: the motels and college towns of the American landscape" (626).[22]

There is no question but that in *Jazz* the City is so vividly alive that it takes on the status of character. Morrison never even mentions Harlem by name, but the descriptions of the streets and avenues, the names of squares and restaurants and the exuberant vigor of the locale leave no doubt as to her setting, the Mecca of black people in the 1920s. The city that has been most vividly reproduced in the work of Chandler, Hammet and Gardner is Los Angeles, however, so if we are looking for a model of a black detective in a "black" city, the most obvious reference would initially be Chester Himes, whose Harlem detectives described the city and its inhabitants memorably. Himes, like Morrison, uses direct textual references to events of the day – the Civil Rights protests and marches, the names of its leaders, for example – though the time-frame is obviously very different. Beyond this "cosmetic" difference, however, Morrison differs from her predecessor in that she deals in *Jazz* with ordinary people, not with the rougher low-life, and that, while there is indeed a great deal of violence in her novel, there is no gore; sex is erotic, but not pornographic or explicit. E. M. Beekman writes that in Himes's novels "violence has a quality of grim delight here, born of a barely repressed hatred" (170). Even though her novel can be classified as a "postmodern" text as can Himes' detective works, Morrison adheres to a certain code of writing more appropriate to the age in which her novel is set in which "explicit sex and strong profanity were taboo" (Sigelman & Jacoby, 18).

Himes first novel, *If He Hollers Let Him Go* (1945), now heralded as a classic of African America fiction, was early dismissed as "social protest" and indeed owes much directly to Richard Wright's *Native Son* (1941), to which his protagonist Bob Jones makes specific reference on pages 87 to 88 of the novel.[23] In fact, however, "the story is related in the hard-boiled, tough-guy style familiar to students of the detective novel of the 1930s and 1940s" (Hodges, vii) and is set in Los Angeles. Himes' indebtedness to the golden age of this type of detective fiction is evident:

---

[22] Sinda Gregory notes that "Chicago and New York were, of course, perfect locations for the hard-boiled stories because of their history of corruption and crime and their reputation for toughness and grit. Yet California, and especially Los Angeles, has produced the most vivid sense of place in the hard-boiled fiction set there.

"But whether Los Angeles or San Francisco or Chicago or New York is the locale, the presence of the city is always felt. It is a perfect physical counterpart to the chaos, the lack of communal feeling, and the loneliness that seem endemic in the private eye's world" (22-23).

[23] Lillian Smith's *Strange Fruit* is also discussed in this drawing room conversation.

Himes's scorching prose is softened by his juxtaposition of descriptions of the people and the terrain of Los Angeles in those times. Through Jones's eyes, we are given a street tour of L.A.'s bars, restaurants, fast-food joints, and party scenes in nearly photographic detail. The novel is a Baedecker of high and low, white and black Angelino life during the 1940's. (Hodges, ix)

Indeed, Morrison "tips her hat" to Himes in a subtle manner in the middle of her book (see below). Nevertheless, while Himes may be a "presence" in the conception of *Jazz*, there are many more reasons to look at a more direct predecessor in Raymond Chandler.

Though Chandler published his first novel, *The Big Sleep,* in 1939, the *description* of Los Angeles in his crime novels is actually of the city during the 1920s when he himself had settled there.[24] Just as Morrison looks back on the Harlem Renaissance with a full understanding of what it meant for the history of African Americans, Chandler looked back on Los Angeles from the point of view in which "the forces that had shaped the Southern California of his mature years [...] could be seen whole." This era in westward movement has been called by some "the greatest internal migration in the history of the United States."[25]

Jazz, too, is set at the time of the culmination of the Great Migration North:

The wave of black people running from want and violence crested in the 1870s; the '80s; the '90s but was a steady stream in 1906 when Joe and Violet joined it. Like the others, they were country people, but how soon country people forget. (*J*, 33)

The urge to forge a new life, a new identity, was as strong in the new arrivals as their desire to forget the past. When Violet asks a neighbor about the Dumfrey women who have not answered the door, she is surprised to learn that they are from Tennesee:

"They need to move on back to Memphis then if daylight is what they want."
"Memphis? I thought they were born here."
"That's what they'd have you believe. But they ain't. Not even Memphis. Cottown. Someplace nobody ever heard of."
"I'll be," said Violet. She was very surprised because the Dumfrey women were graceful citified ladies whose father owned a store on 136th Street, and themselves had nice paper-handling jobs [...]
"They don't like it known" the woman went on. "Why?" asked Violet.
"Hincty, that's why [...] (*J*, 18-19)

David Smith writes that for his part

Chandler would remember these lost souls' cultural deprivation by turning them into

---

[24] Chandler had actually settled in Los Angeles permanently in 1919.

[25] "Distinct by generation, by geographical origin and sociological remove, the immigrants shared the adventure of cultural flux which was compounded of romance and reality, of chicanery and idealism, of a lost past and a projected future, in almost equal measure. [...] Their urban existence was an implicit rejection of their rooted past" (Smith, 424 & 426).

victims [...] the malicious gossip of *Farewell, My Lovely* (1940) is not, as Marlowe surmises, from Sioux Falls, South Dakota, but she is from Mason City, Iowa, where "we had a nice home once, me and George. Best there was" (*FML*, 425).[26]

Both authors, then, focus on "ordinary lives" rather than the flashy well-know celebrities of the age, and their narrators belong to this social milieu as well. Nickerson calls Philip Marlowe "an uncommon common man" (101). Just as Morrison makes many explicit though secondary references to the social injustices of black life at the time, so Chandler makes oblique reference to the fraud and bribery rampant in Southern California. His only allusion to the water scandal of the 1920s in *Farewell, My Lovely*, for example, is the caustic comment that they "brought the water to the Sunny Southland and used it to have a flood with" (*FML*, 172).[27]

Though in Chandler's novels the murderer is always a woman and in *Jazz* it is Joe Trace, in all of them the motives for the crime and the chosen weapon fit "the realities of violence in America: shooting is first, with the handgun the preferred weapon, and bludgeoning or stabbing second. [...] Greed, fear of exposure, and jealousy dominate" as motives (Nikerson, 125 & 126). Joe, of course, murders Dorcas with a handgun out of jealousy, having pawned his hunting rifle. In works by both authors the war is only a backdrop to the narrative in that it frames both a time and a psychological mood: "Alone, yes, but top-notch and indestructible – like the City in 1926 when all the wars are over and there will never be another one" (*J*, 7); "About a hundred yards away from the dam a rope with cork floats barred the pleasure boats from coming any closer. Beyond these details the war did not seem to have done anything much to Puma Lake" (Chandler, *LL*, 19). Even though the action is very much located in the present era of the novel, the 1920s, the importance of the past is pervasive. Many, many critics signal this importance in *Jazz* (Badt, 571; Barnes, 293; Burton, 180; Grewal, 130; Matus, 130; Mayberry, 75; Page, 56), and Margaret B. Wilkerson's comment is a typical response:

> The black people who form her subject matter live on the periphery of large, productive towns and are marginal to the lives of white people. Yet Morrison's focus on their lives reveals a tapestry of attitudes, beliefs, delusions, and fears that tie them to a fertile and sometimes confusing past. In each novel, retrospective (character's memory and perspective) provides more than exposition, and is often deliberately withheld in order to create mystery and suspense which slowly build the tension in the story or plot line. Thus the past is given a crucial role to play – context and motivation for action in present time. (Wilkerson, 183-184)

---

[26] It is delightful to note that the name of this "malicious gossip" is precisely "Mrs. Morrison."

[27] David Smith writes that "Chandler had arrived in Los Angeles in time to see William Mulholland, the city's superintendent of the Water Department, open his 233 mile aqueduct in 1912. It brought water for the growing city and allowed the bare San Fernando valley into which it directed its spout to become highly desirable, irrigated land. It did all this because, in one of the great manipulative scandals of the century, a consortium of the city's elected officials, federal surveyors, bankers, businessmen and newspaper proprietors swindled farmers in the fertile Owens Valley out of their water rights and then, through bribery and deceit, aided by newspaper silence, had public funds voted for their scheme in order to make a private killing on the apparently worthless land they had acquired in the San Fernando valley. A dam built from this crooked deal, which ruined the Owens Valley farming community by 1927, burst in 1928, drowning over 400 people in the Los Angeles area" (426-427).

Yet the past is no less important in the detective story. Marie Rodell writes that "[t]he encroachment of the present plot in the past plot is the conflict in the detective formula. The intensity and suspense involved in this structural element determines the value of a work of this kind" (62; qtd. in Ponder, 172). Anne Ponder adds that "[t]he strongest detective plot weaves past and present inextricably. The unraveling must not come solely from the detection plot but must evolve out of the past" (172). Jameson believes that "[t]he final element in Chandler's characteristic form is that the underlying crime is always old, lying half-forgotten in the pasts of the characters before the book begins" (649).

Nevertheless, in Chandler's detective novels, plot takes a secondary role; his emphasis is on atmosphere and characterization. "The hardboiled novel develops from scene to scene and pays less attention to plot. Its gritty quality allows more realistic developments, and its heroes are simpler men than the noble paper tigers of yore"(Beekman, 153). George J. Thompson agrees: "The plot is finally less important than the scenes, the end less crucial than the process" (124). Certainly the story of *Jazz*, taking its cue again from *The Bluest Eye* in which the "plot" appears in the first pages, concentrates not on what "took place," in Morrison's view, but "what happened."[28] She is interested not in fact, but in "truth," the difference being that "truth" cannot exist without the human mind whereas fact is independent. Early on we know the "facts" of the case; the development of *Jazz* focuses on the atmosphere of "the City" in the 1920s and on the characters who found themselves there at the time.

Ostensibly one might think that the major difference between *Jazz* and Chandler's novels is that in the former the "villain" is revealed on the first pages and is then demonstrated not to be a "villain" at all. That is, the solution to the crime is immediately apparent in *Jazz* whereas Chandler withholds that information until the end of his books. The "investigation" that is initiated is not to find the criminal but to satisfy Violet's need to know everything she can about Dorcas, Joe's eighteen-year-old lover and victim. Since Violet only knew that the girl was "very well thought of in the legally licensed beauty parlor," [...] "she commenced to gather the rest of the information" (*J*, 5) asking questions of the beauticians about the makeup she used and how she did her hair, what music she liked best, how she danced, what her teachers thought of her, even to the point of visiting the dead girl's aunt – all in an effort to understand why Joe needed her. Violet goes about her "careful investigations" (*J*, 28) as a detective would, but not to the same end. It is interesting to note, however, that Gregory believes that at their "most basic level," detective novels are also "allegories about the individual's search for meaning and structure" (13). Jameson concurs: "The initial deception takes place on the level of the book as a whole, in that it passes itself off as a murder mystery. In fact Chandler's stories are first and foremost descriptions of searches" (645). For his part, Joe's tracking of Dorcas is meshed with his frustrated search for his lost mother and ultimately, his "self." Violet as well is involved in a search for the "Me" her mother would have liked and "didn't stay around long enough to see" (*J*, 208). And, of course, Golden Gray is searching not only for the father who never even knew of his existence, but also for wholeness, something to reintegrate his fragmented "self" metaphorically represented as his amputated arm.

---

[28] In her "Introduction" to *Race-ing Justice, En-gendering Power*, Morrison distinguishes between the actual occurrence (what took place) and the circumstances and reasons behind what happened, which "requires multiple points of address and analysis" (xii).

Despite his status as a tough, hard-boiled detective, Philip Marlowe is repeatedly referred to as a "knight errant" (Mawer, 358-9; Ponder, 174; Sigelman & Jacoby, 18; Smith, 432),[29] a hero in a medieval romance.[30] Nikerson refers to Marlowe as a "chavalier in a Chevrolet" (101). In the narrator's envisioning of Golden Gray's state of mind as he recites to himself *his* version of having found Wild, she imagines his view of himself –

> He wants to brag about this encounter, like a **knight errant** bragging about his coolness as he unscrews the spike from the monster's heart and breathes life back into the fiery nostrils. (*J*, 154)

> [...] During the journey he worried a lot about what he looked like, what **armor** he could call on. There was nothing but his trunk and the set of his jaw. But he was ready, ready to meet the black and savage man who bothered him and abused his arm. [...]
> He thought she would be his **lance and shield**; now he would have to be his own.
> (*J*, 160; empahsis mine)

– the difference being that in this section the narrator is thinking of Gray as a liar and a hypocrite, not a true knight of noble stature. (Her attitude changes as she relates the story again immediately thereafter [see below]).

Even in the structure of Jazz we find a "throw-back" to the Chandler novels. Eckard (18), H.W. Rice (129), and Rodrigues (252) all note some of the linguistic links between the ends of Morrison's chapters (which she does not title) and the beginnings of the next, though all three see this feature as belonging to the "improvisational structure" of jazz music:

Chapter I (End):
He is married to a woman who speaks mainly to her birds. One of whom answers back: "I love you." (*J*, 24)

Chapter II (Beginning):
Or used to. When Violet threw out the birds, it left her not only without the canaries' company and the parrot's confession [...] (*J*, 27)

*****

(End):
[...]the right tune whistled in a doorway or lifting up from the circles and grooves of a record can change the weather. From freezing to hot to cool. (*J*, 51)

Chapter III (Beginning):
Like that day in July, almost nine years back, when the beautiful men were cold (*J*, 52)

---

[29] Philip Durham even titles his book *Down These Mean Streets a Man Must Go: Raymond Chandler's Knight.*

[30] Mean as the streets of Los Angeles might be, "it is also a world of quests and ordeals, of knights and fair maidens, of aging kings besieged by the forces of darkness, of magicians [...], witches [...], and mysterious 'helpers' [...]" (Mawer, 359).

*****

(End):

[...] and listened as closely to what she was saying as did the woman sitting by her ironing board in a hat in the morning. (*J*, 87)

ChapterIV (Beginning):

The hat, pushed back on her forehead, gave Violet a scatty look. (*J*, 98)

*****

(End):

[...] that it was spring. In the City. (*J*, 114)

Chapter V (Beginning):

And when spring comes to the City people notice one another in the road; (*J*, 117)

*****

(End):

" [...] And let me tell you , baby, in those days it was more than a state of mind."

(*J*, 135)

Chapter VI (Beginning):

Risky, I'd say, trying to figure out anybody's state of mind. But worth the trouble if you're like me – curious, inventive and well-informed. (*J*, 137)

*****

(End):

The boy knelt down to clean her face, slowly lifting whole patches of blood from her cheek, her nose, one eye, then the other. Golden Gray watched and he thought he was ready for those deer eyes to open. (*J*, 162)

Chapter VII (Beginning):

A thing like that could harm you thirteen years after Golden Gray stiffened himself to look at that girl, the harm she could do was still alive. (*J*, 165)

*****

(End):

But where is *she*? [Refers to Wild] (*J*, 184)

Chapter VIII (Beginning):

There she is. [Refers to Dorcas] (*J*, 187)

*****

(End):

"[...] I don't know who is that woman singing but I know the words by heart."

(*J*, 194)

Chapter IX (Beginning):
> Sweetheart. That's what that weather was called. Sweetheart weather, the prettiest day
> of the year. (*J*, 195)

*****

(End):
> " [...] I drank a lot of water so as not to hurt her feelings. It eased the pain." (*J*, 216)

Chapter X (Beginning):
> Pain. I seem to have an affection, a kind of sweettooth for it. (*J*, 219)

*****

Moreover, the phrase at the end of Chapter V repeated at the beginning of Chapter VI is a direct call to Chester Himes' *If He Hollers Let Him Go*:

> [Leighton]
> ' [...] But as far as the masses, including all of our minority groups, have achieved
> economic security, racial problems will reach a solution of their own accord.' He turned
> to me. 'Won't you agree with me to that extent, Mr. Jones?'
> 'No,' I said. **'It's a state of mind.** As long as the white folks hate me and I hate
> them we can earn the same amount of money, live side by side in the same kind of house,
> and fight every day.' (Himes, 88; emphasis mine)

Himes, however, provides no linguistic links or visible continuity here among his chapters other than strict chronology in this novel, and even in *Run, Man, Run* and *Blind Man With a Pistol* the narrative continuity is not based on this strategy. It is, however, a technique common in Chandler. Though not always reinforced by linguistic repetition, the divisions of the book into chapters in Chandler's novels seem arbitrary, the action proceeding seamlessly from one to the other, emphasized by the fact that the first paragraph of the subsequent chapter is not indented.[31]

Aside from a linking of the chapters which propels the movement rapidly forward (even as in Morrison's case, when there is a change of "voice" or a flashback to another time), reading *Jazz* against the detective novel would explain a problem in the narration. While on pages 121-129 Joe is clearly telling his story to Dorcas (set out in quotation marks as mimesis), and on pages 182-184 he is talking to himself as he looks for her, there is a (con)fusion of the addressee on page 130 as Joe speaks of Dorcas in the third person, lapsing almost unnoticeably into the second person again on the following page. The addressee of Felice's narrative (also mimesis) as she relates her own story and as much as she knows of Dorcas' is unclear (*J*, 198-216). Yet her direct speech must be "directed" at someone, possibly the narrator, who serves as listener while she relates her "confession." Jill Matus ventures that Felice is talking to herself, while other critics see these sections as "jazz solos," stretching a rather over-worked metaphor that much farther.

---

[31] Cf. this transtion from Chapter V to VI in *Farewell, My Lovely*, for example: "I went back to my car and got into it and drove back to the 77th Street Division, and climbed upstairs to Nulty's smelly little cubbyhole of an office on the second floor." "Nulty didn't seem to have moved. He sat in his chair in the same attitude of sour patience." (*FML*, 36 & 37).

If the addressee is the private investigator (the narrator) gathering information from yet another story, however, this technique of direct quotation is more coherent.

The voice of the narrator in *Jazz* has, in fact, been the subject of much discussion and in most cases has been identified either with the book itself, or with jazz music. With both these solutions there are problems, however. In relating the story of Golden Gray, for example, on the one hand, the narrator keeps changing her mind about Gray, and on the other, the features that are said to be characteristic of jazz are not found. (Even Eckard admits that "[w]hen describing rural scenes, the narrator's speech does not contain musical language or jazz imagery"; 15). The self-conscious, intrusive narrator has been around since *Tristram Shandy*, of course, and the *Jazz* narrator's insistence on controlling her own story –

> Bolts of lightning, little rivulets of thunder. And I the eye of the storm. Mourning the split trees, hens starving on rooftops. Figuring out what can be done to save them since they cannot save themselves without me because – well, it's my storm, isn't it? I break lives to prove I can mend them back again.   (*J*, 219)

– has clear antecedents in D.H. Lawrence, for example:

> O thunder-god, god of the dangerous bolts – ! – No, gentle reader, please don't interrupt, I am *not* going to open the door of Johanna's room, not until Mr. Noon opens it himself. I've been caught that way before. I have opened the door for your, and the moment you gave your first squeal in rushed the private detective you had kept in the background. Thank you, gentle reader, you can open your own doors. I am busy apostrophising Jupiter Tonans, Zeus of the Thunder-bolt, the almighty Father of passion and sheer desire. I'm not talking about *your* messy little feelings and licentiousness, either. I'm talking about desire. So don't interrupt. Am I writing this book, or are you?   (Lawrence, 137)

If it is Lawrence's fear of the private detective rushing in here, however, in *Jazz* the private investigator-narrator often takes center stage, expressing an almost narcissistic concern for herself, worried more about herself than the characters and the milieu she is describing:[32]

> I haven't got any muscles, so I can't really be expected to defend myself. But I do know how to take precaution. Mostly it's making sure no one knows all there is to know about me. Second, I watch everything and everyone and try to figure out their plans, their reasonings, long before they do. You have to understand what it's like, taking on a big city: I'm exposed to all sorts of ignorance and criminality. Still, this is the only life for me. I like the way the City makes people think they can do what they want and get away with it.   (*J*, 8)

> Risky, I'd say, trying to figure out anybody' state of mind. But worth the trouble if you're like me – curious, inventive and well-informed.   (*J*, 137)

---

[32] As Katherine J. Mayberry states, the narrator "ends up realizing herself far more successfully" than she does her characters (305).

These statements, with their allusions to secrecy, crime, and the skillfulness of the "investigator," turn out to be contradictory, of course, as the narrator herself later admits to being arrogant and unreliable (*J*, 220-221), but this ironic self-effacement, while much more elaborate in *Jazz*, is also present in Chandler's narrator:

> She misses with three shots. It seems impossible, at such short range, but there it is.
> Maybe it happens all the time. I've been around so little.   (*LL*, 67)

In a different yet related vein, the attention paid to minute details when describing the rooms, for example, is typical of a narration in which the detective must notice absolutely everything, never knowing which observation might come in useful in the future. Marlowe's first look at the mountain cabin in *Lady in the Lake* (25), the last place Kingsley had seen his wife who is now missing, is full of meticulous mental note-taking, as is his visit to the parents of a woman who died under mysterious circumstances:

> The Rossmore Arms was a gloomy pile of dark red brick built around a huge forecourt. It had a plush-lined lobby containing silence, tubbed plants, a bored canary in a cage as big as a dog-house, a smell of old carpet dust and the cloying fragrance of gardenias long ago.
> The Graysons were on the fifth floor in front, in the north wing. They were sitting together in a room which seemed to be deliberately twenty years out of date. It had fat over-stuffed furniture and brass doorknobs, shaped like eggs, a huge wall mirror in a gilt frame, a marble-topped table in the window and dark red plush side drapes by the windows. It smelled of tobacco smoke and behind that the air was telling me they had lamb chops and broccoli for dinner.[33]   (*LL*, 91)

Such a strategy is also a key feature in the first chapter of *Jazz*:

> [...] the parlor needs a struck match to see the face. Beyond are the dining room, two bedrooms, the kitchen – all situated in the middle of the building so the apartment's windows have no access to the moon or the light of a street lamp. The bathroom has the best light since it juts out past the kitchen and catches the afternoon rays. Violet and Joe have arranged their furnishings in a way that might not remind anybody of the rooms in *Modern Homemaker* but it suits the habits of the body, the way a person walks from one room to another without bumping into anything, and what he wants to do when he sits down. You know how some people put a chair or a table in a corner where it looks nice but nobody in the world is ever going to go over to it, let alone sit down there? Violet didn't do that in her place. Everything is put where a person would like to have it, or would use or need it. So the dining room doesn't have a dining table with funeral-parlor chairs. It has a big deep-down chairs and a card table by the window covered with jade, dracena and doctor plants until they want to have card games or play tonk between

---

[33] Chandler, however, had a delightful way of parodying his own scenes, turning a dialogue into a comic book version of the supposedly serious work of clue-finding and of the "tough-talk" of those involved in it. See, for example, *LL* 83 & 84.

themselves. The kitchen is roomy enough to accommodate four people eating or give a customer plenty legroom while Violet does her hair. The front room, or parlor, is not wasted either, waiting for a wedding reception to be worthy of. It has birdcages and mirrors for the birds to look at themselves in, but now, of course, there are no birds, Violet having let them out on the day she went to Dorcas' funeral with a knife. Now there are just empty cages, the lonely mirrors glancing back at them. As for the rest, it's a sofa, some carved wooden chairs with small tables by them so you can put your coffee cup or a dish of ice cream down in front of you, or if you want to read the paper, you can do it easy without messing up the folds. The mantel over the fireplace used to have shells and pretty-colored stones, but all of that is gone now and only the picture of Dorcas Manfred sits there in a silver frame waking them up all night long. (*J*, 12-13)

The immediacy of the first person narration supplying information that may or may not be pertinent to the solution of the puzzle heightens reader participation in the development of the story. [34]

Understanding the reading strategies involved in the unfolding of the detective novel, it becomes clear just why Morrison would choose such a *genre* to write a story about storytelling. The author is extremely concerned with the participation of the reader in the development of the story, which she considers to be a characteristic of true African American fiction.

> So I do a lot of revision when I write in order to clean away the parts of the book that can *only* work as print, but it also must work as a total story because that is one of the major characteristics of black literature as far as I'm concerned – it's not just have black people *in* it or having it be written by a black person, but it has to have certain kinds of fundamental characteristics (one of) which is the participation of the *other*, that is, the audience, the reader, and that you can do with a spoken story.
>
> (Morrison in Davis, 231)

> My writing expects, demands participatory reading [...] It's not just about telling the story, it's about involving the reader. (Morrison in Tate, 125)

Though in 1977 she remarked that when she writes her novels she cannot read the authors that

---

[34] James Guetti explains that "[w]e may know from information theory that the information present in any situation is proportional to the 'resistance' of that situation. We may feel 'informed' [...] because all these separate items, all these details, compose a resistance to our reading efforts, and our response to that resistance is to increase those efforts. We try harder and harder to smooth the story out, to break it down to something handier and neater than this list of details, to reduce it in volume by somehow changing its state from a mixture of separate things to a more homogeneous solution.

"It should be evident, then, that as readers of this story we shall be highly active, constantly working the prose over, altering its form, putting it together in a way that it is not together when we first encounter it. And this continual and intense activity in reading a detective story seems absolutely appropriate, because it is exactly what the fictional detective does himself. [...] This is to say that the act of reading [...] even at moments when nothing more than the furniture of an office is involved, is always an act of detection, that the itemized form of the narrative forces us energetically to manipulate it, reduce it, solve it. Like the detective himself, we must become synthesizers, and compose an agglomeration of bits and pieces, a plethora of 'information,' into something that makes mores sense to us, something more significant than a list of item after visual item" (134 & 135).

she most likes because they interfere with her own creative process and that she has to "read detective stories or things like that " (in Steptoe, 23), clearly all that evasive reading simply settled into her repertoire of styles and strategies for a later and very effective use in *Jazz*.

There is yet another, more "theoretical" reason why the detective novel is an appropriate *genre* for exploring storytelling and language. In his essay entitled "Forms of Time and of the Chronotope in the Novel: Notes toward a Historical Poetics," Mikhail M. Bakhtin posits a theory of the development of the novel, locating its origins in literary works as far back as the ancient Greeks. The major *genres* of the epoch were epic, mythic, and public, the language of literature represented the public man, and its discourse was one and the same as the ruling mythos.

> In general, the ancient world did not succeed in generating forms and unities that were adequate to the private individual and his life. Although personal life had already become private and persons individualized, although this sense of the private had begun to infiltrate literature in ancient times, still, it was able to develop forms adequate to itself only in the minor, lyrico-epic and in the small everyday genres, the comedy and the novela of common life. In the major genres the private life of an individualized person was only externally and inadequately arrayed, and, therefore, in forms that were inorganic and normalistic, either public and bureaucratic or public and rhetorical.
>
> (Bakhtin, *Dialogic*; 110)

There are, however, early signs of the future "privatization" of literature, which will eventually characterize what we denominate the novel, in what Bakhtin calls "the adventure novel of everyday life," particularly in the *Satyricon* of Petronius and *The Golden Ass* of Apuleius (which has survived in its entirety). What is of particular interest at this point is that the protagonist of the latter work, Lucius, is punished by being turned into an ass, thereby becoming a silent observer of the lives going on around him. This is an important literary event because "[t]he position of an ass is a particularly convenient one for observing the secrets of everyday life. The presence of an ass embarrasses no one, all open up completely," enabling Lucius to relate "novelistically" the foibles and lifestyles of the individual members of the community, not just the public voice:

> The everyday life that Lucius observes and studies is an *exclusively personal and private life*. By its very nature there can be nothing *public* about it All its events are the personal affairs of isolated people: they could not occur "in the eyes of the world," publicly, in the presence of a *chorus*. These events are not liable to public reckoning on the open square. Events acquire a public significance as such only when they become cries. The **criminal act** is a moment of private life that becomes, as it were, *involuntarily* public. The remainder of this life is made up of bedroom secrets (infidelities on the part of shrewish wives, husbands' impotence and so forth), secret profiteering, petty everyday fraud, etc. (Bakhtin, *Dialogic*; 122; bold type mine)

According to Bakhtin, in ancient literature there was no necessity of placing a person (or animal, as in the case of Lucius) to eavesdrop because it was a genre of public man and public life.

44

> But when the private individual and private life entered literature [...] *A contradiction developed between the public nature of the literary form and the private nature of its content.* The process of working out private genres began. [...]
>
> The quintessentially private life that entered the novel at this time was, by its very nature and as opposed to public life, *closed.* In essence one could only **spy** and **eavesdrop** on it. The literature of private life is essentially a literature of snooping about, of **overhearing** "how others live."   (Bakhtin, *Dialogic*; 123)

> In the subsequent history of the novel, the criminal trial – in its direct and oblique forms – and legal-criminal categories in general have an enormous organizational significance. **Crimes** play a correspondingly huge and significant role in the actual content of such novels.[35]   (Bakhtin, *Dialogic*; 124; bold type mine)

If, as I propose, Toni Morrison is exploring the ways and means of storytelling, the selection of a *genre* that Bakhtin locates at the very origins of the development of the novel form is a perfect vehicle for the telling of precisely that story.[36]

Apart from the fact that Joe murders his lover and that Morrison's novel relates all sort of "secret activities" of other characters, there are other similarities between this "adventure novel of everyday life" described by Bakhtin[37] and *Jazz.* The themes that Bakhtin locates in this type of early novelistic manifestation, *"metamorphosis (transformation)* — particularly human transformation — and *identity* (particularly human identity), [...] are drawn from the treasury of pre-class world folklore. The folkloric image of man is intimately bound up with transformation and identity. This combination may be seen with particular clarity in the popular folktale" (*Dialogic*, 111-112). Joe Trace, an image of the folk transposed from rural to urban U.S., describes himself specifically in terms of his metamorphosis on pages 123 to 129 of *Jazz* when he talks about becoming "new" seven times[38]: "You could say I've been a new Negro all my live. But all I lived through, all I seen, and not one of those changes prepared me for her. For Dorcas" (*J*, 129). His detailed description of the changes in his life makes Joe almost a prototype for the type of protagonist Bakhtin says is representative of the early everyday adventure novel:

---

[35] Yet Bakhtin goes on to say that "the criminal material itself is not essential for Apuleius; what matters are the everyday secrets of private life that lay bare human nature — that is, everything that can be only spied and eavesdropped upon" (*Dialogic*, 124).

[36] After all, she herself has stated that she is not given to writing other modes of literary expression because she is "trying to perfect the novel form" (Wilkerson, 179).

[37] "At its center is obscenity, that is, the seamier side of sexual love, love alienated from reproduction from a progression of generations, from the structures of the family and the clan. Here everyday life is priapic, its logic is the logic of obscenity. But around this sexual nucleus of common life (infidelity, sexually motivated murder, etc.) are distributed other everyday aspects: violence, thievery, various types of fraud, beatings" (Bakhtin, *Dialogic*, 128).

[38] Though seven is a magic number in the African American tradition, it may also refer to Dante's seven circles of Purgatory in his *Divine Comedy*. These seven changes – though with presumably little progress –, however, occur *before* Joe has met Dorcas, instigating the most profound change in him (number eight), and presumably he changes again when he kills her, throwing him into Dante's nine circles of Hell. His subsequent "redemption" would make ten changes, bringing the reference to Morrison's, if not Dante's, *Paradise* of reconciliation and "blessedness." Tellingly, the insistent number in Morrison's following novel, *Paradise*, is nine, not ten.

> Metamorphosis serves as the basis for a method of portraying the whole of an individual's life in its more important moments of *crisis*: for showing *how an individual becomes other than what he was*. We are offered various sharply differing images of one and the same individual, images that are united in him as various epochs and stages in the course of his life. There is no evolution in the strict sense of the word; what we get, rather, is crisis and rebirth. (Bakhtin, *Dialogic*; 115)

In this sense Bakhtin's sense of sequence (or chronology) in the earliest form of the novel is also applicable to Joe:

> Thus we see that the adventure sequence, governed as it is by chance, is here utterly subordinated to the other sequence that encompasses and interprets it: guilt→ punishment→ redemption→ blessedness. This sequence is governed by a completely different logic, one that has nothing to do with adventure logic. It is an active sequence determining (as its first priority) the very metamorphosis itself, that is, the shifting appearance of the hero. (Bakhtin, *Dialogic*, 118)

Joe's remorse – "Don't get me wrong. This wasn't -Violet's fault. All of it's mine. All of it. I'll never get over what I did to that girl. Never" (*J*, 129) – becomes his own punishment:

> There was never anyone to prosecute him because nobody actually saw him do it, and the dead girl's aunt didn't want to throw money to helpless lawyers or laughing cops when she knew the expense wouldn't improve anything. Besides, she found out that the man who killed her niece cried all day and for him and for Violet that is as bad as jail. (*J*, 4)

Redemption finally appears in the figure of Felice, together with the acceptance by both Joe and Violet of their own faults; the novel itself ends on a note of "blessedness" not found in a typical detective story:

> Breathing and murmuring under covers both of them have washed and hung out on the line, in a bed they chose together and kept together nevermind one leg was propped on a 1916 dictionary, and the mattress, curved like a preacher's palm asking for witnesses in His name's sake, enclosed them each and every night and muffled their whispering, old-time love. They are under the covers because they don't have to look at themselves anymore; there is no stud's eye, no chippie glance to undo them. They are inward toward the other [...]" (*J*, 228)

Even the narrator of *Jazz* fits Bakhtin's description of character-types[39] who can observe the private life of others without their concern or without becoming involved:

> This is the *philosophy of a person who knows only private life and craves it alone*, but

---

[39] Besides the ass, Bakhtin lists the rogue, the tramp, the servant, an adventurer, a parvenue, an actor, the prostitute and the courtesan (*Dialogic*, 125 & 126).

who does not participate in it, who has no place in it – and therefore sees it in sharp focus, as a whole, in all its nakedness, playing out all its roles but not fusing his identity with any one of them.   (Bakhtin, *Dialogic*, 126)

Philip Marlowe might muse over the possibility of house slippers and a stable home life, and even may, as in *Farewell, My Lovely*, be tempted by a love interest, but participation in "normal life" is not an option for the private investigator. In much the same way, the narrator of *Jazz* muses at the end of the novel, "I envy them their public love. I myself have only known it in secret, shared it in secret and longed, aw longed to show it – to be able to say out loud what they have no need to say at all [...]" (*J*, 229). Nevertheless, it must be pointed out that at this point this narrator has "lost control" of her characters, admitting that she has not been so private an eye as she thought:

> I thought I knew them and wasn't worried that they didn't really know about me. Now it's clear why they contradicted me at every turn: they knew me all along. Out of the corners of their eyes they watched me. And when I was feeling most invisible, being tight-lipped, silent and unobservable, they were whispering about me to each other. They knew how little I could be counted on; how poorly, how shabbily my know-it-all self covered helplessness. That when I invented stories about them – and doing it seemed to me so fine – I was completely in their hands, managed without mercy. I thought I'd hidden myself so well as I watched them through windows and doors, took every opportunity I had to follow them, to gossip about and fill in their lives, and all the while they were watching me. Sometimes they even felt sorry for me and just thinking about their pity I want to die.   (*J*, 220)

Morrison's inversion of the position of the narrator/narrated here is one more incidence of her subversion of her readers' expectations. After all, it is the private investigator in the crime novel who has access to knowledge (gnosis) and is meant to reveal it to the rest of us. Yet what this particular "confession" does is to call attention once again to the process of the narration itself. After all, as the narrator has admitted to arrogance and confusion by this time, why or how should she know, and why should we as readers believe, that the characters "feel sorry" for her? Moreover, this conceit will only work if, as argued above, the mimetic direct speech (Joe and Felice in particular) is produced as part of their own "confessions" for the narrator as addressee. Otherwise, there is no indication at all in the text that the characters actually knew anything at all about this "narrator as character."

Notwithstanding all these "co-incidences" and "contra-dictions" in the conception and development of the crime novel, perhaps what Toni Morrison and Raymond Chandler have most in common is their overriding concern with language, with getting it right. For Morrison,

> the best part of it all, the absolutely most delicious part, is finishing it and then doing it over. That's the thrill of a lifetime for me: if I can just get done with that first phase and then have infinite time to fix it and change it. I rewrite a lot, over and over again, so that it looks like I never did. I try to make it look like I never touched it, and that takes a lot of time and a lot of sweat.   (Morrison, "Site"; 2000)

Chandler, too, was distinguished by his preoccupation with "getting it right," and although he wrote only seven novels, he "continued to shape each of his tales with careful exactness, endlessly revising to achieve a final polished draft" (Nolan, 414). Sigelman and Jacoby write that "[i]t is as a stylist that Chandler is acknowledged by all concerned to have been pivotal" (13) and acknowledge his "status as a master of dialogue in general and of the sardonic wisecrack in particular" (22). And it is this preoccupation with language and with style that mark him as an outstanding writer, one that continues to draw readers and serious critics to his work.[40] For Jameson, "it was his distance from the American language that gave him the chance to use it as he did," and likens him to Nabokov: "the writer of an adopted language is already a kind of stylist by force of circumstance. Language can never again be unselfconscious for him; words can never again be unproblematical" (625).[41]

The same fascination with language is also everywhere apparent in Morrison's work, and indeed is a key characteristic of what she considers to be "black" language. What is important to her is

> making a statement on a kind of language, a way to get to what was felt and meant. I always hated with a passion when writers rewrote what black people said, in some kind of phonetic alphabet that was inapplicable to any other regional pronunciation. There is something different about [black] language, as there is about any cultural variation of English, but it's not saying "dis" and "dat." It is the way words are put together, the metaphors, the rhythm, the music – that's the part of the language that is distinctly black to me when I hear it. (Morrison in Ruas, 96)

More than any other of her novels, *Jazz* foregrounds this delight with the possibilities of language, not least in the long "arias" spoken by the narrator (see below).

For David Smith, Chandler's Philip Marlowe is the "urban *flâneur* of Walter Benjamin put onto wheels and given, via a language pieced together as a mosaic from clichés and current idioms, the illusions of control" (436), which is a very interesting analogy when we consider that Gurleen Grewal also draws the same conclusion, but for the narrator of Jazz:

> The anonymous narrator of *Jazz* recalls the *flaneur* (French for *city stroller)* whom Walter Benjamin invoked in his reading of Baudelaire's nineteenth-century Paris. To the leisurely *flaneur*, the city reveals itself in its many capricious forms. The narrator in *Jazz*, captivated by the romance of the city, "watch[es] everything and everyone" (8) [...] Appropriate to the urban spirit of jazz, the novel is interspersed with solos of pure *flanerie*: "I'm crazy about this City" (7) "I like the way the City makes people think they

---

[40] Timothy Steele writes that "[t]he detective story occupies an unusual position among species of popular literature in that it has consistently attracted the attentions of many serious readers and critics" (568). According to Beekman, Chandler's diction is a mixture of colloquial and poetic language, producing a style which is never purely realistic yet always concrete. [...] This is a hallmark of the American style, of course, from Melville to Hemingway: a direct style of communication which is clear and precise without sacrificing poetic beauty (159). (For a summary of Chandler's own views on style, see Calvo, 70.)

[41] Though Chandler was born in the United States, "he spent his school years, from the age of eight, in England, and had an English Public School Education" (Jameson, 625).

can do what they want and get away with it" for "it is there to back and frame you no matter what you do" (9).   (Grewal, 125)

Although Grewal, like so many other critics, intends to draw jazz music into her interpretation of the language, these precise examples feed more readily into the comparison with the detective novel. Consider also the fact that in the first chapter of the novel, in addition to the insistence on "legal" and the metaphorical use of words like "sneak,"[42] Morrison uses the word "frame" (a staple in crime fiction vocabulary) no fewer than four times in the space of eight pages, far too many to be coincidental in the writing of an author so concerned with her use of language:

> Do what you please in the City, it is there to back and frame[43] you no matter what you
> do.   (*J*, 8-9)

> The mantel over the fireplace used to have shells and pretty-colored stones, but all of
> that is gone now and only the picture of Dorcas Manfred sits there in a silver frame
> waking them up all night long.[44]   (*J*, 13)

> And while she sprinkles the collar of a white shirt her mind is at the bottom of the bed
> where the leg, broken clean away from the frame, is too split to nail back.[45]   (*J*, 16)

> [...]and both of them stand in the door frame a moment while the borrower repeats for
> the lender a funny conversation [...]   (*J*, 16)

Like Morrison, Chandler "cared about the choice of words, the rhythm of a sentence, the building of a paragraph, the architecture of a scene and the composition of a novel" (Beekman, 156), and he is famous for his dead-pan irony, startling similes and understated metaphors. "Marlowe's wit is his weapon [...] he actually meets threats of all kinds with his ability to rephrase them" (Guetti, 139), an attribute easily comparable with African Americans' use of

---

[42] "The sun sneaks into the ally behind them" (*J*, 8).

[43] Pam Morris also uses the word to illustrate Bakhtin's theory of "alterity": "In ['Author and Hero in Aesthetic Activity'] it was the author's condition of outsidedness which allowed him to visualize the hero as a unified image *framed* against the surrounding world. The existence of heteroglossia constituted of multiple social discourses allows speakers to achieve a similar position of outsidedness to a language. It is possible to recognize the ideological contours of one social discourse by outlining it against other discourses. In this way any monologic truth claims made by one social language will be relativized by the existence of other views of the world" (p. 16; emphasis added). "This ever-present *excess* of my seeing, knowing and possessing in relation to any other human being, is founded in the uniqueness and irreplaceability of my place in the world" (23; qtd in Morris, 16). In the quote from *Jazz*, it is the City as character that provokes this alterity. The use of "frame" is thus "double-voiced," calling simultaneously to detective fiction and to Bakhtin's theory of the self and the "other."

[44] Note that Chandler, in the description of the room cited above, has also placed a mirror in a "gilt frame" (homophone of "guilt" frame), both words belonging to the semantic field of crime fiction (see page 42 of this text).

[45] The broken bed frame, though not specifically mentioned, turns up again on page 228 of *Jazz* in reference to its being propped up on a 1916 dictionary (see page 52 of this text), possibly the linguistic underpinning of the frame of the novel itself.

language. His sardonic comments[46] are at times turned even on himself:

> Nobody yelled or ran out of the door. Nobody blew a police whistle. Everything was quiet and sunny and calm. No cause for excitement whatever. It's only Marlowe, finding another body. He does it rather well by now. Murder-a-day Marlowe, they call him. They have the meat wagon following him around to follow up on the business he finds.
>
> > A nice enough fellow, in an ingenuous sort of way. (*LL*, 68)

> My face was stiff with thought, or with something that made my face stiff. (*HW*, 26)

David Smith believes that "Chandler turned to a highly-wrought language because he needed a snare to entrap a complex, specific reality that was, in its material existence, insupportable if human integrity was to be preserved" (438). Chandler's use of irony inevitably bring a smile of recognition to the reader's face, a chuckle even. Randall Mawer writes,

> More than anything else, Chandler took *language* seriously. – Virtually everything he wrote, especially early in his career, attests to that fact – the deftly impressionistic descriptions, the truly heard dialogues, the glittering similes, the flatness of tone maintained so strenuously as to suggest much left unsaid. His overall style is necessarily exaggerated, mannered; knowing it to be so, Chandler sometimes pushed it across the bounds of verisimilitude, into a studied playfulness which becomes a part of the style it mocks. (Mawer, 356)

On the other hand, Morrison's use of irony is part of what she considers to be "a black style":

> I can't really explain what makes the irony of Black people different from anybody else's, and maybe there isn't any, but in trying to write what I call Black literature [...] there seems to be something distinctive about it and I can't put it into critical terms. I can simply recognize it as authentic. Any irony is the mainstay. Other people call it humor. It's not really that [...] And taking that which is peripheral, or violent or doomed or something that nobody else can see any value in and making value out of it or having a psychological attitude about duress is part of what made us stay alive and fairly coherent, and irony is a part of that – being able to see the underside of something, as well. (In Jones & Vinson, 175)

Like Chandler's Marlowe, irony seems to be a survival strategy, a way for a clear "underdog" to overcome extreme odds or even tragedy. As the narrator remarks of Joe's murder of Dorcas on the first page of *Jazz*: "He fell for an eighteen-year-old girl with one of those deepdown, spooky loves that made him so sad and happy he shot her just to keep the feeling going"(*J*, 3). Or of Violet's mother, Rose Dear, who committed suicide by drowning:

---

[46] "A siren whined far off, growing louder with great surges of sound. Tires screamed at a corner, and the siren wail died to a metallic growl, then to silence, and the tires screamed again in front of the house. The Bay City police conserving rubber" (*LL*, 82) .

> Slowly but steadily, for about four years, True Belle got things organized. And then Rose Dear jumped in the well and missed all the fun. [...]
> For Rose Dear he brought a silk embroidered pillow to comfort her back on a sofa nobody ever had, but would have been real nice under her head in the pine box – if only he'd been on time. (*J*, 99)

> Maybe it was that: knowing her daughters were in good hands, better hands than her own, at last, and Rose Dear was free of time that no longer flowed, but stood stock-still when they tipped her from her kitchen chair. So she dropped herself down the well and missed all the fun. (*J*, 102)

The absence of Violet's father and the appropriation of Rose Dear's property are explained in understated, unemotional language which drips with irony:

> When she got there all that was left, aside from some borrowed pallets and the clothes on their backs, was the paper Rose's husband had signed saying they could – that the men had the right to do it and, I suppose, the duty to do it, if the rain refused to rain, or if stones of ice fell from the sky instead and cut the crop down to its stalks. Nothing on the paper about the husband joining a party that favored niggers voting. (*J*, 138)

Sometimes the irony is just an offhand comment on human nature, as in Felice's sardonic remark about her friend:

> "Nobody ever caught Dorcas looking for work, but she worked hard scheming money to give Acton things." (*J*, 203)

Or the narrator's acute observation of the nosey Malvonne as she comes across a letter from "Hot Steam" written to "Daddy":

> Perspiring and breathing lightly, Malvonne forced herself to read the letter several times. (*J*, 44)

Joe's ironic comment on the lessons he learned from Hunter's Hunter, however, lends itself to two different readings:

> Taught me two lessons I lived by all my life. One was the secret of kindness from whitepeople – they had to pity a thing before they could like it. The other – well, I forgot it. (*J*, 125)

Although the superficial reading of these lines seems to indicate that Joe has forgotten what he was explaining, in truth the other lesson – not to hurt the young or the female – was what he forgot, leading to tragedy.

Chandler uses metaphor to reinforce the idea of his own rather powerless but highly individualistic position in a society founded on corruption and deceit. E.M. Beekman notes particularly the scene in Chapter 31 of *Farewell, My Lovely,* in which Philip Marlowe notices a little bug crawling across the desk of the investigation police officer, trying to find a way out.[47] Later Marlowe even likens himself to the bug in his dogged determinedness to overcome incredible odds: "I was a pink-headed bug crawling up the side of the City Hall" (*FML*, 272). Beekman also mentions the description in the same novel of a calendar which "serves as an indirect metaphor for his gritty, seedy world, and for his hero who will not bow to its malice," (162) and the greenhouse and the old colonel in *The Big Sleep,* which are "metaphors for claustrophobic artificiality and for a life that is a parasitic death"(163).

Morrison's metaphorical passages are often more lyrical, particularly when she ventures into the past of her characters, into the South. In her imagining of the conflicting emotions of Golden Gray as he searches for his unknown father, the narrator compares his pampered "self" to a flower ready to bloom with all its consequences:

> He needs courage for that, but he has it. He has the courage to do what Duchesses of Marlborough do all the time: relinquish being an adored bud clasping its future, and dare to open wide, to let the layers of its petals go flat, show the cluster of stamens dead center for all to see.   (*J*, 160)

She sees the power born of self-confidence that "flicks like a razor and then hides":

> But once the razor blade has flicked – he will remember it, and if her remembers it he can recall it. That is to say, he has it at his disposal.   (*J*, 161)

The open flower, a pastoral image, eloquently depicts Gray's vulnerability as he faces the consequences of his new-found life as the son of a black man; the power resides in a street image of hidden brutality, ready to snap at a moment's notice. But the sharp blade also calls to the previous metaphor of the father Gray never knew he had as an amputated arm:

> Only now, he thought, now that I know I have a father, do I feel his absence: the place where he should have been and was not. Before, I thought everybody was one-armed, like me. Now I feel the surgery. The crunch of bone when it is sundered, the sliced flesh and the tubes of blood cut through, shocking the bloodrun and disturbing the nerves. They dangle and writhe. Singing pain. Waking me with the sound of itself, thrumming when I sleep so deeply it strangles my dreams away. [...] I am not going to be healed, or to find the arm that was removed from me. I am going to freshen the pain, point it, so we both know what it is for.   (*J*, 158)

---

[47] "When he is leaving, Marlowe picks the bug up and carries him down eighteen floors to put him gently among some vegetation. By referring indirectly to the helplessness of the insignificant insect as a counterpoint to the brutality of the conversation [about a murder investigation], Chandler implies the inhumanity of the world Marlowe inhabits and, in the final act of off-handed tenderness, he depicts Marlowe's concern for life much better than could many pages of discursive prose. It is a chivalrous act just a touch insane, since anyone else in that room would have squashed the bug, not necessarily with malice but simply because it would be bothering somebody" (Beekman, 162).

In the City, however, the tone is much closer to that of the caustic private eye. Music, of course, is Morrison's main metaphor in *Jazz*, and the "tracks" of the hunted animal or the criminal become the City plan and the grooves of a record as well:

> Take my word for it, he is bound to the track. It pulls him like a needle through the
> groove of a Bluebird record. Round and round about the town. That's the way the City
> spins you.   (*J*, 120)

Sometimes the metaphor used plays on "double-voicedness" (see Bakhtin, below) to call to circumstances not directly related to the context, but never very far away from the consciousness. When Alice becomes distracted and leaves her iron too long on the dress, "the black and smoking ship burned clear through the yoke" (*J*, 113), which, as Rodrigues points out, is not only a metaphor for the iron, but also a reminder of a painful past — the middle passage, the slave ships, the branding irons, and the yoke of slavery (264, note 8). At others, it is just an innovative new use of a common image to evoke a sensation, as when Violet, discovering that she is more tired that she had thought, finds her tiredness interrupted by "a soft, wide hat, as worn and dim as the room she sat in, descending on her" (*J*, 225). As Jill Matus points out, jazz music, recently arrived on the scene, was also a symbol for crime, though jazz as metaphor will be discussed in more detail below. Dorcas is almost always identified with the candy and sweets that she loves, Joe's "private candy box" (*J*, 121), a weakness that flaws her skin with "tracks" like "hoof-marks," and the metaphor of sugar returns time and again in Morrison's work as a reference to the destructive work of capitalism on working-class people.[48] Morrison's more subtle metaphors, much like Chandler's, have much to do with the imposition of the effects of greed and wealth on the "little people" of society.

The trope that Raymond Chandler is most famous for, however, is the simile, a figure of speech he uses with startling clarity precisely because his comparisons are so unusual and yet so masterful. Beekman believes that often "critics have denigrated these similes simply because they don't expect to find them in this genre of fiction" but finds them "no less fittingly-preposterous than Pope's [...], Dickens' famous descriptions or such similes as Conrad's in *The Secret Agent*: [...]" (16). One of the author's most famous remarks is about a man dressed so as to be "about as inconspicuous as a tarantula on a piece of angel food cake" (*FML*, 4) but this is only one of many that make his style so memorable. The versatility that marks Chandlers as a master of the simile, however, is remarkably similar at times to that of Morrison. Sometimes they reflect a more lyrical mode:

> Beyond the gate the road wound for a couple of hundred yards through trees and then
> suddenly below me was a small oval lake deep in trees and rocks and wild grass, like a
> drop of dew caught in a curled leaf.   (*LL*, 20)

---

[48] Wallerstein explains in *The Modern World System* [that] sugar production in the New World was essential to the rise of capitalism. [...] Capable of providing increased energy output at the expense of long-term health, sugar is the opiate of the working class under capitalism (Willis, 42, Note 8).

I let the remark fall to the ground eddying like a soiled feather.   (*LL*, 72)

As does Morrison when she is refers more to life in a more pastoral past:

He forgets a sun that used to slide up like the yolk of a good country egg. [...]   (*J*, 34)

In his company forgetfulness fell like pollen.   (*J*, 100)

After a light rain, when the leaves have come, tree limbs are like wet fingers playing in wooly green hair.   (*J*, 118)

Or even in the City, when the music calls up its roots in the Deep South:

The clarinets had trouble because the brass was cut so fine, not lowdown the way they love to do it, but high and fine like a young girl singing by the side of a creek, passing the time, her ankles cold in the water.   (*J*, 195)

Or the migrants to the City recall their former deprivations there:

Even if the room they rented was smaller than the heifer's stall and darker than a morning privy, [...]   (*J*, 32)

More often, however, Chandler uses a flat tone more in accord with Marlowe's tough guy diction:

He reared back as if I had hung a week-old mackerel under his nose.   (*LL*, 3)

The roar of his laughter was like a tractor backfiring. It blasted the woodland silence to shreds.   (*LL*, 21)

At the cash desk a pale-haired man was fighting to get the war news on a small radio that was as full of static as the mashed potatoes were full of water.   (*LL*, 37)

She caught her voice and snapped it in mid-air like a rubber band.   (*LL*, 65)

A style that Morrison can imitate admirably –

A poisoned silence floated through the rooms like a big fishnet that Violet alone slashed through with loud recriminations.   (*J*, 5)

(Of Violet's dancing Dorcas's steps) It was like watching an old street pigeon pecking the crust of a sardine sandwich the cats left behind.   (*J*, 6)

No day to wreck a life already splintered like a cheap windowpane, [...]   (*J*, 197)

> Under the ceiling light pairs move like twins born with, if not for, the other, sharing a
> partner's pulse like a second jugular. *(J*, 65)

> Later, and little by little, feelings, like sea trash expelled on a beach – strange and
> recognizable, stark and murky – returned. *(J*, 75)

> Your wit surfaces over and over like the rush of foam to the rim. The laughter is like
> pealing bells that don't need a hand to pull on the rope; it just goes on and on until you
> are weak with it. You can drink the safe gin if you like, or stick to beer, but you don't
> need either because a touch on the knee, accidental or on purpose, alerts the blood like
> a shot of pre-Pro bourbon or two fingers pinching your nipple. *(J*, 187)

– and in which images of violence and weapons and allusions to sex abound.

At the beginning and end of *Jazz*, however, there are references to Morrison's own black
religious culture, obviously not present in Chandler —

> [...] and that sheets impossible to hang out in snowfall drape kitchens like the curtains
> of Abyssinian Sunday-school plays. *(J*, 11)

> Breathing and murmuring under covers both of them have washed and hung out on the
> line, in a bed they chose together and kept together nevermind one leg was propped on
> a 1916 dictionary, and the mattress, curved like a preacher's palm asking for witnesses
> in His name's sake, enclosed them each and every night and muffled their whispering,
> old-time love. *(J*, 228)

— and, of course, her signature type of comparison so strikingly used in *Beloved* with her
"crawling-already? baby," also recurrent in *Jazz*,

> Here comes the new. Look out. There goes the sad stuff. The bad stuff. The things-
> nobody-could-help stuff. *(J*, 7)

> (About Dorcas) Cream-at-the-top-of-the-milkpail face of someone who will never work
> for anything; [...][49] *(J*, 12)

> (on the train) the green-as-poison curtain separating the colored people eating from the
> rest of the diners.[50] *(J*, 31)
> [...] she admired those ready-for-bed-in-the-street clothes. *(J*, 55)

> The dirty, get-on-down music the women sang and the men played [...] *(J*, 58)

> [...] Dorcas thought of that life-below-the-sash as all the life there was. *(J*, 60)

---

[49] A reference to the mulatto class of African Americans who were privileged in white society because they
were lighter-skinned ...

[50] ... and to the Jim Crow laws that governed the South from Reconstruction to the Civil Rights Era.

> [...] a week after he put the engagement ring on Neola's finger, the soon-to-be-groom
> at her wedding left the state. (*J*, 62)

> And maybe it was her head-of-a-seamstress head that made what you thought was a
> cheerful dress turn loud and tatty next to hers. (*J*, 71)

> For Joe she felt trembling fury at his snake-in-the-grass stealing of the girl in her charge;
> [...] (*J*, 76)

> [...] Wild was not a story of a used-to-be-long-ago-crazy girl [...] (*J*, 167)

— which, apart from acute descriptive devices, make social comments.

These figures of speech do more that demonstrate the virtuosity of these writers; they reinforce the stories told by their authors, and sometimes contain other stories within themselves. The language is controlled, studied, but calculated for maximum empathetic response as when Morrison's narrator, speaking of Rose Dear's emotional exhaustion and her final decision to commit suicide, includes the story of a young black choir member who has been castrated by whites:

> Or had it been the news of the young tenor in the choir mutilated and tied to a log, his
> grandmother refusing to give up his waste-filled trousers, washing them over and over
> although the stain had disappeared at the third rinse. They buried him in his brother's
> pants and the old woman pumped another bucket of clear water. (*J*, 101)

The restraint with which Morrison relates this story of whites' brutality and heart-rending loss simply heightens its poignancy. All that needs to be said is expressed in only two sentences. David Smith writes that "Chandler never despaired of the arousal of human sympathy that could be achieved through the skill of the written word" (441); it is clear that these words are equally applicable to the work of Toni Morrison.

I do not mean to press the similarities of Morrison and Chandler too far, only to demonstrate that understanding the detective novel as a storytelling strategy is useful for the exegesis of *Jazz*. Given Morrison's technique of using a popular genre as a base-text in order to subvert its premises, the above observations also enable us to examine what it is exactly she is subverting/rewriting. There are obvious differences in that, as Mayberry remarks, the "exclusively narrating function (of the 'voice' of *Jazz*) precludes an interaction with the characters at the level of plot" (305) while Marlowe, of course, is very much involved with the development of the action and the resolution of the crime. Nonetheless, both narrating voices maintain, in the words of Dubey, "an immediacy and continuity between narrator and audience" (312), just as in oral storytelling. Both are deeply involved in the description of their social milieu, and both develop the city as one of the main characters. Like *Jazz*, Chandler's novels are concerned with "an intellectual content as well: [...] the converse, the darker concrete reality, of an abstract intellectual illusion about the United States," and "the presentation of social reality is involved immediately and directly with the problem of language" (Jameson, 631 & 635).

Though some critics have called Chandler's novels "romances" because "the action and violence more or less covered up the fact that everything came out all right in the end" (Durham, 96-97), most remark upon the lack of clear resolution:

> Marlowe [...] is in a long line of Romantic heroes. [...] If Marlowe were an archetype he would be a somber knight on a never finished quest, recharging his faith by adversity. A Romantic Hero, to be sure, but one who has been mired in reality. [...] outsider, [...]archetypical hero of American fiction [...] That is why these novels are not simply crime fiction: at their close little has been resolved despite the fact that the murderer has been found. All of them end on a note of dissatisfaction. (Beekman, 166)

Although the crime may have been solved, the corruption of the society at large remains unchanged,[51] and often the perpetrators of the crimes enjoy Marlowe's sympathy as he reveals them to have been caught in a web from which they could not escape. There is a controlled sadness in the last paragraphs of *Farewell, My Lovely* evident despite Marlowe's flat tone, yet it contains a reference to the jagged determination of the individual idealist against overwhelming odds. And though the crime is solved, as Beekman notes, "the purported solution does not tidy things up since there is no end to a waking nightmare"(164). Chandler's hero "untangles nothing, he only exposes a mess that is far from a naive, passive construction and which no simple morality can banish" (Smith, 432).

Perhaps herein lies the major difference between Morrison's and Chandlers novelistic conceptions. In spite of the narrator's predictions at the beginning of the novel – "What turned out different was who shot whom" (*J*, 6) – she is forced to recognize her error:

> So I missed it altogether. I was sure one would kill the other. I waited for it so I could describe it. I was so sure it would happen. That the past was an abused record with no choice but to repeat itself at the crack and no power on earth could lift the arm that held the needle. I was so sure, and they danced and walked all over me. Busy, they were, busy being original, complicated, changeable – human, I guess you'd say, while I was the predictable one, confused in my solitude into arrogance, thinking my space, my view was the only one that was or that mattered. (*J*, 220)

Though Joe and Violet have hurt each other and themselves immeasurably, somehow their search for themselves and each other has healed their wounds and brought them back together. Here in truth is the "romance," an ode to reconciliation and the possibility of personal redemption. But Morrison is not content with only personal resolution, believing that each reader has it in his/her hands to mold the future, to tell the story. The responsibility for this change is passed on in the final words of the narrator:

---

[51] Nickerson writes that the three great hard-boiled detective novelists "have set forth, in their portrayals of villainy and the milieu which sustains it, a serious indictment of a whole society. Further, they have offered their readers only a small portion of hope, because their heroes of detection win only temporary victories over these formidable adversaries" (132).

> If I were able I'd say it. Say make me, remake me. You are free to do it and I am free
> to let you because look, look. Look where your hands are. Now.   (*J*, 229)

By passing on the responsibility for telling stories, Morrison foregrounds the importance of the way in which language is used and in which narratives shape our lives. In choosing a riddle *genre* she provokes readers and critics not only to find solutions but also to participate in the unfolding of the story. Moreover, she sets out to examine the uses and *genres of language* and their roles in the development of narration – particularly in the development of the novel as an answer to the authoritarian nature of official discourse. For a look at this aspect and as hermeneutic tool for the specific analysis of the discourse in *Jazz*, we turn now to the theories of M. M. Bakhtin.

The Enabler

VI. BAKHTINIAN THEORY AND THE MEANING(S) OF "JAZZ"

The rise in importance of the theories of Mikhail M. Bakhtin has coincided dramatically with the emphasis on the "linguistic turn" in a wide range of disciplines and the postmodern preoccupation with language stimulated by Foucault, Lacan, and Derrida, among others. As Pam Morris puts it in her introduction to *The Bakhtin Reader*,

> Perhaps what is most striking about the work of Mikhail Bakhtin is the diversity of areas and range of disciplines across which it is invoked. His ideas are being utilized not just in literary studies but also in philosophy, semiotics, cultural studies, anthropology, feminist and post-colonial studies, Marxism, ethics and, of course, Russian and Slavic studies. Apart from the accessibility of his ideas, there are two main reasons for this. At the centre of all his thinking is an innovative and dynamic perception of language. [...] A concern with language as production of meaning has been pushed to the centre of twentieth-century Western epistemology. (Morris, 1)

That this preoccupation with language is everywhere present in Morrison's thinking and writing, particularly in the 1990s, has been discussed previously in this study. Making use of Bakhtinian theory for an analysis of *Jazz* as an exploratory discussion of language and storytelling is therefore both fruitful and to the point. This is particularly true if we consider, as does Tvzetan Todorov, that Bakhtin's theories of language are gestated within his ideas of "philosophical anthropology" which "recur in strikingly stable form throughout the course of his career. [...] These ideas have to do with otherness." Bakhtin posits "a general conception of human existence, where the *other* plays a decisive role. [... This is his] fundamental principle: it is impossible to conceive of any being outside of the relations that link it to the other" (94). The "other" as concept has been foregrounded in much of modern critical inquiry, particularly as it applies to women's, post-colonial and "minority" literature. Michael Holquist writes that these contemporary critical approaches "have in common the need to rethink an otherness that always founds its effects on a binary opposition: "imaginative geography" (Occident/Orient), gender (male/female), race (white/black, non-Jew/Jew) or of a power alignment that assigns privilege according to whether the subject is either a colonializer [*sic*] or one of the colonialized [*sic*]." He finds "certain parallels between Bakhtin's attempt to theorize his way out of dialectical habits of thought [...] and the attempts of blacks, feminists, and anti-colonialist thinkers to rethink the categories of alterity." His position that the "self cannot coincide with itself" and that it is "less a static locus of privilege than it is a specifically structured worksite for the dynamic and all-encompassing activity of alterity" (Holquist, "Stereotyping"; 454 & 455), has given impetus to inquiry which works to expose the linguistic basis for the structures of "designation and division."

It is therefore hardly surprising that the widespread introduction of Bakhtin into literary studies in the 1980s caused quite an impact on many intellectuals in the African American community.[52] Indeed, his double concerns of language and alterity have taken a preeminent place in both the literary and critical work that Toni Morrison has developed to date, especially emphasized in the last decade of the twentieth century. Her exploration of the very genesis of American literature in *Playing in the Dark* (1992), for example, demonstrates just how the development of the American identity and the literary expression it received at the hands of our "classic" writers (mostly male, all white) depended heavily on what she denominates "the Africanist presence" – the American "other" *par excellence*.[53] Like Bakhtin, Morrison posits the very definition of the self in opposition to the "other," though in this particular work she is discus-sing the general concept of a white self as only possible in the context of a large black (and en-slaved) presence. Bakhtin, however, goes even further: for him there is no self at all without an "other," and it is through this other that the individual "self" comes into being.[54] This takes place precisely through language, which is always open-ended and dialogic, and always social. From this perspective he could take issue with such major figures of his early era as Saussure and Freud: The one for pretending to isolate language from its social environment via analyses of *langue*, the other for locating the development of the self in the *id* rather than in the *other*. For Bakhtin the crucial issue is always the social interaction of language which gives meaning to the utterance, and it is the social interaction of human beings via their discourse that gives an identity to the "self."

Though Pam Morris traces what she considers to be a development in the theories of this great Russian theorist, Tzvetan Todorov emphasizes the consistency of his thought with respect to the development of what he denominates a "Poetics of the Utterance" (x). For Bakhtin language is essentially radical. Although he acknowledges the "centripetal" forces which provide the coherence in language that is necessary for communication, he also insists on the "centrifugal" forces (those of linguistic and ideological centralization and decentralization) that constantly force its renewal (Holquist in Bakhtin, 1981; xviii). According to Michael Holquist, "[t]his extraordinary sensitivity to the immense plurality of experience more than anything else distinguishes

---

[52] For a discussion of the impact of Bakhtinian theory on African American critics, see Dale E. Peterson's "Response and Call: The African American Dialogue with Bakhtin."

[53] Morrison's critical analysis also deftly supports Bakhtin's assertion that each age will undertake different readings of literary texts precisely because of the heteroglossia found in them. Her interpretation of these "founding" texts from an African-American position have proved to be valuable re-readings, shedding light on puzzling contradictions and certain strained discourse in the novels she studies.

[54] Contrast this approach with Richard Hardack, who argues that "true desire is involuntary [...] a violent possession, double-consciousness itself: the desire for an other as the self." (454) For Bakhtin, it is through a dialogue with the other that the self comes into being.

Bakhtin from other moderns who have been obsessed with language" (xx). It is this *plurality* of experience that is reflected in the term Bakhtin uses to describe the constant struggle between the centripetal and centrifugal forces: heteroglossia. And it is precisely the *plurality* of experience, manifest in language, which Morrison has insisted is necessary to combat the ossification of authoritarian discourse; that is, we very much *need* the Babel of competing narratives to combat an oppressive, dominant social myth that privileges some human beings over others. This is, in fact, what the current "multi-cultural" movement in the United States is all about.

For Bakhtin, language is always double-voiced and always reflects an ideological point of view; it is the constant interaction of voices (and therefore, of ideologies) that struggle against an authoritarian imposition of a single, unitary voice: "It is necessary that heteroglossia wash over a culture's awareness of itself and its language, penetrate to its core, relativize the primary language system underlying its ideology and literature and deprive it of its naive absence of conflict" (Bakhtin, *Dialogic;* 368). Holquist notes that Bakhtin is developing his theories of the struggle of language against a unitary discourse and its reflection in the novels of Rabelais precisely at the moment that Stalin is waging a campaign of terror against any expression of dissent in the Soviet Union, thereby reading Bakhtin's own theoretical work as "double-voiced" and ideologically charged (see Holquist, 1982-83). For ideological, and hence political, change to come about, a national culture must undergo a "verbal-ideological decentering" which will occur

> only when a national culture loses its sealed-off and self-sufficient character, when it becomes conscious of itself as only one among *other* cultures and languages. It is this knowledge that will sap the roots of a mythological feeling for language, based as it is on an absolute fusion of ideological meaning with language; there will arise an acute feeling for language boundaries (social, national and semantic), and only then will language reveal its essential human character; from behind its words, forms styles, nationally characteristic and socially typical faces begin to emerge, the images of speaking human beings.   (Bakhtin, *Dialogic*; 370)

This theory of language as a decentering force in the culture is one that would complement Morrison's own concern with political change.

But this is not the only aspect of language that is of interest with respect to Morrison's work. Many critics have remarked on the importance of memory for Morrison, even when they center their critique around a "jazz aesthetic," as does Eusebio Rodrigues: "Morrison adapts the oral/musical mode of storyteling that relies on listening and memory" (257). And Deborah Barnes notes that memory in *Jazz* is absolutely crucial:

> As in all Morrison novels, memory is the saving grace. Without memories of a historical, cultural, and personal foundation, the sojourner will have no identity, no point of orientation, no way to proceed and nowhere from which to begin anew. Even an evolving identity must be rooted in a past.   (Barnes, 293)

Jill Matus quotes psychologist Pierre Janet, saying that "[m]emory, like belief, like all psychological phenomena, is an action; essentially it is the action of telling a story" (qtd. in Matus, 25). And Gurleen Grewal cites Michael Lambek's study of "The Past Imperfect: Remembering as Moral Practice": memory is "a culturally mediated expression [...] of social commitments and identifications" (qtd. in Grewal, 61). Bakhtin, however, charges that what we call "collective memory" is in fact contained in linguistic expressions preserved in the culture. For an author who is exploring the relationship of history, memory and story, this aspect of language is absolutely crucial. Writes Bakhtin:

> Cultural and literary traditions (including the most ancient) are preserved and continue to live not in the individual subjective memory of a single individual and not in some kind of collective "psyche," but rather in the objective forms that culture itself assumes (including the forms of language and spoken speech), and in this sense they are inter-subjective and inter-individual (and consequently social); from there they enter literary works, sometimes almost completely bypassing the subjective individual memory of their creators.   (Bakhtin, *Dialogic*; 249, note 17)

Thus, the novel, via its incorporation of heteroglossia, is in fact the almost inadvertent preserver of cultural memory, of social difference, and of ideological struggle. "The decentralizing of the verbal-ideological world that finds its expression in the novel begins by presuming fundamentally differentiated social groups, which exist in an intense and vital interaction with other social groups" (368), all of which deconstruct the presumption of a unitary language and undermine any authoritarian ideology. Certainly this function would be vitally important for a work that dealt with stories and how they are told. While Morrison may take her cue for *Jazz* from the discussion of the "criminal act" which propels the private life into the public pages of literature, it is the novel form itself which becomes vitally important as the expression of "multivocality" (and "multiple realities") so necessary for political change:

> The novel begins by presuming a verbal and semantic decentering of the ideological world, a certain linguistic homelessness of literary consciousness, which no longer possesses a sacrosanct and unitary linguistic medium for containing ideological thought; [...] What is involved here is a very important, in fact a radical revolution in the destinies of human discourse: the fundamental liberation of cultural-semantic and emotional intentions from the hegemony of a single and unitary language, and consequently the simultaneous loss of feeling for language as myth, that is, as an absolute form of thought. Therefore it is not enough merely to uncover the multiplicity of languages in a cultural world or the speech diversity within a particular national language – we must see through to the heart of this revolution, to all the consequences flowing from it, possible only under very specific sociohistorical conditions.   (Bakhtin, *Dialogic*; 367)

The language of the novel for Bakhtin is a living language; "[t]he forces that define it as a genre are at work before our very eyes: the birth and development of the novel as a genre takes place in the full light of the historical day" (*Dialogic*, 3), incorporating the vitality and mutability of semantic expressions even as they are evolving. This dynamic process is one that fascinates Bakhtin and leads him to another observation which is particularly pertinent for our discussion of *Jazz* —

> The novel is the only developing genre and therefore it reflects more deeply, more essentially, more sensitively and rapidly, reality itself in the process of its unfolding. Only that which is itself developing can comprehend development as a process.
>
> (Bakhtin, *Dialogic*, 7)

— or as David Lodge so succinctly puts it: "Narrative consists essentially in the representation of process" (146).[55]

Many critics of *Jazz* have commented precisely on its self-conscious reflection of *process*, leading them, indulgently, I believe, to insist on the structural and strategic affinity of the novel with the music. In his detailed and effective refutation of Morrison's "jazz critics," Alan Munton meticulously reviews these critics' basic misinterpretations of jazz music as their basis for a literary analysis, locating the origin of the "mishearing" in Henry Louis Gates' *The Signifying Monkey: A Theory of African-American Literary Criticism* (1988). In his refutation of Gates appropriation of terminology from jazz, Munton comes to the conclusion that "[m]esmerised by the beat, Gates seems to be unaware that every jazz performance is a 'signification' upon, or revision of, something already in existence, whether the melody or theme, or the chord sequence. If all jazz is Signifyin(g), then the term becomes redundant" (248). Picked up by subsequent critics of African American literature, Gates' "mishearing" of jazz music has inadvertently become an example of one type of language that Morrison protested against in her Nobel acceptance speech: " the proud but calcified language of the academy" (319). What Munton also collaterally demonstrates is what happens when suspect or equivocal critique makes its way into "authoritative" academic discourse.[56]

This insistence on looking at jazz as the underlying aesthetic for *Jazz* is, in fact, a distraction from another, much more useful approach. As Alan Munton has already effectively refuted these "jazz critics'" arguments, I wish to examine jazz not as the structure, strategy or aesthetic behind the creation of the novel, but as a perfect metaphor for the underlying theme of the novel: stories and the language used to tell them.

A. JAZZ AS METAPHOR

It would be unfair to "blame" Gates entirely for what Munton declares to be a "misreading" of *Jazz*. Morrison herself is quoted on various occasions as comparing her novel to the music. Carolyn M. Jones cites Morrison's interview in the *Paris Review* –

---

[55] Though Lodge in his chapter on "Indeterminacy in Modern Narrative" is specifically discussing Rudyard Kipling's short story "Mrs. Bathurst" (1904), the words he uses to describe this particular narrative are equally illuminating when applied to *Jazz*: "The consequence of all this is to displace the attention of the reader from the story to the discourse – not merely to the rhetoric of the discourse (though this is certainly the case, and a characteristic effect of modern narrative) but also to what might be called the story of the discourse: that is, the story of the interaction [...]" (147).

[56] Gates has since distanced himself from some of the theories he first elaborated in *The Signifying Monkey*.

The novel *Jazz* "predicts its own story" (117), containing, like jazz music, a melodic line that the narrator returns to time after time, "seeing it afresh each time, playing it back and forth" Morrison continues: "[...] the jazz-like structure wasn't a secondary thing for me – it was the raison d'être of the book" (110) .

– to justify her opinion that "this novel [...] Morrison consciously constructs as jazz" (491). Jill Matus quotes Morrison from her interview with Angeles Carribí –

> So when I was thinking who was going to tell this story, the idea of "who owns jazz" or who knows about it, came up... I decided that the voice would be one of assumed knowledge, the voice that says "I know everything". [...] Because the voice has to actually imagine the story it's telling [...] the story [...] turns out to be entirely different from what is predicted because the characters are evolving [...]. It reminded me of a jazz performance [...] Somebody takes off from a basic pattern then the others have to accommodate themselves.   (Carribí, 42)

– to support her theory that "Morrison shows that narrative improvisation means taking risks, responding spontaneously to what emerges in the process of creation. This is one of the ways in which Morrison's novel approximates jazz music" (123-124).

However, precisely because of the "double-voicedness" found in all literary language, David Lodge states that an author's comments "do not have absolute authority." In fact, he writes:

> Most writers are in fact chary of giving unequivocal answers to direct questions about what they meant or intended by a particular work or part of a work, because of an intuitive sense that by doing so they might be impoverishing, limiting, closing down the possible meanings that their writing might produce.   (Lodge, 145)

> It is the nature of texts, especially fictional ones, that they have gaps and indeterminacies which may be filled in by different readers in different ways, and it is of the nature of codes that, once brought into play, they may generate patterns of significance which were not consciously intended by the author who activated them, and which do not require his "authorization" to be accepted as valid interpretations of the text.   (Lodge, 159)

Michael Sprinkler concurs, saying that "[n]othing in the signifying or communicational potential of language as such can prevent one from interpreting an utterance in a way not intended by the author, which is to say that intentions cannot ever determine or absolutely predict meaning" (126). In fact, however, Morrison has couched her statements with the words "like jazz," "jazz-like," "reminded me of," and in no way believes that the narrative is "improvisational." Indeed, in her interview with Alan Rice, Morrison specifically states that "[t]he point in black art is to make it look as a jazz musician does, unthought out, unintellectual as it were, so the work doesn't show, to be able to do it on the spot ... And the jazz musician's the classic person" (Morrison in A. Rice, 424).

But this is a far cry from "improvisation." On the contrary, this is an art so elaborate that it appears to be effortless, but that nonetheless obeys its own strict internal logic and development. Bakhtin affirms that "[e]very creative act is bound by its own special laws, as well as by the laws of the material with which it works." An artistic image, of whatever sort, cannot be invented, he continues, "since it has its own artistic logic, its own norm-generating order. Having set a specific task for himself, the creator must subordinate himself to this order" (Bakhtin, *Dostoevsky*; in Morris, 94). Narrative is indeed like jazz, but not for the reasons espoused by Morrison's "jazz critics." In *Jazz* the music in effect becomes the perfect metaphor for language and its development in literature.

It is a common assumption that the great American contribution to world music has been jazz, an amalgamation of African music and style played on Western instruments, but the appreciation of this art form was not always a given. Said to have originated in "Storyville," an area of New Orleans with a reputation for prostitution and "low living," jazz was early associated with moral anarchy, cultural backwardness and illicit sexuality, particularly black female sexuality.[57] "During the 1920s [people] often cast it as a low-down, gutbucket form stigmatized by its association with the cultural backwardness of Southern migrants" (Dubey, 301 & 99; 299; see Ogre, 114-38; Peretti, 58-63). Alice Manfred in *Jazz* is appalled by how it

> made her aware of its life below the sash and its red lip rouge. She knew from sermons and editorials that it wasn't real music – just colored folks' stuff: harmful, certainly; embarrassing, of course; but not real, not serious.   (*J*, 58-59)

The ascendancy of jazz from an intimate association with the "lower" classes of society to a world-renowned high art form closely parallels the views of language held by the German philosopher, historian, and folklorist, Johann Gotfried von Herder (1744-1803). Herder believed that "the highest cultural values can be derived from what cultivated classes often describe condescendingly as the vulgar, lowest levels of society" and argued, together with other more modern American critics, "that the lower layers of society are not at all devoid of cultural significance. In fact they are conceived to be the major source of materials which sophisticated society uses to fashion its literary expression; and these original materials are acknowledged to be esthetically valid in their own terms" (Bluestein, iii). Herder's theory of literature

> ran counter to the major assumptions of enlightenment thinkers [... whose] conception of cultural progress was predicated upon the eradication of myth and superstition from the minds of the peasantry, whose subjugation by the church prevented them from responding to the new light of rationalist philosophies.   (Bluestein, 4)

In Herder's view, which became widely accepted in the nineteenth century, it is precisely the folk songs and folklore that nourish and renew "higher" forms of art and provide a distinctly

---

[57] "No one is exactly certain how the word jazz originated. Emerging sometime around 1910, the term is usually associated with the folk mores of black men, and therefore its roots have been linked to Africa" (Lewis, 272). *The Dictionary of Word Origins* says that jazz "originated in a West African language, [and] was for a long time a Black slang term in America for 'strenuous activity,' particularly 'sexual intercourse'" (John Ayto, [New York: Arcade Publishing, 1990], 307; qtd. in Lewis, 277).

nationalist flavor to culture of a given country:

> It will remain eternally true that if we have no *Volk*, we shall have no public, no
> nationality, no literature of our own which shall live and work in us. Unless our
> literature is founded on our *Volk*, we shall write eternally for closet sages and disgusting
> critics out of whose mouths and stomachs we shall get back what we have given.
>
> (Herder in Bluestein, 6)

According to Gene Bluestein, what his theory suggests is "the growth of a literary tradition from the lowest levels of the culture to the highest," revealing "the startling assumption that the major literary values of a nation are defined by the lowest strata of the culture"(Bluestein, 6).

Although Herder's views were later misinterpreted as providing a basis for a nationalistic, xenophobic stance, in reality, "it was not blood but *language* which Herder regarded as the essential criterion of a *Volk*" (9; emphasis added). Rather than supporting the ideologies which were later mis-accredited to him,

> Herder provided a major and unique justification for a democratic ideology. It was based
> on the concrete demonstration of the creative powers of the lower classes. [...] Herder's
> *volk* ideology made it possible to offer empirical proof that the major values of a national
> literature resided in the abilities of common men to create a folk tradition from which a
> formal, sophisticated literature developed. (Bluestein, 11)

He also believed that it was the music of the folk which displayed "the internal character of the people" even in its "most imperfect form"(8). Bluestein notes, however, that folklorists believe the folk process to be a highly conservative activity, on the one hand, and that if language "makes it possible to conceptualize experience, in its written form it also freezes it" (12). Herder "never reconciled this contradiction," but Bakhtin, obviously drawing on Herder's work,[58] solves the problem by posing all language, most certainly including written language, as "double-voiced," at once absorbing and reflecting the semantics and ideologies from whence it is derived, thereby providing renewal in literature (most specifically the novel) by virtue of its heteroglossia. Bluestein relates Herder's theory to what he calls a "peculiar form of American anarchism" in which

> the individual is all, yet his culture has been shaped by processes that can only be
> understood in terms of the anonymous movement of the folk. The attempts to control
> this delicate balance between the individual and the mass have often exhibited what
> seems to be a major inconsistency in American thought, an inconsistency that seems to

---

[58] Though Bakhtin does not openly acknowledge Herder's influence in the development of his own theory of language, he does cite him in his work several times. (See "Forms of Time and of the Chronotope in the Novel: Notes toward a Historical Poetics," in *The Dialogic Imagination*; 139 & 205.) In *Rabelais and His World* (1965) Bakhtin criticizes Herder for what he considered to be a limited view: "The narrow concept of popular characters and of folklore was born in the pre-Romantic period and was basically completed by von Herder and the Romantics. There was no room in this concept for the peculiar culture of the marketplace and of folk laughter with all its wealth of manifestations" (in Morris, 195-196). See below for an elaboration on his own theory of folk and the marketplace.

stem from our cultural immaturity.   (Bluestein, 14)

Bakhtin, of course, would not look upon this phenomenon as "inconsistent" in that he posits the individual self as only possible in "dialogue" with the other. That is, there is no "text" without context.

The discussion of the appropriateness of using jazz as a basis for "higher art forms" such as poetry and fiction was particularly acute during the Harlem Renaissance. Many black intellectuals of the time echoed W.E.B. Du Bois' opinion that it was the Negro spirituals that were the true source of black cultural expression. And although Langston Hughes defended the new music as "authentic" black expression, jazz and blues as art forms were considered to be suspect, as indicated in Countee Cullen's attack on Hughes' poem "The Weary Blues." Hughes' response to Cullen in "The Negro Artist and the Racial Mountain" attempts to formulate a "manifesto" against the proletarian world of "work, work, work" and celebrates jazz as a struggle for individuality in the face of American standardization. However, perhaps because of the music's connection to the "low life" of the Negro community at the time, on the one hand, and the fact that it was "compromised" in its performance in some Harlem night clubs by being often restricted to white audiences, on the other, the "acceptability" of jazz as a true folk art and source for "higher" cultural expression was questioned by many blacks determined to carve a place for their race in "respectable circles." Drawing on jazz for art in both music and literature made many uncomfortable precisely because of its association with lower class blacks and because of its appropriation by whites looking to rebel against social norms. This discussion, moreover, also parallels the one underway at the time, on the use of black dialect in poetry and literature. While many poets and writers from Paul Dunbar onward preferred to use a more standardized English in their work, and even felt that their artistry was greater in doing so, whites were demanding more and more of the "primitive" Negro manifest in language that was a "throw-back" to plantation times. This "mediation" of white audiences in what was "allowed" or "expected" of black artists, coupled with a desire to leave a degrading past behind, caused more than a little consternation among blacks during the 1920s, when the "New Negro" was being touted and racial equality was insisted upon. The desire for assimilation into mainstream America and for individual artistic excellence conflicted with the need to retain strong links with precisely the sources of black creativity.[59]

This tension between "the individual and the mass" in questions of cultural development is perfectly reflected in jazz. As Elizabeth Cannon and other critics rightly point out, though the jazz soloists are spotlighted and seemingly develop their own individual interpretation of the melody, the individual player cannot exist without the ensemble. Cannon links this fact directly to Morrison's development of the novel (237).[60] Gene Bluestein notes that

---

[59] Charles Chesnutt's well-know short story, "The Wife of His Youth," deals specifically with these counter-impulses, though his emphasis is on black dialect and folk traditions more than on music.

[60] Interestingly, descriptions of jazz music have drawn upon metaphors of language and storytelling. Grewal notes that Paul Berliner "links jazz and storytelling by showing how musicians adopt metaphors of storytelling to convey the meaning of jazz oratory" (128). H.W. Rice quotes Gunther Schuller as saying, "within the loose framework of European tradition, the American Negro was able to preserve a significant nucleus of his African

Luis (Armstrong) [...] is positively and deeply associated with the cultural sources of his art. For if jazz provides an outlet for individual expression it also demands an allegiance to the group as well, and [Ralph] Ellison employs this circumstance thematically as a way of defining the relationship of the individual to his society, thus raising the issue from a purely esthetic to a political level as well. [...]

[T]he will to achieve the most eloquent expression of idea-emotions through the technical mastery of their instruments [...] the give and take, the subtle rhythmical shaping and blending of idea, tone and imagination demanded of group improvisation. The delicate balance struck between strong individual personality and the group during those early jam sessions was a marvel of social organization.   (Bluestein, 135 & 136)

The precise interplay of the musicians in a jazz ensemble is often remarked upon as "call and response," one instrument listening and then picking up on the notes played by another. Again, as the metaphor for language in Bakhtinian terms, jazz is appropriate. In "The Problem of Speech Genres" Bakhtin elaborates on the importance of response in communication and its place in defining the "utterance":

Sooner or later what is heard and actively understood will find its response in the subsequent speech or behavior of the listener. In most cases, genres of complex cultural communication are intended for this kind of actively responsive understanding with delayed action. Everything we have said here also pertains to written and read speech [...] Thus, all real and integral understanding is actively responsive, [...] the speaker himself is oriented precisely toward such an actively responsive understanding. [...] Any utterance is a link in a very complexly organized chain of other utterances.

The boundaries of each concrete utterance as a unit of speech communication are determined by a *change of speaking subjects,* [...] its beginning is preceded by the utterances of others, and its end is followed by the responsive utterances of others (or, although it may be silent, others' active responsive understanding, or, finally, a responsive action based on this understanding). The speaker ends his utterance in order to relinquish the floor to the other or to make room for the other's active responsive understanding.   (Bakhtin, *Speech*; 69)

Bakhtin pushes this emphasis on the ensemble and inter-subjective interdependence into ethical considerations. Response to the other means, in effect, response-ibility to and for the other.[61]

---

heritage. And it is that nucleus that has made jazz the uniquely captivating *language* that it is" (*Early Jazz,* 63; in H.W. Rice, 128; emphasis added). No one, however, insists on the imposition of a theory of narrative in order to understand the music.

   [61] "Thus the world, is, in its most basic constitution an ethical space, a space structured by an irreducible difference between *I* and *other.* [...] 'Responsibility' means grasping this uniqueness and the obligation to act toward others that flows from it. [...] Once you have grasped the architectonics of the world, its ineluctable division into *I* and *other,* you become responsible, obligated, because you simultaneously grasp the fact that your *own* consciousness can neither satisfactorily ground your acts nor provide your life with certain meaning and significance. For that, you must depend on the community of *others* around you and on the faith that they will sense their obligations toward you as surely as you acknowledge your obligations toward them. With the end of solipsistic individualism comes, so Bakhtin believed, the beginning of an ethical life" (Hirschkop, 586).

Bakhtin's concern with the responsibility of the individual to his community perfectly reflects Morrison's (and other African Americans') insistence on the inherent values of the village for black life (see Morrison, 1981, "City"). The individual may soar, but s/he is never alone; the subject only acquires meaning within the group. Holquist emphasizes Bakhtin's basic thesis that

> men define their unique place in existence through the responsibility they enact, the care they exhibit in their deeds for others and the world. Deed is understood as meaning word as well as physical act: the deed is how meaning comes into the world, how brute facticity is given significance and form, how the Word becomes flesh.
>
> (Holquist, "Politics"; 176)

In the essay on "Speech" cited above, Bakhtin later reiterates the social interdependence of language, much as jazz musicians play within the context of the ensemble:

> Utterances are not indifferent to one another, and are not self-sufficient; they are aware of and mutually reflect one another. [...] Each utterance is filled with echoes and reverberations of other utterances to which it is related by the communality of the sphere of speech communication.
>
> (Bakhtin, *Speech*; 91)

A jazz ensemble is a perfect musical metaphor for the "echoes" and "reverberations" of this speech "communality."

At the same time, however, "one of the fundamental principles of alterity," in this "dialogue" which is on-going between the self and other, "is that one can never perceive himself as finished, complete, one can only see others as already having become what they are":

> My "I" lives in an "absolute future," thus my self is a project never to be completed by me.[...] What consciousness is always conscious of is the incompleteness of self. In temporal terms what this means is that I answer the present by projecting a future. My self then performs itself as a denial of any given (specific) category's power fully to comprehend it.
>
> (Holquist, "Carnival"; 228)

This "incompleteness" of the self manifest in language is also represented in jazz music. Consider Morrison's words: "Jazz always keeps you on the edge. There is no final chord. There may be a long chord, but no final chord. [...] I want my books to be like that – because I want that feeling of something held in reserve and the sense that there is something more" (in McKay, 411).

In the last chapter of his book, *The Voice of the Folk: Folklore and American Literary Theory,* Gene Bluestein in fact turns his attention to the use of "Negro folklore and folksong" in American literature, expressing a special interest in jazz. He notes that F. Scott Fitzgerald in *The Great Gatsby* refers to a specific piece of music played at the gala as Vladimir Tostoff's *Jazz History of the World* in pejorative terms, since a "jazz history of the world" would have been "an assault on the very idea of history itself. [...] The important point is that jazz is defined in essentially negative terms as a way of identifying the chaos and libertinism of Gatsby's world

[...] " (p. 119). [62] This critic also notes that

> Jazz carried clear associations with a level of culture decidedly outside the stream of
> middle-class white morality and rooted essentially in the attitudes and expression of the
> Negro. For the writers of the twenties and thirties jazz carried strong connotations and
> was associated with stereotypes of the Negro as fantastically virile and barbarously
> effective in his sexual life.   (Bluestein, 120)

He later emphasizes the close relationship of this type of music as emblematic of freedom, even licentiousness, ideas also echoed in Alice Manfred's head:

> It was the music. The dirty, get-on-down music the women sang and the men played and
> both danced to, close and shameless or apart and wild. Alice was convinced and so were
> the Miller sisters as they blew into cups of Postum in the kitchen. It made you do unwise
> disorderly things. Just hearing it was like violating the law.   (*J*, 58)

Alice struggles against the new-fangled music because she aspires to middle-class respectability; jazz represents what is base, low and vulgar in black people, while she strives for assimilation into the mainstream culture, adopting the dominant white view. For Susan Willis this tension is a key concept in Morrison's fiction:

> When Morrison remarks that the black community tolerates difference while the white
> bourgeois world shuts difference out, she underscores the fact that for the white world,
> under capitalism, difference, because it articulates a form of freedom, is a threat and
> therefore must be institutionalized or jailed.   (Willis, 40)

In the *Paris Review* interview, Morrison states that jazz music "reinforced the idea of love as a space where one could negotiate freedom"(qtd. in Jones, 113). This negotiation of a freedom from oppressive authority once again reinforces the idea of jazz as metaphor and returns us to Bakh-tin's theory of language in the novel. H.W. Rice asserts that "to some extent Morrison uses jazz (a musical idiom from popular culture) just as Bakhtin asserts that Rabelais used 'popular-festive elemental imagery.'[...] It enables her to undercut the clearly defined and rigidly conceptualized world of tradition" (120). I would argue that this comparison is much stronger than Rice would allow. Bakhtin speaks of popular styles in language and literary expression in combating authoritarian discourse, and not only located in the Rabelaisian era:

> In other periods as well, when the task was to destroy traditional official styles and world
> views that had faded and become conventional, familiar styles became very significant
> in literature. Moreover, familiarization of styles opened literature up to layers of langu-

---

[62] Michael Nowlin remarks that *Jazz* is "a text haunted [...] by powerful precursor texts, an obvious one being *The Great Gatsby*, white America's landmark tale of the jazz age" (160). Michael Holquist ("Stereotyping") also uses the latter novel as a case study for "examining the role played by otherness in giving shape to the past" (453).

age that had previously been under speech constraint.   (Bakhtin, *Speech*; 97)

Perhaps the most well-known of this critic's theories, the disruption of official discourse by the disempowered populace, is seen as a means of rebellious expression at the same time that it revises and renews both spoken language and literary expression. It is precisely in Bakhtin's notion of 'carnival' that we find the same usurping of authority in language that jazz came to represent in music: "Regarded as an epidemic of moral anarchy, jazz became the prime signifier of a new urban culture that was perceived as threatening to social stability and order" (Dubey, 300). Alice Manfred, paragon of social respectability in *Jazz*, is irrationally disturbed by the music:

> Yet Alice Manfred swore she heard a complicated anger in it; something hostile that disguised itself as flourish and roaring seduction. But the part she hated most was its appetite. Its longing for the bash, the slit; a kind of careless hunger for a fight or a red ruby stickpin for a tie – either would do. It faked happiness, faked welcome, but it did not make her feel generous, this juke joint, barrel hooch, tonk house, music. It made her hold her hand in the pocket of her apron to keep from smashing it through the glass pane to snatch the world in her fist and squeeze the life out of it for doing what it did and did and did to her and everybody else she knew or knew about. Better to close the windows and the shutters, sweat in the summer heat of a silent Clifton Place apartment than to risk a broken window or a yelping that might not know where or how to stop.   (*J*, 59)

B. BAKHTIN'S THEORY OF CARNIVAL

It is a given in political science as well as in psychology that the desire or need for authority will manifest itself in an effort to control the discourse, to set the terms of the discussion and to govern the language that it deems admissible. Hence the need of the church to dictate and control religious dogma and the frequency with which dictatorships resort to control of the media and outright censorship in an effort to eliminate dissent. For Holquist, "political power is ultimately an authority, the power to interdict. The most pervasive form of interdiction is, of course, censorship, control over words," and this fight for the language is essentially a concern with values. "Censorship, like literary criticism, is a form of axiology, the science of values," and "it always believes that there is *one* way to say things and declares any other way of saying it officially meaningless. It is monologue erected into a principle" ("Dissidence," 32). It is notable, however, that absolute control over language is subject to disruption precisely because, as Bakhtin insists, "language is riddled with the messiness of history and the vagaries of individual performance" (33). This is why Holquist states that rather than the dissidents and the idealists, "it is the censors who are the utopians" (Holquist, "Dissidence"; 34):

> They dream a social order that requires for its realization two conditions that the structure of language will simply not permit: a monologic meaning (everyone says and thinks the same thing and there is no gap between what they say and what they think); or – silence. [...] Repression loves the fantasy of Eden; dissent knows the truth of Babel.

71

Or as Pam Morris puts it,

> Any ruling class will attempt to monologize the word, imposing an eternal single
> meaning upon it, but a living ideological sign is always dialogic. Any word can be
> reaccentuated – a curse can be spoken as a word of praise – and any word can provoke
> its counter-word. (Morris, 13)

While our "official consciousness" may "accord with the stable, fully fledged values of our community and class – its laws, its morality, its world outlook" (9), our "unofficial consciousness"[63]
may rebel against the authority of an unquestioned imposition of values.

> Authoritative discourse [...] is not usually experienced as truly persuasive but rather
> demands *unconditional* allegiance simply because it derives from an authoritative source.
> By contrast, innerly persuasive discourse is denied such authority or privilege. Its
> importance comes only from its persuasiveness. (Moreson, 268)

This conflict of ideology, according to Bakhtin, will determine (undermine or reinforce) the
conception of the self and the course of individual, and perhaps, collective action. "The struggle
and dialogic interrelationship of these categories of ideological discourse are what usually
determine the history of an individual ideological consciousness" (*Dialogic*, 342).[64] All this
struggle of ideology will be manifest in language, for the word is always dialogic, that is, it
always embodies the ideologies of those who use it.

> Language invokes the political concept of freedom because language is struggle against
> the necessity of certain forms. Language is a unitizing noun developed for the action of
> what is a scattered and powerful array of social forces. Whether or not social interaction
> is conceived as class struggle, social forces are never conceived otherwise than as being

---

[63] In his work *Freudianism, a Marxist Critique*, Bakhtin argues that Freud's distinction between the
"conscious" and the "unconscious" is incorrect. They are "both variants of the same phenomenon: both are aspects
of consciousness. He perceives the distinction as differing degrees of ideological sharing: the unconscious is a
suppressed, relatively idiosyncratic ideological realm [...] whereas the conscious is a public world whose ideologies
may be shared openly with others." He calls Freud's unconscious the "unofficial conscious," as opposed to the
ordinary "official conscious" (Holquist, "Politics"; 177). The former is "inner speech," the latter "outer speech."

[64] Though official consciousness always has an enormous impact on members of the society, the struggle
of the unofficial consciousness will also take its toll: Bakhtin writes that "in the depths of behavioral ideology
accumulate those contradictions which once having reached a certain threshold, ultimately burst asunder the system
of the official ideology;" but, on the other hand, he also warns that "the wider and deeper the breach between the
official and unofficial conscious, the more difficult it becomes for motives of inner speech to turn into outward
speech [...] wherein they might acquire formulation, clarity and vigor" (*Freudianism*; in Holquist, "Politics"; 179
& 180; see also Vološinov, *Freudianism: A Critical Sketch, 1927*, in Morris, ed.; 38-48). Holquist believes that
Bakhtin is speaking here of his own dilemma, the "gap between his religious and metaphysical ideas and the Soviet
government's ever more militant insistence on adherence to Russian Communism." Bakhtin worries that "the gap
between official and unofficial conscious can become so great that finally the content of the unofficial conscious is
snuffed out" (Holquist, 1981; 180 & 181), a phenomenon that Morrison would recognize as "internal colonization"
in which the colonized adapts the language of the colonizer, thereby forgetting his own. See her "Friday on the
Potomac" in *Race-ing Justice, En-gendering Power*.

in conflict, except in utopias, which is why the word utopian has come to mean "unreal."
Bakhtin argues that language is where those struggles are engaged most comprehensively
and at the same time most intimately and personally.

(Clark & Holquist, 220; qdt. in Sprinkler, 123)

Bakhtin finds that it is in the work of Dostoevsky that the novel begins to reflect precisely
this struggle of ideology manifest in language; that is, Dostoevsky refuses to impose a line of
argument, a closed discourse, upon his characters, thereby giving them the freedom to express
conflicting ideas. This new-found freedom of expression in the novel Bakhtin denominates
"polyphony" – the simultaneous expression of multiple voices, hence multiple ideologies, which
he says the author allows to speak for themselves. Morris notes that it was the "special historical
conditions of Dostoevsky's own time which provided him with the optimal conditions for this
new perception."

> The impact of capitalism upon Russian ways of life maximized social and ideological
> contradictions so that the epoch itself became a creative borderzone between opposing
> historical consciousnesses. For Bakhtin such dialogic moments are always charged with
> the potential of creative change. (Morris, 18)

The idea of a "creative borderzone" is captured perfectly in the use of jazz as a metaphor. The
1920s in the United States were a time of multiple contradictions, a time both of prohibition and
of the attempt at legislation of morality, and of excessive wealth, ostentatiousness and
licentiousness, a time when whites held captive by day in Victorian modes of thinking escaped
to Harlem by night to revel in the freedom afforded by association with the more "primitive,"
more "instinctual" ways of behavior as represented by blacks. It was actually F. Scott Fitzgerald
who, looking back from the 30s upon a decade of libertine behavior, denominated it "the Jazz
Age," ("an age *defined* by Afro-American art and culture" [Morrison, "Un-speakable"; 26]), a
name which provocatively combined creative artistry with rebellion against established norms.
Even the term Bakhtin selects — "polyphony" — conjures up the jazz experience:

> Polyphony is an approach to narrative that embodies a dialogic sense of truth. [... T]hat
> truth is the sort of thing that can be represented not by a proposition but only by an
> unfinalizable conversation. [...I]n a polyphonic work, the reader is asked to engage
> directly with the ideas of the characters, much as the reader engages with the ideas of the
> author. [...] The tendency to engage characters this way is itself indicative of polyphony
> at work, because only in polyphonic works do (major) characters possess the power to
> mean directly. [...T]he author expresses his own position in *two* ways. As the creator *of*
> the work he embodies [...] a dialogic sense of truth. [...]
> *Polyphony is therefore a way of representing human freedom.*
>
> (Moreson, 258 & 259; emphasis added)

The use of a musical term for describing literary processes reflects Bakhtin's preoccupation with
voice and discourse in the novel. Because of the technical difficulty posed by some of the
vocabulary this author uses, Holquist provides a glossary at the end of *The Dialogic Imagination*

in which he defines a different yet related term. His definition is illustrative of yet another aspect of the jazz metaphor in Morrison:

> ORCHESTRATION [*orkestrovka*]
> Bakhtin's most famous borrowing from musical terminology is the "polyphonic" novel, but orchestration is the means for achieving it. Music is the metaphor for moving from seeing (such as in "the novel is the encyclopedia of the life of the era") to hearing (as Bakhtin prefers to recast the definition, "the novel is the maximally complete register of all social voice of the era"). For Bakhtin this is a crucial shift. In oral/aural arts, the "overtones" of a communication act individualize it. Within a novel perceived as a musical score, a single "horizontal" message (melody) can be harmonized vertically in a number of ways, and each of these scores with its fixed pitches can be further altered by giving the notes to different instruments. The possibilities of orchestration make any segment of text almost infinitely variable. The literary CHRONOTOPE [...], with its great sensitivity to time [...] finds a natural kinship with the overwhelmingly temporal art of music. (Bakhtin, *Dialogic*; 430)

The examples cited build a strong case for underscoring jazz as a perfect metaphor for writing about language, but there are yet others. In his analysis of the work of Rabelais, Bakhtin continues to explores the relationship of the folk with high literary arts, elaborating his theory of "double-voicedness" and moving toward a conception of "heteroglossia." Though the official church dominated the ideology of the Middles Ages with its authoritarian discourse, it more or less wisely accommodated to the populace's need for "release" from moral strictures once a year through its unofficial recognition of carnival. As Holquist describes it,

> Carnival is best conceived dialogically: i.e. as the interaction of differences in a simultaneity, [...] difference between official and unofficial worlds. The normal state of society is one in which relatively rigid hierarchies and hard-edged divisions separate social classes: what is and what is not permissible in personal relations and sexual politics. It is a state intolerant of ambiguities and semantic fluidity; it erects institutions, such as legal canons and dictionary-writing-academies, to stopper up the leaks in meaning. It is a world of human bodies that are closed to each other: the appropriate symbol of the state being the uniforms with which its armies and its churches homogenize the differences between bodies. Carnival celebrates the opposite of all these values. It promotes indeterminacy. (Holquist, "Carnival"; 222)

Such is Bakhtin's idea of the "unofficial" language of the folk, the market-place, and the carnivalesque: a permissible parodying of the "official," authoritarian discourse which signals a break-down in hierarchy, a "democratization" in which official powers are rendered less powerful, in which the power of discourse renders all men equal.

> The ruling power and the ruling truth cannot see themselves in the mirror of time, therefore they do not see their own beginnings, boundaries, and ends; they do not see their old and ridiculous face, the comic character of their pretensions to eternity and immutability. And the representatives of the old power and the old truth finish playing

74

their roles, in serious tones and with very serious faces, after their audience has already been laughing for a long time. They continue to speak in the serious, majestic, threatening, terrible tone of kings or heralds of "eternal truths," not noticing that time has already rendered this tone ridiculous in their mouths and transformed the old power and truth into a Shrovetide carnival dummy, into a comic scarecrow which the people tear to pieces with their laughter in the public square.

(Bakhtin, *Tworchestvo*, 236; in Hirschkop, 583)

For Bakhtin, carnival "laughter" or canivalesque discourse undermined the powers of authority; nothing was sacred or exempt except laughter itself, a powerful social leveler and democratic force. Bodily functions are celebrated, not denied, in their representation of birth, life, death, regeneration and transformation:

[C]arnival's symbol is the mask and the costume that decertify identity and enable transformation. Far from seeking to conceal the body, carnival dramatizes flesh as the site of becoming, and flaunts the orifices which in their activity of ingesting and defecating enact connections between the individual person and the whole world he is not, between inner and outer, the self and non-self. At this level the hierarchies erected by the state fall away as a kind of biologically ordained democracy takes over. This democracy breaks down not only class and political barriers, but the borders between generations as well. (Holquist, "Carnival"; 222)

The suspension of all hierarchical precedence during carnival time was of particular significance. Rank was especially evident during official feasts; [...]It was a consecration of inequality. On the contrary, all were considered equal during carnival. Here, in the town square, a special form of free and familiar contact reigned among people who were usually divided by the barriers of caste, property, profession, and age. The hierarchical background and the extreme corporative and caste divisions of the medieval social order were exceptionally strong. Therefore such, free, familiar contacts were deeply felt and formed an essential element of the carnival spirit. [...]
This temporary suspension, both ideal and real, of hierarchical rank created during carnival time a special type of communication impossible in everyday life. This led to the creation of special forms of marketplace speech and gesture, frank and free, permitting no distance between those who came in contact with each other and liberating from norms of etiquette and decency imposed at other times. A special carnivalesque, marketplace style of expression was formed which we find abundantly represented in Rabelais' novel. (Bakhtin, *Rabelais*; in Morris, 199-200)

For Holquist and others, carnival represents freedom in that it "becomes an exploration of alterity in social, political and religious mechanisms, a celebration that nurtures the liminality needed to keep such institutions from dying of a structural hardening of the arteries" (1985, "Carnival"; 230). Bakhtin himself signaled the striking "peculiarity" of carnival; that is, "its indissoluble and essential relation to freedom" (qtd. in Holquist, "*Rabelais*"; 16).

According to Bakhtin's theories of discourse, it is with Rabelais that this democratic irreverence enters the novel via the parody of all that is in authority and deemed sacred by the social structures. And with the entry of the folk diction, the discourse of the marketplace, the novel becomes truly multi-vocal. (Bakhtin discusses this innovation, particularly in *Pantagruel*, at some length.) The contact among cultures and religions produced at the end of the Middle Ages by the crusades and pilgrimages to the Holy Land also hastened the breakdown in the authority of the church; other conceptions of poetry and musical instruments were introduced to Renaissance Europe. And this "dialogic moment" saw the incorporation of voices from across cultures and social strata and produced the major changes in discourse that Rabelais reflected in his work. According to Todorov,

> [Bakhtin's] *Rabelais* provides a list of characteristic features of popular and comic culture: a material and corporeal principle of life; disparagement and debasement, hence parody; ambivalence: confusion of death with rebirth; the necessary relation to time and becoming: In the book on Dostoevsky, nearly the same table can be found; its elements are: free and familiar contact between persons; the attraction of the eccentric, the surprising, the bizarre; misalliances, the reunion of opposites; profanation and debasement [...] The essence of carnival lies in change, in death-rebirth, in destructive-creative time; carnivalesque images are basically ambivalent. (Todorov, 79)[65]

Bakhtin's work on Rabelais revealed to him a theory of discourse in the novel that he considered applicable to other novels in other eras.

> Though he led the popular chorus of only one time, the Renaissance, he so fully and clearly revealed the peculiar and difficult language of the laughing people that his work sheds its light on the folk culture of humor belonging to other ages.
> (Bakhtin, *Rabelais*; in Morris, 244)

That it is also applicable to the "infiltration" of the black vernacular into popular language and the discourse of the novel in the United States, particularly during the first part of the twentieth century (though, in fact, the phenomenon continues to the present), is apparent.

That jazz music represented a breakdown in dominant structures during another "dialogic moment," both for blacks and for rebellious whites, has been mentioned above, but its relationship with the folk is illustrative in other ways. As discussed previously, some critics have seen jazz, in its northward movement from its origins in New Orleans to its development in large northern cities, as representative itself of the Great Migration of black people from the rural south to the urban north. Dubey goes so far as to say that "the Great Migration constituted an enabling condition for jazz," insomuch as its introduction to major audiences was facilitated by this trajectory. "Neither a pure folk form in the South, nor suddenly commercialized by the migration, jazz was productively transformed by its passage into Northern cities during the 1920s" (298).

---

[65] Some critics have objected to describing the language of Dostoevsky's work as "carnivalesque." René Wellek complains that Dostoevsky represents "the opposite of the carnival spirit. He was a man of deep commitment, profound seriousness, spirituality and strict ethics, whatever his lapses were in his life" (239). Actually, however, Bakhtin defined the term as simply the undermining of the official discourse by the folk; "Carnivalesque," is "applied by synecdoche to the whole of this culture" (Todorov, 79).

She goes on later to add that "even the early jazz played in Southern cities was characterized by its fusion of diverse cultural sources. Jazz during the 1920s represented a unique cultural form that scrambled the boundaries between folk and classical, low and high cultural traditions" (299).[66] Dubey uses these arguments to refute Morrison's stated objective of transposing the oral culture of Southern blacks into her novel.

> The novel's conflicted inscription of a lost oral tradition as the constitutive basis of its own fictional language destabilizes a central claim of Morrison's (as well as other) vernacular criticism. Even as it is invoked to authorize the black fictional text, the black oral tradition gains its value in being produced as the absent condition of novelistic discourse.[67]   (Dubey, 307)

But, of course, it is not absent at all. In fact, as we shall see (Chapter VII), Morrison's use of the vernacular in *Jazz* precisely parallels Bakhtin's theories of "carnivalization" of the novel via heteroglossia. Jazz is once again an appropriate metaphor for this process. What is more, other critics pay their respects to the fact that jazz is, in fact, a hybrid form, even at its inception. Jazz is a "mixed race" aesthetic which – despite its popular association with black culture – is neither a wholly white nor wholly black tradition. During the 1920s jazz was regarded as "a New Orleans music played in somewhat different styles by both blacks and whites" (Collier, 332; qtd. in Burton,175).[68] Burton uses this musical "hybridity" to further her argument that Morrison is highlighting the theme of miscegenation in her novel, but it is no less certain that it also, and to even a greater extent, showcases the "dialogue" between two races as well as between "high" and "low" culture. Jazz works as a hybrid construction which corresponds to hybridity in discourse, that is, "an utterance which belongs, by virtue of its grammatical synactic (*sic*) and compositional markers to a single speaker, but which actually contains mixed within it two 'languages,' two semantic and axiological belief systems" (Holquist, "Politics"; 168). Hazel Carby notes the hybridity of *culture* as a whole which she describes as "the terrain of struggle between groups, 'a continuous and necessarily uneven and unequal struggle' and there is no whole, authentic, autonomous black culture which lies outside of these relations of cultural power and domination" (43).

---

[66] Dubey quotes Dan Morgenstern who argues that jazz cuts through the "artificial dichotomy between 'serious' and 'popular' art that was the creation and legacy of nineteenth-century European bourgeois culture" ("The Evolution of Jazz" in *New Perspectives on Jazz: Report on a National Conference Held at Wingspread, Racine, Wisconsin, September 8-10, 1986.* Ed. David N. Baker. Washington: Smithsonian Institute, 1990; 47; qtd. in Dubey, 299).

[67] Writes Dubey: "*Jazz*, for example, italicizes its narrator's failure to assume the voice of Southern oral tradition. [... I]t forces a recognition of the fact that novelistic communication is inevitably mediated by the material object of the book, a commodity that cannot transcend its conditions of production and reaction. The necessary gap between oral and novelistic modes distinguishes narration in the wake of migration, and constitutes the unique achievement of the vernacular novel, ... [and it] produces moments of formal stress (such as the concluding paragraphs of *Jazz*) that expose the contradictory status of history in vernacular theory" (309). Bakhtinian theory takes issue with this conclusion, as will be discussed below.

[68] Munton also insists that we acknowledge that there have been many contributions to jazz made by white interpreters as well as black.

Let us return for a moment to the understanding of "alterity," or "otherness," which is "the defining condition of all perception and therefore of all representations." Without the other, there can be no "self," and no self is finite in the discourse:

> There is no first or last discourse, and dialogical context knows no limits (it disappears into an unlimited past and in our unlimited future). Even *past* meanings, that is those that have arisen in the dialogue of past centuries, can never be stable (completed once and for all, finished), they will always change (renewing themselves) in the course of the dialogue's subsequent development, and yet to come. At every moment of the dialogue, there are immense and unlimited masses of forgotten meanings, but, in some subsequent moments, as the dialogue moves forward, they will return to memory and live in renewed form (in a new context). Nothing is absolutely dead: every meaning will celebrate its rebirth. The problem of the *great temporality*.
>
> (Bakhtin, "Methodology"; qtd. in Todorov, 110)

It is for this reason, and because of the heteroglossia found in the genre, that Bakhtin praises the quality of being unfinished as the "secret of the novel's superiority over other genres," a fact which "guarantees the possibility of others entering into dialogue with it: the loop hole guarantees freedom for the reader, and thus future life for the text."[69] Bakhtin even "concludes that the distinguishing feature of his [own] works is a certain unfinished quality" (Holquist, "Introduction"; 8), an aspect that invites dialogue and revision and the constant interchange of ideas. Indeed, Todorov laments the fact that because Bakhtin was censored and unpublished for so long in his native country, he himself never enjoyed a proper dialogue concerning his own theories. As the critic himself wrote, "For discourse (and, therefore, for man) nothing is more frightening than the *absence of answer*" (qtd. in Todorov, 111).

These considerations return us to the question of the "response-ibility" of the individual to the group, to the tradition, to the culture, an undeniable characteristic of jazz itself. Writes Bluestein:

> For jazz is a uniquely American expression and when we understand it as Ellison does, it encompasses just that sense of individualism directed toward communal concerns which we have already encountered in Emerson and Whitman. The metaphor of the jazzman illustrates the relationship better than any analogy we have seen. [...] Jazz values improvisation, personal vision, an assault on the conventional modes of musical expression, but it will not allow the individual to forget what he owes to tradition — [...] the legacy shaped by a whole people. [...] The authentic sources of a nation's culture lie in the lower levels and if they are developed sensitively, not only the poet speaks but his nation also finds its expression. (Bluestein, 136)

Just as the music at the turn of the century migrated both geographically and socially, amalgamating features from black and white, high and low, insinuating the vulgate into the higher

---

[69] Wolfgang Iser, in his *Implied Reader: Patterns of Communication in Prose Fiction from Bunyan to Beckett* (John Hopkins Univ. Pr., 1978), made this quality a central point in his reader response aesthetics.

forms of art, so black oral expression made its way from South to North, absorbing the ways and means of narrative from the most devalued members of the society, only to find its way into the much applauded literary canon scarcely one hundred years later. With the language, as with the music, comes the history, the "collective memory," the ideologies, the pain and the truths that Morrison so arduously searches for in her fiction. For "cultures, whether silenced or monologistic, whether repressed or repressing, seek meaning in the language and images available to them" (Morrison, "Unspeakable"; 8). For the exploration of storytelling and the black folk language and lore used to transmit an indescribably rich oral tradition, Toni Morrison could have chosen no more appropriate metaphor than jazz for *Jazz*.

PART TWO

STORYTELLING IN *JAZZ*

The Analysis

VII. STORYTELLING IN *JAZZ*

In the last section of her ground-breaking essay, "Unspeakable Things Unspoken: The Afro-American Presence in American Literature," Toni Morrison explicitly examines her own writing (from *The Bluest Eye* to *Beloved*) to demonstrate that the way in which she "practices language" is "a search for and deliberate posture of vulnerability to those aspects of Afro-American culture that can inform and position my work" (33):

> What makes a work "Black"? The most valuable point of entry into the question of cultural (or racial) distinction, the one most fraught, is its language – its unpoliced, seditious, confrontational, manipulative, inventive, disruptive, masked and unmasking language. Such a penetration will entail the most careful study, one in which the impact of Afro-American presence on modernity becomes clear and is no longer a well-kept secret. (Morrison, "Unspeakable"; 11)

Morrison's experimentation with the ways and means of language and storytelling is therefore contingent upon and indivisible from her concern with what make specifically her a *black* writer because, as Hazel Carby has stated, "we have defined the boundaries of an authentic culture in a language which can define authenticity because it is itself authentic" (41). The authenticity of the language, however, stems not only from its form in the utterance but also, and especially, in its dialogic exchange with the discourse that surrounds it, precedes it, and is expected to respond to it. Even though Briggs and Bauman recur to Bakhtin to sustain their work on linguistic anthropology, their affirmation that the process of producing and receiving discourse "lies in its interface with at least one other utterance" seems at best conservative. For Bakhtin the social nature of discourse simultaneously calls into play extensive referential information subsisting in cultural forms (other discourses) which are the basis for both communication and potential disruption. "There is no utterance without relation to other utterances, and that is essential" (Todorov, 60).

Nowhere is this more clearly seen than in the novel, for Bakhtin is convinced that "every literary work is sociological, and that it is so internally, immanently" (Bakhtin, *Dostoevsky*; qtd. in Todorov, 34):

> In the authentic novel, one can feel behind every utterance the nature of social languages
> with their internal logic and necessity. [...] The image of such a language in the novel is
> the image of the social horizon, of the social ideologeme, welded to its discourse, to its
> language.   (Bakhtin, "Discourse"; qtd. in Todorov, 62)

Moreover, in the novel, "language does not merely represent: it is itself an object of representation. Novelistic discourse is always self-critical" (Bakhtin "Prehistory"; qtd. in Todorov, 66). It is also, in *Jazz* particularly, self-referential – an exploration of just how language at once constitutes and defines the specificity of black culture and how it is used to tell stories. But the stories contained are not only the ones explicitly set out in the text. It is by means of intertextuality (Julia Kristeva's term) that the stories are expanded to include a wider cultural arena. Bakhtin refers to the novel as a "secondary" or "complex" genre which, in the case of the "pictorial" style of writing (Voloshinov, *Marxism,* in Morris, 65; or "pictural" in Todorov, 69) is a "powerful means of creatively exploiting intertextual gaps," in the dialogic nature of the word and, more particularly, in the deliberate blurring of the boundaries between different types of speech and literary genres (see below). So important is this aspect, in fact, that for Bakhtin

> [t]he plot itself is subordinated to the task of coordinating and exposing languages to
> each other. The novelistic plot must organize the exposure of social languages and
> ideologies, the exhibiting and experiencing of such languages: the experience of a
> discourse, a world view. [...] What is realized in the novel is the process of coming to
> know one's own language as it is perceived in someone else's language, coming to know
> one's own horizon within someone else's horizon.   (Bakhtin, *Dialogic*; 365)

And so concerned is *Jazz* with this interaction of discourse and with the intertextual gaps that are produced in this interaction that the careful analysis of the text comes close to revealing it as Morrison's attempt to explicate and enact Bakhtin's theory of the novel.

Morrison refers to the possibility of these "gaps" (or "spaces") as the basis for her choice of language ("speakerly, aural, colloquial") which calls upon "codes embedded in black culture," necessary, she believes, for the "full comprehension" of the meaning of the text and which are an attempt to "transfigure the complexity and wealth of Afro-American culture into a language worthy of culture" ("Unspeakable," 23). Bakhtin would probably take issue with Morrison at this point, in that for him "comprehension" and "full" interpretation will vary according to the historical condition of the reader/interpreter. For him, it is precisely readers standing outside the chronotope and the culture of the author who will provide ever more enriching readings – an "authorization" of non-black, non-American, non-female (etc.) critics.

> To be sure, to enter in some measure into an alien culture and look at the world through
> its eyes, is a necessary moment in the process of its understanding. [...] Creative
> understanding does not renounce its self, its place in time, its culture; it does not forget
> anything. The chief matter of understanding is the exotopy of the one who does the
> understanding – in time, space, and culture – in relation to that which he wants to
> understand creatively.   (Bakhtin, "Response"; qtd. in Todorov, 109)

In fact, Morrison's own innovative reading of texts from the so-called "American Renaissance" in *Playing in the Dark* constitutes an excellent example of Bakhtin's theory. What is necessary as far as Bakhtin is concerned is that the critic immerse him/herself within the culture and historical time of the novel and the author, to learn as much as possible, and then *return* to his/her own culture/time-frame to provide a deeper, more thoughtful interpretation. (Thus, the question of the appropriation of black female texts by white female or male critics for Bakhtin is a moot point.) Morrison is not unaware of, nor unreceptive to, other readings:

> These spaces, which I am filling in [with "black cultural meanings"], and can fill in because they were planned, can conceivably be filled in with other significances. That is planned as well. The point is that into these spaces should fall the ruminations of the reader and his other invented or recollected or misunderstood knowingness.
>
> (Morrison, "Unspeakable"; 29)[70]

It is precisely these intertextual gaps or spaces that constitute a fundamental aspect of Morrison's concern with storytelling. In his influential essay entitled "The Storyteller," Walter Benjamin complains that with the arrival of the novel on the cultural scene, the art of storytelling has been progressively lost, and he decries the fact that, as a solitary act, novel reading could no longer involve the participation of the listener in the story (87). Linguistic research confirms that in the African-American community, "participation in oral storytelling and other forms of verbal art afforded children great acuity in creating intertextual relations, particularly as based on metaphorical and fictionalized links" (Briggs & Bauman citing Heath, 160). In fact, one of Henry Louis Gate's arguments in the *Signifying Monkey* is that intertextuality lies at the very heart of African-American aesthetics. As has already been remarked upon, however, a clear Morrison objective is to involve the reader in the unfolding of her story (stories); certainly one of her foremost strategies is to ensure these "intertextual spaces" for readerly participation.

A close examination, therefore, of the ways in which language is used to fabricate stories, both narratively and intertextually, is the focus of this last chapter. By using Bakhtin's theory of the dialogic nature of language, moreover, it will become ever more apparent that the "orality" of black culture is everywhere present, thereby providing a direct refutation of Dubey's argument that there is no black vernacular culture in *Jazz* (307).[71] Drawing on Bakhtin's considerations of speech acts, speech genres, and narrative formation, moreover, it becomes apparent that with each new chapter of *Jazz*, Morrison is experimenting with language to elucidate the many and varied ways in which stories are told. Just as the characters search for understanding, so the reader (the literary critic and sleuth) participates in the unfolding of their stories via the myriad ways and means of storytelling.

---

[70] What is clear in this statement and becomes ever more so in an analysis of her text is that nothing in *Jazz* is left to improvisation and that the "spontaneity" alleged by so many of Morrison's "jazz critics" is carefully wrought and constructed.

[71] Morrison herself in an interview with Salman Rushdie stated, "I want to merge vernacular with the lyric, with the standard and with the biblical, because it was part of the linguistic heritage of my family, moving up and down the scale, across it, in between it (BBC "The Late Show," [Summer, 1992]).

A. "Sth. I know that woman."

In "Unspeakable Things Unspoken" Morrison goes into great detail in explaining her choices for the opening of each of her first five novels. I have suggested elsewhere that *Jazz*, her sixth novel, could be read as a reworking of certain themes present in *The Bluest Eye* (Tally, "Specter"), and the author's comments on the opening of that novel are most certainly pertinent to the beginning of the text under consideration. With "Quiet as it's kept [...]" Morrison has here and in a recorded video interview with A. S. Byatt made explicit her allusion to an opening ritual for gossip which was typical among the black women in her home town of Lorraine, Ohio. There is in these four words the

> suggestion of illicit gossip, of thrilling revelation, there is also, in the "whisper," the assumption (on the part of the reader) that the teller is on the inside, knows something others do not, and is going to be generous with this privileged information. The intimacy I was aiming for, the intimacy between the reader and the page, could start up immediately because the secret is being shared at best, and eavesdropped upon, at the least. (Morrison, "Unspeakable"; 21)

As in the case of the relationships between the endings of the chapters and the beginnings of the next (see above), the emphasis on "sound" in the epigraph of *Jazz* ("I am the name of the sound and the sound of the name") turns up in the first "word" which is itself a sound (an unusual strategy, much as in *Beloved*, which intentionally begins with a number: 124).[72] To the strategy of immediacy and involvement of the reader is added the "illicitness" of what is about to be mentioned, reinforced on the following pages by the insistence on the "legally licensed beauty parlor," and the "legally licensed beauticians" (*J*, 5 & 18), which correlates to and conjures up the opposite. Even the opening phrase from *The Bluest Eye* turns up on page 17 of *Jazz*: "It never happened again as far as I know - the street sitting - but quiet as it's kept she did try to steal that baby although there is no way to prove it." (*J*, 17)

The "illicitness" of the gossip (and of the theft) indicated by the hush-hush, disapproving quality of the opening sound also immediately contextualizes and qualifies the simple sentence that follows it: "I know that woman." Given the dubious nature of this "knowledge" it should come as little surprise at the end of the novel that the narrator acknowledge just how little she knows of the characters. What follows is a brief run-down of the scandalous affair (Joe's murder of Dorcas and Violet's attempt to desecrate the corpse), complete on the first page of the text, which makes Morrison's reference to her first novel again completely relevant:

> I hoped the simplicity was not simple-minded, but devious, even loaded. And that the process of selecting each word, for itself and its relationship to the others in the sentence, along with the rejection of others for their echoes, for what is determined and what is not determined, what is almost there and what must be gleaned, would not theatricalize itself,

---

[72] Moreover, if one is looking for "clues" to relate Jazz to the former novel in the trilogy, as Jennifer Fitzgerald has pointed out, "Sth" is "Sethe" without the vowels.

would not erect a proscenium – at least not a noticeable one. So important to me was this unstaging, that in this first novel I summarized the whole of the book on the first page.   (Morrison, "Unspeakable"; 20)

That the "whole" story is set out on the first page of *Jazz* immediately signals that the "facts"of the event (which will be repeated and elaborated upon throughout the novel) are much less important that the nature of the telling. It is, indeed, the narrator's narration (the gossipy style and viewpoint) that constitute the first mode of storytelling in the book. Even in the narrator's description of the City, she specifically refers to people (obviously like herself) who "find themselves butting in the business of people whose names they can't even remember and whose business is none of theirs" (*J*, 11), or later in the chapter to Violet as "a hardworking young woman with the snatch-gossip tongue of a beautician" (*J*, 23).

Apart from the questionable reliability of this narrator, it is clear that s/he is claiming center stage for herself in the story and to do so s/he resorts to various storytelling strategies: (1) the slow, teasing divulging of information, (2) the continuous repetition of terms and phrases, (3) the interruption into the narrative of personal observation, and (4) a narrative line based on free association and circularity that brings the narrative back to where it started. What it has in common with many other chapters (see below) is (5) a penchant for pseudodiegesis and (6) a vibrant intertextuality

1. The Delaying of Critical Information

Although both Joe and Violet are specifically named in the opening synopsis, Dorcas' identity is delayed even as Violet initiates a search to find out as much as possible about her. Initially she is referred to only as "the girl" (*J*, 3), "the dead girl" (twice on page 4), "the eighteen-year-old," "the girl" (on three occasions), "that girl" and the more personalized "whose child she was" (all on page 5). Page six refers to her again as "the girl" and "the dead girl" (and a generic reference to "a colored girl"), though with the introduction of "the aunt" she also becomes "the niece." As the narrator takes over with her own personal observations, "the deal girl['s face]" is not mentioned again until page 11, and only on page 12 is Dorcas finally named, "Dorcas? Dorcas," as if the name gave some finality to Violet's search. Page 13 repeats her name three times and finally gives her a last name, "Dorcas Manfred," though she is only a picture in a silver frame "waking them up all night long." "Dead" is picked up several times as well after that (on pages 14 & 15), even in the "City interlude" (... "nothing was safe --- not even the dead" [*J*, 9]), the insistence on the word somehow emphasizing the fact that Dorcas is more present than absent and that her physical death is far from final ("[her picture ...] seems like the only living presence in the house" [*J*, 10-11]); Violet even has "whispered conversations with the corpse in her head" (*J*, 15). Indeed both Joe's and Violet's search for Dorcas — or for understanding her life and death — will dominate the rest of the text. In the words of one of the prostitutes, "Can't rival the dead for love. Lose every time" (*J*, 15).

Violet's attempt to steal the baby is set out in certain detail, through both mimesis and diegesis, though again it is introduced in a conspiratorial manner: "What is known is this [...]" (*J*, 17). But this first chapter also "drops" elliptical information concerning other stories which will only be complemented in later chapters, a technique we usually refer to as foreshadowing:

85

her mother's suicide (insinuated in reference to the "brightness" which could be "Distributed [...] into places dark as the bottom of a well" [*J*, 22], and "[...] the children of suicides are hard to please and quick to believe no one loves them because they are not really here" [*J*, 4]); the story of Joe's first encounter with Dorcas and her love of sweets ("Long before Joe stood in the drugstore watching a girl buy candy [...]" [*J*, 23]; the reference to Alice, the "dead girl's aunt" and Violet's visits to her (*J*, 6) the future appearance of Felice ("another girl with four marcelled waves," [*J*, 6], the story of Violet's grandmother and Golden Gray; Malvonne, "an upstairs neighbor"; and mention of Violet's cracks and her "renegade tongue." And, of course, the hint once again of illicitness in the "scandalizing threesome on Lenox Avenue" and of future information that never materializes: "What turned out different was who shot whom" (*J*, 6). Even the "seep of rage. Molten. Thick and slow moving (*J*, 16)" anticipates the interlude on pages 74-75 of women fighting back, the anger Alice hears in jazz, and her own feelings of fury over her husband's desertion which she had smothered for so long to keep herself from losing control. The number "eight," appearing not only in Violet's lottery combination (J, 22) but also in the sum of the numbers of 134[th Street] (*J*, 4) is prescient to Joe's own account of his metamorphoses in that before he met Dorcas he affirms he had been "made new" seven times; presumably the eighth time he changes is on his encounter with his eighteen-year-old lover (see *J*, 123ff).

2. Repetition

Apart from the terms discussed above ("dead girl," "legal," "frame"), the narrator frequently uses the storyteller's technique of heightening attention through the repetition of other, more colloquial terms: the repetition of "baby," "baby buggy," "baby brother," and the fact that she will "bathe" him as soon as she gets him home. Later the narrator will mention the dark fissures in "globe light of the day," a " globe light holds and bathes each scene," or the "daylight" of the discussion of the Dumfrey women, later to be "a kind of skipping, running light traveled her veins" (*J*, 19) which returns in the "memory of light" (*J*, 22), with "lightness" and "brightness," or that she first saw Joe in the "early light" of day; and repeated references to "cracks" and "crevices" return the reference to the "fissures." Violet's "laugh" is emphasized (J, 20, 21, 22) to heighten the effects of the different versions of her attempted theft; but there are other, much more subtle repetitions as, for example, the appearance of "okay" in the careless sister's account of her conversation with Violet when she left her baby brother to go upstairs to get a record: "A woman! I was gone one minute. Not even one! I asked her ... I said ... and she said okay ...!" (*J*, 20), and in Joe's male friends who discreetly asked about Violet: "How *is* Violet? Doing okay, is she?" Both recall the arrival of the other girl with four marcelled waves, "coming into the building with an Okeh record under her arm" (*J*, 6). The birdcages left empty after Violet lets the birds out are repeated in the description of the Traces' apartment: "the rooms are like the empty birdcages wrapped in cloth" (*J*, 11).

3. Intrusiveness

Early on in this chapter (pages 7 to 9) the narrator introduces "the City" (guided in by a mention of "spring came to the City" at the end of page 6), which takes on the guise of one more character in the novel as its overwhelmingly new, urban presence makes itself felt on all the characters, including the narrator herself. It is, however, a very personal account of how the narrator feels about and describes its many facets. It is also here an excuse for explicitly making what Bakhtin calls the "hidden polemic" of the text transparent through the quibbling voice of the narrator:

> Any speech that is servile or overblown, any speech that is determined beforehand not to be itself, any speech replete with reservations, concessions, loopholes and so on. Such speech seems to cringe in the presence, or at the presentiment of, some other person's statement, reply, objection. (Bakhtin, *Dostoevsky*; qtd. in Lodge, 37)

It "senses its own listener, reader, critic, and reflects in itself their anticipated objections, evaluations, points of view. In addition, it senses alongside itself another discourse, another style" (Bakhtin, *Dostoevsky*; 196; qtd in Lodge, 86), which David Lodge explains as "the style of peers, rivals and precursors, which it rejects, competes with, seeks to supplant" (86). The narrator in *Jazz* grovels, vacillates, tries to anticipate any possible criticism she thinks might be leveled at her:

> I haven't got any muscles, so I can't really be expected to defend myself. But I do know how to take precaution. Mostly it's making sure no one knows all there is to know about me. Second, I watch everything and everyone and try to figure out their plans, their reasonings, long before they do. You have to understand what it's like, taking on a big city: I'm exposed to all sort of ignorance and criminality. (*J*, 8)

Yet she revels in the vibrance of the City and sets it up as indispensable background for her story. At the same time, however, this passage is another indication of the narrator's contradiction. Although she insists that she makes sure that "no one knows all there is to know about me," she uses these interludes to divulge more about herself than about anyone else. And though she boasts here that "you have to be clever to figure out how to be welcoming and defensive at the same time," or else risk ending up "out of control or controlled by some outside thing" (*J*, 9), by the end of the book she will be lamenting her own carelessness.

By far the most noticeable characteristic of this narrator is her intrusiveness; she is constantly insinuating herself into her own narrative by way of personal comments and appraisals. Just to give a few examples:

> So she commenced to gather the rest of the information. Maybe she thought she could solve the mystery of love that way. Good luck and let me know. (*J*, 5)

> The aunt showed all the dead girl's things to Violet and it became clear to her (as it was to me) that this niece had been hardheaded as well as sly. (*J*, 6)

> I don't know who was more ambitious — the doomsayers or Violet—but it's hard to match the superstitious for great expectations. (*J*, 9)

> You know how some people put a chair or a table in a corner where it looks nice but

87

nobody in the world is ever going to go over to it, let alone sit down there?   (*J*, 12)

This notion of rest, it's attractive to her, but I don't think she would like it.   (*J*, 16)

It is true that, like Philip Marlowe, we never learn what the narrator looks like or even where she lives, or any of the other defining characteristics she is careful to give about her characters. We do, however, come to know a good deal about her "personality": she is gossipy, of course, a bit arrogant (as supposed insiders will be) about how much she knows and can inform us, by her own account very clever (and therefore, questionably so), ostensibly very observant, mostly solitary by her own admission, and quite a romantic, judging from her description of the man in the straw hat seducing a girl in the space between two buildings (*J*, 8). She is intrusive, never missing an opportunity to comment on the story as she tells it, but she is also a skillful storyteller given the way she melds one section right into the next.

4. Free Association and Circularity

The narrator's use of associative ideas in this chapter is clearly based on the often rambling discourse of oral storytellers. One of the techniques that most effectively integrates a sense of "orality" and immediacy in the text, in fact, is precisely the flow of the narrative into seemingly unrelated (yet highly pertinent, *a posteriori*) stories or anecdotes. The interlude on the City, which sets the *topos*, for example, ends in its mention of the "signs" during "last winter" and setting of the *chronos* ("Barely three days into 1926"), refers back to the so-called "scandal" ("a message sent to warn the good and rip up the faithless"), and continues with Violent's disruption of the funeral by relating the Armistice with the veterans who were "still wearing their army-issue greatcoats" (*J*, 9).

It is her washing of "*gray* hair, soft and interesting as a baby's" (*J*, 17) that leads to the mention of True Belle's Baltimore stories (about Miss Vera Louise and the little golden-haired boy we will later be introduced to as Golden *Gray* [emphases added]), and later leads into the story of "baby-snatching," whose mimetic section echoes the nature of gossip already described:

> "Daylight," said Violet. "Have some daylight get in there."
> "They need to move on back to Memphis then if daylight is what they want."
> "Memphis? I thought they were born here."
> "That's what they'd have you believe. But they ain't. Not even Memphis. Cottown.
> Someplace nobody ever heard of."
> "I'll be," said Violet.   (*J*, 18)

As mentioned above, the memory of the light and Violet's "craziness" move the narrator into a discussion of her "cracks" and the "disconnect" which sometimes occur in her conversation. Violet's uncontrollable tongue leads her to keep silence, but the narrator brings her narrative deftly back to where she began with references to birdcages and the attempt to cut Dorcas' dead face: "Less excusable than a wayward mouth is an independent hand that can find in a parrot's cage a knife lost for weeks" (*J*, 24). Also closing the chapter is the parrot who "answers back: 'I love you,'" which not only completes the circle but points to two major themes in the book: 1) the obvious question of love (or lack of it) in all its facets; and 2) the question of dialogue (or lack of it), since the parrot can never love or even "other" Violet because it offers no real response. For a time Violet feels "othered" by the picture of Dorcas on her mantelpiece: "You are there, it says, because I am looking at you" (*J*, 12). But only with the creation of "Violent" can this protagonist work on finding the self her mother would have liked (*J*, 208).

5. Quasi-direct Discourse (Free Direct Speech, Free Indirect Speech) and Pseudodiegesis ("Hybridization")[73]

The overt intrusiveness of the narrator in the text tends to obscure another technique of authors/narrators for creating a sense of "live," orally-spoken language — *quasi-direct discourse* (which Lodge breaks down into free direct speech and free indirect speech) and *pseudodiegesis*. While the intrusive narrator in *Jazz* offers her own opinions, comments gratuitously on events of the narration or asks rhetorical questions of the reader, the use of free direct speech or free indirect speech involves different criteria. In this strategy the narrator slides more or less unobtrusively from straight-forward diegesis into another "voice," either of a character or of an anonymous public, without bothering to signal mimetic reproduction of the discourse. David Lodge summarizes Bakhtin's typology of literary discourse as:

> 1. *The direct speech of the author*. This corresponds to Plato's diegesis.
> 2. *Represented speech*. This includes Plato's mimesis – i.e. the quoted direct speech of the characters; but also reported speech in the pictorial style.
> 3. *Doubly-oriented speech*, that is, speech which not only refers to something in the world but refers to another speech act by another addresser.
> Bakhtin subdivides this third type of discourse into four categories, stylization, parody, *skaz* (the Russian term for oral narration), and what he calls "dialogue." Dialogue means here not the quoted direct speech of the characters, but discourse which alludes to an *absent* speech act. In stylization, parody and *skaz*, the other speech act is "reproduced with a new intention"; in "dialogue" it "shapes the author's speech while remaining outsides its boundaries."
> (Lodge, 33)

Closer reading, of the text reveals that what is being related under the guise of narrative is actually the appropriated discourse of another who may or may not be specifically designated.

(a) Quasi-direct Discourse

At then end of *The Bakhtin Reader,* Pam Morris includes a glossary of what she considers to be key terms, one of which concerns "speech":

> Forms of speech discussed by Bakhtin include 'pryamaya' ('direct') speech, 'kosvenna-ya' (indirect') speech and 'nesobstvenno-pryamaya' ('quasi-direct'); this latter is a

---

[73] Todorov states that Bakhtin uses the term "hybridization" to mean "a generalization of free indirect style" (73) as seemingly does Pam Morris (249), but from my understanding of Bakhtin's discussion of the term in "Discourse in the Novel" (as translated by Michael Holquist), he is apparently closer to Lodge's interpretation of "pseudodiegesis." For further discussion, see below.

transitional, explicitly 'double-voiced" speech type, since it contains linguistic and cognitive features taken both from the narrator's and from the character's speech [...]

(Morris, 251)

In his glossary at the end of *The Dialogic Imagination*, Michael Holquist also defines the term:

> Between the two traditional grammatical categories of DIRECT SPEECH *[prjamaja rec']* and INDIRECT SPEECH *[kosvennaja rec']* Bakhtin posits an intermediate term, QUASI-DIRECT SPEECH *[nesobstevenno-prjamaja rec']*. (This category is given very detailed treatment in chapter 4 of V.N. Voloshinov's *Marxism and the Philosophy of Language* [tr. Matejka and Titunik, New York, 1973]:141-159.) Quasi-direct speech involves discourse that is formally authorial, but that belongs in its "emotional structure" to a represented character, his "inner speech transmitted and regulated by the author" [319], where the passage cited is an internal monologue of Nezhdanov's from Turgenev's *Virgin Soil*].
>
> Quasi-direct speech is a threshold phenomenon, where authorial and character intentions are combined in a single intentional hybrid. Measuring the relative strength of these competing intentions is a major task of novel stylistics.

(Holquist, *Dialogic*; 432)

In his practical analysis of a short section of D. H. Lawrence's *Ulysses*, however, Lodge distinguishes between "focalized narrative," "interior monologue," "free direct speech," and "free indirect speech" (34-35). In an effort to be more specific, I will use Lodge's additional classification:

[i] Free Direct Speech

In free direct speech the requisite quotation marks are dispensed with to secure the flow of the narrative, but these could easily be added to the text to indicate specific speakers (italics added):

> Up in those big five-story apartment buildings and the narrow wooden houses in between people knock on each other's doors to see if anything is needed or can be had. *A piece of soap? A little kerosene? Some fat, chicken or pork, to brace the soup one more time? Whose husband is getting ready to go see if he can find a shop open? Is there time to add turpentine to the list drawn up and handed to him by the wives?* (*J*, 10)

[Although the women in the apartment building are not specified, their voices are present in this example.]

> There was gentle soap in the sample case already so she could bathe him in the kitchen right away. *Him? Was it a him?* Violet lifted her head to the sky and laughed with the excitement in store when she got home to look. (*J*, 20)

[This is clearly Violet's interior monologue.]

[ii] Free Indirect Speech

Lodge argues that the device of free indirect speech allows the narrator, without absenting himself entirely from the text, to communicate the narrative to us

> coloured by the thoughts and feelings of a character. The reference to this character in the third-person pronoun, and the use of the past tense [...] still imply the existence of the author as the source of the narrative; but by deleting the tags which affirm that existence, such as "he said," "she wondered," "she thought to herself," etc., and by using the kind of diction appropriate to the character rather than to the authorial narrator, the latter can allow the sensibility of the character to dominate the discourse, and correspondingly subdue his own voice, his own opinions and evaluations. The device is an extremely flexible one, which allows the narrator to move very freely and fluently between the poles of mimesis and diegesis within a single paragraph, or even a single sentence; and its effect is always to make the reader's task of interpretation more active and problematic.　　　　　　　　　　　　　　　　　　　　　　　　　(Lodge, 49)

Consider this example from *Jazz*:

> Besides, she found out that the man who killed her niece cried all day and *for him and for Violet that is as bad as jail.*　　　　　　　　　　　　　　　　(J, 4)

[Although there is no break in the narrator's sentence, the *voice* of this section is obviously the opinion of Alice Manfred.]

Lodge states that free indirect speech "allows the novelist to give the reader intimate access to a character's thought without totally surrendering control of the discourse to that character" (126), but at times the strategy is used to include voices of "people on the street" who are not necessarily involved in the novel except as dialogic backdrop. Consider the following:

> Regardless of the grief Violet caused, her name was brought up at the January meeting of the Salem Women's Club as someone needing assistance, but it was voted down because *only prayer — not money — could help her now, because she had a more or less able husband (who needed to stop feeling sorry for himself)*, and because a man and his family on 134ᵗʰ Street had lost everything in a fire.　　　　　(J, 4)

[Again there is no direct quotation but the collective voice of this discourse is the anonymous members of the Women's Club discussing, with some disapproval, Violet and Joe. The rest of the sentence not in italics belongs to the narrator's diegesis.]

> The woman had left her bag and was merely walking the baby while the older sister — *too silly to be minding a child anyway* — ran back in her house for a record to play for a friend. *And who knew what else was going on in the head of a girl too dumb to watch a baby sleep?*　　　　　　　　　　　　　　　　　　　　　　　(J, 21)

[In this example the voice is most probably that of the people who gathered around to find out what had happened to the "stolen baby," criticizing the sister's negligence.]

> From the legally licensed beauticians she found out what kind of lip rouge the girl wore; the marcelling iron they used on her *(though I suspect that girl didn't need to straighten her hair);* the band the girl liked best *(Slim Bates' Ebony Keys which is pretty good except for his vocalist who must be his woman since why else would he let her insult his band).*
> (*J*, 5)

[While the first italicized phrase is clearly another intrusion on the part of the narrator, the second is not so clear. Although it might simply be yet another opinion of the narrator, it is much more likely that the comment in parenthesis is fruit of some collective gossip. Lodge writes that "paradoxically, indeterminacy of meaning leads to an increase of meaning, because it demands more interpretative effort by the reader than does traditional narrative" (143).]

(b) Pseudodiegesis

The question of pseudodiegesis poses yet another type of authorial device. For Lodge, pseudodiegesis is neither diegesis nor mimesis, nor a blend of the two, but characterized by "the mimesis not of a character's speech but of a discourse [...]" (36), appropriated for effect directly into the narrative. "When such narration has the characteristics of oral discourse, it is designated *skaz* in the Russian critical tradition, though Bakhtin argues that the 'oral' quality is less important than the adoption of another's discourse for one's own aesthetic and expressive purposes" (60). Nevertheless, in the following example, the oral quality of the discourse plays an extremely important part in conveying the mood and dynamic voice of black people in the neighborhoods and on the streets of the City:

> The smart ones say so and people listening to them and reading what they write down agree: *Here comes the new. Look out. There goes the sad stuff. The bad stuff. The things-nobody-could-help stuff. The way everybody was then and there. Forget that. History is over, you all, and everything's ahead at last.*
> (*J*, 7)

[This pseudodiegesis — the appropriation of a style of discourse rather than the words of a character — will become dominant in the third chapter of *Jazz* (See below).]

It can be argued that these insertions into the narrative effected by the use of free direct discourse, free indirect discourse and pseudodiegesis are paralleled by the "disconnects" in Violet's "cracks"
—

> "Got a mind to double it with an aught and two or three others just in case who is that pretty girl standing next to you?"
> (*J*, 24)

> Like the time Miss Haywood asked her what time could she do her granddaughter's hair and Violet said, "Two o'clock if the hearse is out of the way."
> (*J*, 24)

— perhaps Morrison's way, once again, of explicitly highlighting the use of authorial strategies in the process of narration.

(6) Historical Reference and Intertextuality

History in *Jazz*, far from being over, is everywhere present, either in specific references or via the double-voicedness of intertextuality. Apart from the geography of what is clearly New York, principally Harlem (Lenox Avenue and the Tenderloin district, Lexington and Park Avenue, etc.) and the reference to the UNIA men, Armistice, Okeh records, the Ebony Keys, *Modern Homemaker*, the Lafayette, and such, the positive attitude of the Harlem Renaissance with its newly instilled pride is signaled in new social attitudes:

> The A&P hires a colored clerk. [...] Nobody wants to be an emergency at Harlem Hospital but if the Negro surgeon is visiting, pride cuts down the pain. And although the hair of the first class of colored nurses was declared unseemly for the official Bellevue nurse's cap, there are thirty-five of them now – all dedicated and superb in their profession. (*J*, 8-9)

And in addition to the pride in what the black population sees as the advancement of the race, tributes to "regular people" of the City are interspersed in the narrative:

> A last courtship full of smiles and little presents. Or the dedicated care of an old friend who might not make it through without them. Sometimes they concentrated on making sure the person they had shared their long lives with had cheerful company and the necessary things for the night. (*J*, 11)

Eric Forner had earlier been highly critical of Morrison's depiction of history in her previous book, *Beloved*:

> Nor does Morrison present anything but a pessimistic picture of the post-emancipation society her black characters inhabit. *Beloved* is set in 1873, in the midst of Reconstruction. The world outside Sethe's house plays a secondary role in the story, but when it appears, it does so in tales of Klan violence, in evidence of the continuing exploitation of blacks and flagrant disregard for their rights. As one who has studied this period for many years now, I see Reconstruction in a rather different light — as a remarkable time of hope, of accomplishment, of dreams, soon to be shattered, of a brighter future. Nothing that Morrison relates is "untrue," but she offers the reader no hint of the remarkable achievements of black in the *public* world in these years, of how the former slaves' quest for individual and community autonomy and for equal rights as citizens of the American republic helped to shape the nation's political agenda, and helped them leave behind the legacy, although not the memory, of slavery.
>
> (Forner, 48-49)

The references to the public and more positive world of *Jazz* look like the author's attempt to respond to his objections — a clear instance of dialogue between the author and critic via the text and an assumption of "response-ibility." Morrison does not dwell on the persistent and pervasive racism of the era — no high schools nor banks in Harlem, for example, — but neither does she ignore it. Even though Alice Manfred knows who murdered her niece she does not prosecute Joe because she "didn't want to throw money to helpless lawyers or laughing cops when she knew the expense wouldn't improve anything" (*J*, 4).

Though the explicit historical references serve to ground and enrich the narrative, the intertextual references (the "spaces" for interpretation) are at once more intricate and more rewarding. Besides Violet's own surmising that she became a hairdresser because of her grandmother's Baltimore stories about Golden's beautiful blonde hair, Violet's job as an extralegal beautician and Joe's as a salesman of cosmetics is a direct reference to Madame Walter, the first black female millionaire, whose fortune was made in beauty products during the era.[74] I would argue as well that Violet's obsession with Golden Gray's beautiful locks calls even more directly to a poem also published during the Harlem Renaissance, Jessie Fausset's "Touché," in which the female voice interprets her lover's fascination with her own black hair as a conscious rejection of the fascination he felt as a youth for exactly the opposite - an attitude she divines precisely because she had experienced the same emotions. This rejection of the obsession with blonde curls is exactly what Violet must effect on her way to wholeness.

It also seems to me that the repeated references to "bird cages" in this first chapter subtly but insistently call to Josephine Baker, who also became wildly popular in Paris during the 1920s, one of her more widely acclaimed performances enacted in a "birdcage."[75]

B. "Or used to."

The second chapter in *Jazz* is divided almost equally into two main parts (13 pages and 11 pages, respectively) and both include interludes on the City seamlessly worked into the narrative. The first section concerns Joe's reverie of the past (including thoughts about Dorcas, Violet and their migration to the north, and his and Dorcas' confidences shared in secret) and is framed by Joe's lying awake in bed:

> He remembers his memories of her; how thinking about her as he lay in bed next to
> Violet was the way he entered sleep.   (*J*, 28)

> On those nights Joe does not mind lying awake next to his silent wife because his
> thoughts are with this young good God young girl who both blesses his life and makes
> him wish he had never been born.   (*J*, 40)

That the subsequent narration will be filtered through Joe's voice is emphasized in the repetition of terms related to memory, ten times in the course of two pages (*J*, 28 & 29): "[...] the girl's memory is a sickness in the house [...]"; "[...] he remembers his memories of her [...]"; "[...] the

---

[74] Though Walker was a generous patron of the Harlem Renaissance artists, there is some historical irony in the fact that she made her fortune selling beauty products to help black people look more like whites with hair straighteners and skin lighteners, etc.

[75] And a nod to Maya Angelou's *I Know Why the Caged Bird Sings*, the first book in this author's autobiographical series.

possibility of his memory failing to conjure up the dearness [...]"; "Now he lies in bed remembering every detail of that October afternoon [...] over and over"; "[...] because he is trying to sear her into his mind [...]"; "[...] when Joe tries to remember the way it was [...]"; "He recalls dates [...]"; "[...] old age would be not remembering what things felt like"; "[...] you could not retrieve the fear"; "That you could replay in the brain the scene of ecstasy, of murder, of tenderness [...]" On the following page Victory, who will always be associated with memory, is mentioned for the first time.

This is not a straight-forward narrative technique, however; it is full of all of the hybrid forms mentioned above but complicated to yet a larger degree. Initially the narrator omnisciently relates his first encounter, but, then, unobtrusively recurs to an appropriation of Joe's voice in free direct speech:

> Then, suddenly, there in Alice Manfred's doorway, she stood, toes pointing in, hair braided, not even smiling but welcoming him in *for sure. For sure.* Other wise he would not have had the audacity, the nerve, to whisper to her at the door as he left.
> (*J*, 29; emphasis added)

Joe's "decision" to court Dorcas reminds him (free association) of other decisions from the past including his name, the walnut tree, the decision to emigrate from the South, as opposed to his union with Violet (her decision) which helped him escape from redwings and silence — the first mention of Wild, the woman he supposes to be his mother — all strategies of foreshadowing the coming chapters. The brief summary of his first meeting with Violet leads into their train ride to the City and provides more space for the social commentary initiated (also in the City section) in the first chapter. That the table cloths are "foamy white" (*J*, 31) in the segregated (until the North) dining car calls to the "raving whites" who "had foamed all over the lanes and yards of home" (*J*, 33). The almost imperceptible mention of the "colored section of the Southern Sky" (*J*, 30) feeds into the memory of the southern sun, "thick and red-orange at the bottom of the sky" (*J*, 34), a sky to be reduced to a "tiny piece of information" (*J*, 35), and opens up the eloquently lyrical passage on the "unbelievable sky" of the City, mention of which occurs another ten times in the course of two pages (*J*, 35-36).

Against this backdrop the "illegal love of sweethearts" unfolds (and the consequences of the illicit or illegal in abortion and theft, remains of which lie under the ocean), the windows where "sweethearts, free and illegal, tell each other things" (*J*, 36) — "Important things" like Joe's fruitless attempt to receive a sign from his mother. Here Joe's voice takes over once again in an interior monologue related in both free direct and free indirect speech often given to repetition and allusion:

[...] say some kind of yes, even if it was no, so he would know.　　(Line 2)

Just a sign, he said, just show me your hand, he said, and I'll know don't you know I have to know?　　(Lines 9-11)

Her hand, her fingers poking through the blossoms, touching his [...]　　(Line 5)

[...] in light so small he could not see his knees poking through the holes in his trousers

(Lines 25- 26)

Just a sign, he said [...]   (Line, 9)

All she had to do was give him a sign [...]   (Line 16)

[...] maybe he missed the sign [...]   (Line 27)

(all on *J*, 37)

The repetition Joe uses here reinforces the idea of his voice in the "monologue," but when he turns to his memories of Dorcas' confession of her memories of her own mother and the fire that killed her, the voice changes not only to that of Dorcas herself, but Dorcas reliving the experience and speaking as she would have responded as a child, again in both free direct and free indirect discourse:

> How it burned, she told him. And of all the slaps she got, that one was the one she remembered best because it was the last. She leaned out the window of her best girlfriend's house because the shouts were not part of what she was dreaming. They were outside her head, across the street. Like the running. Everybody running. For water? Buckets? There was no getting in that house where her clothespin dolls lay in a row. In a cigar box. But she tried anyway to get them. Barefoot, in the dress she had slept in, she ran to get them, and yelled to her mother that the box of dolls, the box of dolls was up there on the dresser can we get them? Mama?   (*J*, 38)

Giving the narrative over to Dorcas' child-like voice obviously intensifies the pathos of the story, on the one hand, and on the other the depth of their relationship and the strength of the ensuing passion in their love-making. Dorcas' voice will continue to pepper the narrative ("One for me, she says, and one for you. One for me and one for you. Gimme this, I give you that. Gimme this. Gimme this" [*J*, 39]), reinforcing her youth and impatience with his caution, and laying the groundwork for her later dissatisfaction with their relationship. Her free direct discourse figures prominently in Joe's reverie right up until "he opens his eyes" on page 40. Given the additional framing of this narrative (the narrator [Joe's memory/voice {Dorcas' memory/voice}]), this phrase, "And he opens his eyes," creates a certain ambiguity: This could be the narrator's voice or Joe's; Joe could be remembering the end of his conversation with Dorcas — which he sustained with his eyes closed, opening them at her last words about the apple, or the narrator could be relating the intensity of the memory for Joe as he lies silent next to Violet, causing him to open his eyes at this point in his reverie. It should be pointed out, however, that the "framing" of Joe's memories is an unusual one, even though they take place with his lying in bed: the opening of the frame refers to Joe's memories after he has killed Dorcas, while the ending of the section refers to his thinking of her while their relationship is still going on.

The free direct discourse included on page 39 as a remembered conversation between Joe and Dorcas concerning their "trip to Mexico" (itself an ambiguous reference the first time it is mentioned, only cleared up by the subsequent exchange between the two) also brings into play another form of discourse based on the "other": *hearsay*. As Bakhtin points out, "the weight of 'everyone says' and 'it is said' in public opinion, public rumor, gossip, slander and so forth" is "enormous." In fact, he asserts that "the majority of our information and opinions is usually not communicated in direct form as our own, but with reference to some indefinite and general source: 'I heard,' 'it's generally held that ...,' 'It is thought that ...' and so forth" (*Dialogic*, 338). This different but extremely important way of communicating information, of forming another type of "story-line," is made explicit in Dorcas' insistence on how wonderful a place Mexico is:

> Mexico, she whispers. I want you to take me to Mexico. Too loud, he murmurs. No, no she says, it's just right. How you know? He demands. I heard people say, people say the tables are round and have white cloths over them and wee baby lampshades. [...] Mexico people sleep in the day, take me. They're in there till church time Sunday morning and no whitepeople can get in, and the boys who play sometimes get up and dance with you. (*J*, 39)

While hardly as malicious as gossip can be, information gathered from an indeterminate source plays an important role in developing a story. Joe is hesitant, concerned that "people can see us," also an important consideration for Bakhtin, since "one must also consider the psychological importance in our lives of what others say about us, and the importance, for us, of understanding and interpreting these words of others," a concept that this critic calls "living hermeneutics" (*Dialogic*, 338).

After the finalization of the memory section, Morrison makes a clear break before beginning with the narrator's introduction of Malvonne in diegesis and continuing with the mimetic reproduction of Malvonne and Joe's conversation, which leads into another interlude about the City. As character, Malvonne unites the themes of the gossip/busybody, illicitness and storytelling, explicit in the opening lines of her presentation in the text:

> Malvonne lived alone with newspapers and other people's stories printed in small books. When she was not making her office building sparkle, she was melding the print stories with her keen observation of the people around her. Very little escaped this woman who rode the trolley against traffic at 6:00 p.m.; who examined the trash baskets of powerful whitemen, looked at photographs of women and children on their desks. Heard their hallway conversation, and the bathroom laughter penetrating the broom closet like fumes from her bottle of ammonia. She examined their bottles and resituated the flasks tucked under cushions and behind books whose words were printed in two columns. She knew who had a passion for justice as well as ladies' undergarments, who loved his wife and who shared one.
> [...] But Malvonne was not interested in them; she simply noticed. Her interest lay in the neighborhood people. (*J*, 40-41)

This interest in the neighborhood people is what leads Malvonne to read each of the letters her nephew had stolen, "including those Sweetness had not bother to tear open" (*J*, 42), and it is these letters that provide yet a different focus in this chapter. While the first "Dear Helen Moore" letter provides more in the way of insinuating Malvonne's voice into the narration by way of free indirect discourse, it is Winsome Clark's plaintive letter that is of interest for the present analysis. Since Clark's letter is set off by quotation marks, rather than a hybrid form of discourse or pseudodiegesis, it is more reminiscent of the "collage" effects of incorporating other genres (newspapers, letters, etc.) into literary works that were an important innovation in the 1920s in the work of John Dos Passos and others.

In "Speech Genres" Bakhtin considers *genre* to be of maximum importance in human communication: as Emerson and Holquist write in their introduction to these essays, for Bakhtin "what distinguishes one human undertaking from another, one science from another, is the roster of genres each has appropriated as its own" (xvi). He distinguishes between what he calls primary and secondary genres and defines the relationship of the two:

> Secondary (complex) speech genres – novels, dramas, all kinds of scientific research, major genres of commentary, and so forth – arise in more complex and comparatively highly developed and organized cultural communication (primarily written) that is artistic, scientific, sociopolitical, and so on. During the process of their formation, they absorb and digest various primary (simple) genres that have taken form in unmediated speech communion. These primary genres are altered and assume a special character when they enter into complex ones. They lose their immediate relation to actual reality and to the real utterances of others. [...] ex. Rejoinders of everyday dialogue or letters found in a novel retain their form and their everyday significance only on the plane of the novel's content.   (Bakhtin, "Speech"; 62)

The letter, as a personal and privatized form of communication, retains much of its primary discourse, as is easily discerned in Clark's letter in that she "writes" in the particular form of English typical of the inhabitants of the West Indies. For Bakhtin the incorporation of the "familiar and intimate genres" into secondary genres "gives rise to a certain candor of speech" precisely because they lie "more or less outside the framework of the social hierarchy and social conventions, 'without rank,' as it were":

> [W]hen the task was to destroy traditional official styles and world views that had faded and become conventional, familiar styles became very significant in literature. Moreover, familiarization of styles opened literature up to layers of language that had previously been under speech constraint.   (Bakhtin, "Speech"; 97)

In fact, Bakhtin includes the specific integration of the letter under the third "basic type" of "compositional-stylistic unities into which the novelistic whole usually breaks down: [...] (3) Stylization of the various forms of semiliterary (written) everyday narration (the letters, the diary, etc.)" (*Discourse*, 262). For him the "special relationship" between the novel and "extraliterary genres, with the genres of everyday life and with ideological genres," constitutes an important phenomenon in the history of the development of the novel (33). These "incorporated genres" become "one of the most basic and fundamental forms for incorporating and organizing heteroglossia in the novel":

> The novel permits the incorporation of various genres, both artistic (inserted

short stories, lyrical songs, poems, dramatic scenes, etc.) and extra-artistic (everyday, rhetorical, scholarly, religious genres and others). In principle, any genre could be included in the construction of the novel [...]   (Bakhtin, *Dialogic*; 320)

Todorov, however, states that

Bakhtin seems unaware of the problem posed by the use of the same term ("genre") for linguistic and translinguistic reality on one hand, and a historical one on the other [... because] the notion of genre is not the exclusive prerogative of literature; it is rooted in the everyday use of language.   (Todorov, 80)

But I would argue that this apparent "confusion" of the term may be more intentional than not. For Bakhtin genre in discourse simply differentiates it from another type of discourse, and the literary work, or "secondary genre," is simply a particular author's stylized way of addressing a certain public. Therefore, the distinction among genres is often one of degree not of quality, for "these secondary genres of complex cultural communication *play out* various forms of primary speech communication" ("Speech," 98; emphasis in original). In fact, Bakhtin complains that the study of stylistics in the novel slights precisely this aspect of discourse:

It is this idea that has motivated our emphasis on "the stylistics of genre." The separation of style and language from the question of genre has been largely responsible for a situation in which only individual and period-bound overtones of a style are the privileged subjects of study, while its basic social tone is ignored. [...] More often than not, stylistics defines itself as a stylistics of "private craftsmanship" and ignores the social life of discourse outside the artist's study, discourse in the open spaces of public squares, streets, cities and villages, of social groups , generations and epochs. Stylistics is concerned not with living discourse but with a histological specimen made from it, [...]
                    (Bakhtin, *Dialogic*; 259)

To return to Winsome Clark's letter, there are two extremely important aspects contained therein. The first is what Bakhtin has referred to as "social ideologemes":

A social language [...] is a concrete socio-linguistic belief system that defines a distinct identity for itself within the boundaries of a language that is unitary only in the abstract. [...] The image of such a language in a novel is the image assumed by a set of social beliefs, the image of a social ideologeme that has fused with its own discourse, with its own language. [...] In the novel formal markers of languages, manners and styles are symbols for sets of social beliefs.   (Bakhtin, *Dialogic*; 356-357)

Nowhere could this be more manifest that in Clark's letter to her husband in the Canal Zone:

"I don't know what to do," she wrote. "Nothing I do make a difference. Auntie make a racket about everything. I am besides myself. The children is miserable as me. The money you sending can not keeping all us afloat. Us drowning here and may as well drown at home where your mother is and mine and big trees."   (*J*, 43)

99

The letter contains both a double protest and a different "world view." We can infer that Clark had moved his wife and children to New York in search of a better life, but that the work he found — menial labor building the Panama Canal — was not enough to keep his family afloat, in spite of Winsome's job which obviously pays little as well. Once the money is no longer a factor to be counted on ("Us drowning here and may as well drown at home"), the quality of life hinges on family ("your mother and mine") and a return to the beauty of natural environs ("big trees"),[76] things unavailable in the City. (Malvonne remarks that "Must be jungle for sure.")

The second aspect dramatized in this (sub)section is Bakhtin's consideration of the *chronotope* of the literary expression, that is, "the set of distinctive features of time and space within each literary genre" (Todorov, 83). In addition to defining literary genres by determining their specific chronotope, Bakhtin locates the literary expression outside the chronotope of its perception:

> If I tell (orally or in writing) an event that I have just lived, insofar as I *am telling* (orally or in writing) this event, I find myself already outside of the time-space where the event occurred. [...] However realistic or truthful it may be, the represented universe can never be chronotopically identical with the real universe where the representation occurs, and where the author-creator of this representation is to be found.   (Todorov, 52)

Nor, of course, is the reader. This discrepancy of chronotopes is made explicit in Malvonne's preoccupation with the intercession of Winsome's letter, originally meant to reach her husband in the Canal Zone by a certain date:

> The point now was to get Winsome's notice of departure, already two pay envelopes ago, to Panama before any more cash went to Edgecombe where the aunt might get hold of it, and who knows, if she was as hateful as Winsome told it [...] she might keep the money for herself.   (*J*, 43)

In dramatizing Malvonne's reading of the letter much later than was intended by the author for her husband, Morrison in effect calls attention to the fact that any reading *about* or listening *to* a story a priori belongs to a different chronotope. The represented world can never coincide with the real world, no matter how "realistic" the art form. Nevertheless, and as Malvonne's reaction to Winsome's letter makes clear,

> [h]owever forcefully the real and the represented world resist fusion, however immutable the presence of that categorical boundary line between them, they are nevertheless indissolubly tied up with each other and find themselves in continual mutual interaction; [...]   (Bakhtin, *Dialogic*; 254)

Reading the letter creates in Malvonne the need of resolving the problem; it demands "response-ibility" of her.

---

[76] This longing for the rural setting will be picked up later by Violet who remembers her life in the South as a time when "life made sense."

One more letter is included as narrative strategy simply to return the focus of the story to Joe and his "illicit" proposal to rent Malvonne's rooms for his rendezvous with Dorcas. Malvonne's fascination with "Hot Steam's" letter is written with ironic comic relief, emphasized with the repetition of related associative fields: "one letter to sweat over," "delivering her heat," "perspiring and breathing lightly," "lowdown sticky things" (*J*, 43 & 44). Joe's knock on her door and the ensuing conversation (in mimesis) ends in Joe's profession of "I ain't like that. I ain't" (*J*, 49), giving the narrator a lead into her musings on "Thursday men" in the City: "Of course he wasn't, but he did it anyway. Sneaked around, plotted, and stepped out every night the girl demanded" (*J*, 49).

Different from the discourse of the letters previously described, the language of this last section becomes so stylized that it could well be considered hybridization, the intromission of one discourse into another:

> But for satisfaction pure and deep, for balance in pleasure and comfort, Thursday can't be beat — as is clear from the capable expression on the faces of the men and their conquering stride in the street. (*J*, 50)

[or]

> The regrettable things, the coarse and sour remarks, the words that become active boils in the heart — none of that takes place on Thursday. (*J*, 50-51)

This specific inclusion seems to initiate the discussion of genre which will become so important in the next chapter. For Bakhtin,

> the simplest genre but one that is important for Rabelais – the street cries, especially the cries of Paris. The cris were loud advertisements called out by the Paris street vendors [...] certain versified form each cry had four lines offering and praising a certain merchandise. (Morris, 218)

Both these instances can be rephrased into lines of "advertising" for Thursday in the City, though one might also argue that the reworking of the phrases also recalls the free verse of poetry which was coming into prominence during the modernist era:

But for satisfaction pure and deep,
for balance in pleasure and comfort,
Thursday can't be beat
— as is clear from the capable expression
on the faces of the men
and their conquering stride in the street.

The regrettable things,
the coarse and sour remarks,
the words that become active boils in the heart
— none of that takes place on Thursday.

Aside from the historical references to the Panama Canal and the allusions to developments in literary expression during the Modernist era, there is also a specific *intertextual* reference which once again returns us to Morrison's first novel, *The Bluest Eye*: "The woman who churned a man's blood as she leaned all alone on a fence by a country road might not expect even to catch his eye in the City" (*J*, 34), recalls Pauline's first encounter with Cholly but also alludes to the progressive destruction of their relationship once they migrate north. Within the novel itself (*intra*textual, if you will), just like Violet's "cracks" in the first chapter, we are introduced to Joe's "tracks" here in the second, first with respect to the train ("And like a million others, chests pounding, tracks controlling their feet, [...]" [*J*, 32]), and then in the allusion to Dorcas' scarred face: "Somebody called Dorcas with hooves tracing her cheekbones [...]" (*J*, 37).[77]

C. "Like that day in July, almost nine years back, when the beautiful men were cold."

Many of the characteristics described in the previous two chapters again make their appearance in Chapter III, but its true *raison d'être* lies in its underlying discussion of semiotics and heteroglossia. Alice Manfred may be the topic which maintains the coherence of the storyline, but the indisputable theme of this section is the struggle between authoritative and disruptive language, between monologic and dialogic discourse, represented metaphorically in the tension and the ambivalence Alice feels when she hears jazz.

That this chapter will deal with the opposition of official and unofficial discourse is signaled on the very first page, which juxtaposes the "promises from the Declaration of Independence" with the meaning of the drums and the cold faces (*J*, 53), and continues with the semiotics of signs and discourses that challenge the status quo. In fact, the introduction of so many unofficial or non-literary *genres* turn this chapter into a fascinating dialogue on the nature of the *carnivalesque* so basic to Bakhtinian theory, heavily dependant on what he calls the "stratification of language":

> This stratification is accomplished first of all by the specific organisms calls *genres*. Certain features of language (lexicological, semantic, syntactic) will knit together with the intentional aim, and with the overall accentual system inherent in one or another genre: oratorical, publicistic, newspaper and journalistic genres, the genres of low literature (penny dreadfuls, for instance) or, finally, the various genres of high literature. Certain features of language take on the specific flavor of a given genre: they knit together with specific points of view, specific approaches, forms of thinking, nuances and accents characteristic of the given genre. (Bakhtin, *Dialogic*; 288)

By incorporating these different speech genres into the novel, the literary work becomes enriched both linguistically and ideologically:

> [T]hese languages are primarily significant for making available points of view that are

---

[77] I have already noted (Tally, "Specter"), with the help of Tyler McMahon, that Dorcas' name actually means "gazelle" in ancient Greek, reinforcing the notion of tracks and prey.

generative in a material sense, since they exist outside literary conventionality and thus have the capacity to broaden the horizon of language available to literature, [...]

(Bakhtin, *Dialogic*; 323)

In addition, the introduction of this *heteroglossia* into the novel means that the era's multiple and diverse languages will be represented as equals in the literary terrain. Like Bakhtin's understanding of carnival, in which "the suspension of all hierarchical precedence [...] was of particular significance" and during which "all were considered equal," the inclusion of genres high and low has the effect of leveling the linguistic playing field. Authoritative language is questioned, reexamined in light of other popular genres; monologic discourse is challenged by dialogue and heteroglossia. But it is not just the novel which will be expanded by the entry of non-literary language into the text; as it is taken into the text, this stratification of language "establishes its own special order within it, and becomes a unique artistic system, which orchestrates the intentional theme of the author" (299).

Perhaps the most obvious demonstration Morrison makes of this point is her explicit inclusion of street signs, playing specifically on the dialogic nature of the term itself. Voloshinov/Bakhtin write that

a sign does not simply exist as a part of a reality – it reflects and refracts another reality.[...]Wherever a sign is present, ideology is present, too. *Everything ideological possesses semiotic value* [...] Idealism and psychologism alike overlook the fact that understanding itself can come about only within some kind of semiotic materia (e.g., inner speech) that sign bears upon sign, that *consciousness itself can arise and become a viable fact only in the material embodiment of signs.*

("Marxism" in Morris, 50; emphasis in the original)

Morrison goes out of her way to indicate that the dialogic sign is indeed the crux of the matter in this chapter, first by capitalizing the letter in a seemingly incidental place ("The stomach-jump Dorcas and Felice have agreed is the *Sign* of real interest and possible love surfaces and spreads as Dorcas watches the brothers" (*J*, 66); secondly, by effectuating a change in Joe's perception through the teasing from Alice's friends ("But that day in Alice Manfred's house, as he listened to and returned their banter, *something in the wordplay took on weight*" (*J*, 71; emphasis added); and thirdly, and most explicitly, by including a specific section on actual signs found in the City:

The City is smart at this: smelling and good and looking raunchy; sending secret messages disguised as public signs: this way, open here, danger to let colored only single men on sale woman wanted private room stop dog on premises absolutely no money down fresh chicken free delivery fast. (*J*, 64)

After the first two "signs," she deliberately drops the separating commas so that the ambiguity of their dialogic nature becomes even more transparent. Obviously, we are meant to toy with the alternatives in the messages.

While the standard interpretation is likely: Other possible ones could read:

this way	this way
open here	open here
danger	danger to let colored only sin-
to let	gle men
colored only	[or] danger to let colored
single men	single men on sale
on sale	woman wanted - private room
woman wanted	[or] wanted: private room
private room	stop, dog
stop	absolutely no money
dog on premises	down, fresh
absolutely no money down	chicken free
fresh chicken	delivery
free delivery fast.	fast

According to Voloshinov/Bakhtin, "the word is the most sensitive index of social changes" and "has the capacity to register all the transitory, delicate momentary phases of social change." As *signs*, these words dialogically comment upon the social conditions of black people — the fear (by whites) of black men, the fear of white men by black women, the lack of proper living space, poor economic conditions, hunger. In Morrison's twist on the language, she deftly demonstrates the subversive nature of the sign. In the words of Voloshinov/Bakhtin,

> Every sign, as we know, is a construct between socially organized persons in the process of their interaction. Therefore, *the forms of signs are conditioned above all by the social organization of the participants involved and also by the immediate conditions of their interaction.* When these forms change, so does sign. [...]
>
> Class does not coincide with the sign community, i.e., with the community which is the totality of users of the same set of signs for ideological communication. Thus various different classes will use one and the same language. As a result, differently oriented accents intersect in every ideological sign. Sign becomes an arena of class struggle.[...]
>
> The very same thing that makes the ideological sign vital and mutable is also, however, that which makes it a refracting and distorting medium. The ruling class strives to impart a supraclass, eternal character to the ideological sign, to extinguish or drive inward the struggle between social value judgments which occurs in it, to make the sign uniaccentual.
>
> (Voloshinov/Bahktin, "Marxism"; in Morris, 55; emphasis in original)

It is this drive "to make the sign uniaccentual" that fuels the authoritarian need for censorship, which "always believes that there is *one* way to say things and declares any other way of saying it officially meaningless. It is monologue erected into a principle."

The useless struggle of authoritative discourse to monopolize the meanings of signs is also demonstrated in the story of the Neola Miller, whose fiance left her only a week after their engagement. "The pain of his refusal was visual, for over her heart, curled like a shell, was the hand on which he had positioned the ring" (*J*, 62). Neola reads Psalms from the Old Testament to her young charges, but when she tires she tells them stories of waywardness and human degradation, "of moral decay, of the wicked who preyed on the good," ostensibly with the religious intent of instigating the young to a moral life. "Her stories, however, of the goodness of good behavior collapsed before the thrill of the sin they deplored" (*J*, 62). What Dorcas read into these stories, however, was the irresistible power of passion:

> The children scratched their knees and nodded, but Dorcas, at least, was enchanted by the frail, melty tendency of the flesh and the Paradise that could make a woman go right back after two days, two! Or make a girl travel four hundred miles to a camptown, or fold Neola's arm, the better to hold the pieces of her heart in her hand. Paradise. All for Paradise. (*J*, 63)

Like the drums that disrupt the authoritative discourse of the Declaration of Independence, the dialogic nature of the sign/language will tend to subvert any attempt to impose a unitary interpretation of language. Hence Alice, who receives her information from newspapers and documents rather than from the living word on the streets, is representative of the monologic discourse of the dominant culture (and of a Victorian sense of morality); she becomes disgruntled and disquieted over the pervasive influence of jazz. Jazz is consistently thrown into contrast with the precepts of religious dictates:

> They did not know for sure, but they suspected that the dances were beyond nasty because the music was getting worse and worse with each passing season the Lord waited to make Himself known. Songs that used to start in the head and fill the heart had dropped on down, down to places below the sash and the buckled belts. Lower and lower, until the music was so lowdown you had to shut your windows and just suffer the summer sweat when the men in shirtsleeves propped themselves in window frames, or clustered on rooftops, in alleyways, on stoops and in the apartments of relatives playing the lowdown stuff that signaled Imminent Demise. (*J*, 56)

On the one hand, the repeated references to the "life below the sash and its red lip rouge" of jazz call to the purported origins of the music in the "lowlife" of Storeyville (see above) and the prevailing opinion during the 1920s that jazz was not a true form of artistic expression. In its early era jazz was looked down upon and disparaged by the "middle and upper class society"[78] that Alice represents: "She knew from sermons and editorials that it wasn't real music — just colored folks' stuff: harmful, certainly; embarrassing, of course; but not real, not serious" (*J*, 59).

---

[78] In "Blue Note: the Story of Modern Jazz," the documentary makes clear that the innovative work of Alfred Lion, who founded and promoted the Blue Note label, was absolutely crucial in the promotion of the artists who we now consider to be "all-time-greats" in jazz and in the documentation of its development. It is also extremely relevant to note that Lion was a German immigrant to the United States who became fascinated with the first jazz performance he heard in Berlin, precisely in 1926, and that as a "foreigner" he brought with him no racial bias nor class snobbery that interfered with his total appreciation of this new art form.

On the other hand, and more importantly, these literary descriptions of the new music link it ever more firmly to the concept of jazz as metaphor for the "carnivalesque" discourse which Bakhtin argues has always irrupted into the dominant monologic language, both to renew the language and to subvert the authoritarian nature of the ideology it entails. During official celebrations in the Middle Ages rank and hierarchy were especially on display; but during Carnival, not only was everyone considered equal, but also the "people's laughter" parodied the imposition of "officialdom." Moreover, "the people's laughter which characterized all the forms of grotesque realism from immemorial times was linked with the bodily lower stratum. Laughter degrades and materializes"(Bakhtin, Rabelais; in Morris, 206). Thus, jazz's relation to "life below the sash" directly parallels the carnivalesque link with "the bodily lower stratum," an idea reinforced in *Jazz* by Violet's preoccupation with developing her hips.

For Bakhtin, the carnivalesque (or "laughter") had three important characteristics: first, its "universalism," in that all were considered equal during Carnival; second, its "freedom," in that authority could be questioned and parodied; and third, "its relation to the people's unofficial truth":

> The serious aspects of class culture are official and authoritarian; they are combined with violence, prohibitions, limitations and always contain an element of fear and intimidation. [...] Laughter, on the contrary, overcomes fear, for it knows no inhibitions, no limitations. Its idiom is never used by violence and authority.
>
> (Bakhtin, *Rabelais*; in Morris, 209)

Authoritarian discourse "demands our unconditional allegiance," manifest in the figure of Alice Manfred, as representative of these "serious aspects of class culture." This chapter repeatedly insists on her fear and on the confining attitudes of her parents toward her (as representative of class and societal oppression) which she herself adopts in her up-bringing of Dorcas.

> The drums and the freezing faces hurt her, but hurt was better than fear and Alice had been frightened for a long time [...]   (*J*, 54)

> From then on she hid the girl's hair in braids tucked under, lest whitemen see it raining round her shoulders and push dollar-wrapped fingers toward her. She instructed her about deafness and blindness — how valuable and necessary they were in the company of whitewomen who spoke English and those who did not, as well as in the presence of their children. Taught her how to crawl along the walls of buildings, disappear, into doorways, cut across corners in choked traffic — how to do anything, move anywhere to avoid a whiteboy over the age of eleven.   (J, 54-55)

Though Alice finds that the drums have formed a "rope cast for rescue [...] reliably secure and tight — most of the time," the sound of jazz breaks the rope, "disturbing her peace, making her aware of flesh and something so free she could smell its bloodsmell [...]"(*J*, 58), and she begins to associate the music with the anger in the marchers on Fifth Avenue and the insistent sound of the drums. She "swore she heard a complicated anger in it, something hostile that disguised itself as flourish and roaring section" (*J*, 59), but it is its "appetite" that most worries her. She prefers to "sweat in the summer heat of a *silent* Clifton Place apartment that to risk a broken window or a yelping that might not know where or how to stop" (J, 59; emphasis added). Moreover, Alice refuses to enter into the banter of her friends when Joe comes to deliver cosmetics at her house: "They sang their compliments, their abuse, and only Alice confined herself to a thin smile, a closed look and did not joint the comments with one of her own" (J, 70). This "abuse" is what Bakhtin calls "the other side of market place hawking":

> Abuses, curses, profanities, and improprieties are the unofficial elements of speech. They were and are still conceived as a breach of the established norms of verbal address; they refuse to conform to conventions, to etiquette, civility, respectability.[79]
> (Bakhtin, *Rabelais*; in Morris, 220)

Fear and the imposition of monologue breeds silence; "carnival, by contrast, expresses a utopian belief in a future time in which fear and authority are vanquished" (Morris, 207). Only through dialogue (see below) will Alice come to understand the repression of her own anger into the socially acceptable (monologic) thinking and behavior which has led her to repress her niece in the same way.

These intentions, however, prove useless as Dorcas responds to the sensuousness of the music:

> While her aunt worried about how to keep the heart ignorant of the hips and the head in charge of both, Dorcas lay on a chenille bedspread, tickled and happy knowing that there was no place to be where somewhere, close by, somebody was not licking his licorice stick, tickling the ivories, beating his skins, blowing off his horn while a knowing woman sang ain't nobody going to keep me down you got the right key baby but the wrong keyhole you got to get it bring it and put it right here, or else. (J, 60)

Again the irruption of the vernacular "blues lyrics" within the same sentence (with no differentiating punctuation) reinforces not only the sensuality of the description of the music and the musicians (and Dorcas' own budding sexuality), but also, given its pervasiveness, the impossibility of keeping jazz (or the language of the "lower classes," the carnival laughter) out of the text.

There are various other forms of intromission into the text which slide into the authorial narrative almost imperceptibly. Take for example Morrison's "nod" to the radio serial so popular at the time —

> Taller than most, she gazes at them over the head of her dark friend. The brothers' eyes seem wide and welcoming to her. She moves forward out of the shadow and slips

---

[79] "These elements of freedom [...] exercise a strong influence on the entire contents of speech, transferring it to another sphere beyond the limits of conventional language. Such speech forms, liberated from norms, hierarchies, and prohibitions of established idiom, becomes themselves a peculiar argot and create a special collectivity, a group of people initiated in familiar intercourse, who are frank and free in expressing themselves verbally. The marketplace crowd was such a collectivity, especially the festive, carnivalesque crowd at the fair" (Bakhtin, *Rabelais*; in Morris, 220).

through the group. The brothers turn up the wattage of their smiles. The right record
is on the turntable now; she can hear its preparatory hiss as the needle slides toward its
first groove.   (*J*, 66-67)

— in which the short, declaratory sentences are reminiscent of the oral storytelling broadcast
daily over the waves. Or notice how easily another form of *skaz* (colloquial speech) incorporates
the vernacular folk sayings, thereby reinforcing once again the orality of the narration: "They
know that *a badly dressed body is nobody at all*, and Felice had to chatter compliments all the
way down Seventh Avenue to get Dorcas to forget about her clothes and focus on the party" (*J*,
65; emphasis added).

Perhaps the most easily recognizable mixing of genre in this chapter is the parody of the
black sermon which, given the repeated references to monologic religious discourse (Judgement
Day, the Imminent Demise, or the reading of Pslams), again recalls the carnival disruption
described by Bakhtin:

> The primary instance of appropriating another's discourse and language was the use
> made of the authoritative and sanctified word of the Bible, the Gospel, the Apostles, the
> fathers and doctors of the church This word continually infiltrates the context of
> medieval literature and the speech of educated men (clerics). (Bakhtin, *Dialogic*; 69)

This "parodia sacra" would correspond to Bakhtin's fourth type of "compositional-stylistic
unities into which the novelistic whole usually breaks down: "[...V]arious forms of literary but
extra-artistic authorial speech (moral, philosophical or scientific statements, oratory ethnographic
descriptions, memoranda and so forth)" (*Dialogic*, 262). These instances constitute what Bakhtin
calls an "intentional hybrid," that is, "the perception of one language by another language, its
illumination by another linguistic consciousness" (*Dialogic*, 359).[80] In *Jazz*, Alice's reverie turns
the traditional black sermon into a "parodia sacra" on the position of "unarmed" black women
"who found protection in church and the angry God whose wrath in their behalf was too terrible
to bear contemplation":

> He was not just on His way, coming, coming to right the wrongs done to the, He was
> here. Already. See? See? What the world had done to them it was now doing to itself.
> Did the world mess over them? Yes but look where the mess originated. Were they
> berated and cursed? Oh yes but look how the world cursed and berated itself. Were the
> women fondled in kitchens and the back of stores? Un huh. Did police put their fists in
> women's faces so the husbands'spirits would break along with the women's jaws? Did
> men (those who knew them as well as strangers sitting in motor cars) call them out of
> their names every single day of their lives? Un huh. But in God's eyes and theirs, every
> hateful word and gesture was the Beast's desire for its own filth. The Beast did not do

---

[80] [In an] intentional novelistic hybrid [...] the important activity is not only (in fact not so much) the mixing
of linguistic forms – the markers of two languages and styles - as it is the collision between different points of views
on the world that are embedded in these forms. Therefore an intentional artistic hybrid is a semantic hybrid; not
semantic and logical in the abstract (as in rhetoric), but rather a semantics that is concrete and social (Bakhtin,
Dialogic; 360).

what was done to it, but what it wished done to itself: raped because it wanted to be raped itself. Slaughtered children because it yearned to be slaughtered children. Built jails to dwell on and hold on to its own private decay. God's wrath, so beautiful, so simple. Their enemies got what they wanted, became what they visited on others.

(J, 77-78)

It then continues to consider their vulnerability in another "sacra" form, the litany[81]:

> Who else were the unarmed ones? The ones who thought they did not need folded blades, packets of lye, shards of glass taped to their hands. Those who bought houses and hoarded money as protection and the means to purchase it. Those attached to armed men. Those who did not carry pistols because they became pistols; did not carry switchblades because they were switchblades cutting through gatherings, shooting down statutes and pointing out the blood and abused flesh. Those who swelled their little unarmed strength into the reckoning one of leagues, clubs, societies, sisterhoods designed to hold or withhold, move or stay put, make a way, solicit, comfort and ease. Bail out, dress the dead, pay the rent, find new rooms, start a school, storm an office, take up collections, rout the block and keep their eyes on all the children. Any other kind of unarmed black woman in 1926 was silent or crazy or dead. (<i>J</i>, 78)

This rather long passage is a perfect example of Bakhtin's hybridization, "the collision between different points of view on the world": A religious genre based on the book of Revelations is turned into a social commentary on the position of black women in a violent society. While the sacred text of the Apocalypse is "dialogized" by the traditional "call and response" of the black sermon, its deeper exchange is enacted between the promises of an avenging God (someone to look out for the women and justify their existence in difficult conditions) and the possibility of self-defense, either through the violence of "folded blades, packets of lye, and shards of glass," through money, or though the more socially acceptable banding together of women to help each other; that is, the choice is between relying on God's help or self-help (help from men does not seem to figure in here, a fact which also enters the dialogue). The "in-between" is no option at all: silence, madness or death. The dialogue of different discourses foregrounds the possibility of choice, which of itself is a form of freedom.

What has brought on this reverie is Alice's refusal to talk to any policeman, black or white (her understanding that what grants a policeman power is "the blue steel that made him a man" [<i>J</i>, 74]), and the recognition of the violence associated with being a black woman in America. The headlines of the newspapers Alice reads — another (semi-)literary genre incorporated directly into the text — tell stories of violence all over the country —

> Man kills wife. Eight accused of rape dismissed. Woman and girl victims of. Woman commits suicide. White attackers indicted. Five women caught. Woman says man beat. In jealous rage man. (<i>J</i>, 74)

---

[81] Also reminiscent of this form is Margaret Walker's prize-winning poem, "For My People" (1942).

— and prompt Alice to "respond" to the fact that many women were forced into defending themselves because no one was going to protect them. The "dialogue" with these texts opens the way for her entering into a more meaningful dialogue with Violet.

It is no surprise, then, that the chapter that deals most explicitly with the pervasive influence of speech genres and the irruptions of the carnivalesque (skaz, parody, and other forms of hybridization) into the literary text should lead into a fairly long section (pages 79 to 85) of textual dialogue (mimesis) between Alice and Violet/Violent and end with Alice's meditation on and acceptance of long-suppressed feelings (86-87). This dialogue becomes a meaningful exchange of ideology in which Alice begins to free herself of an "authoritarian," hence monologic, point of view.[82] Certain exchanges between Alice and Violet specifically reinforce the characteristics of carnival as expressed above. First is the breakdown in "hierarchy" which positions some people over others. Violet forces Alice to recognize her kinship to all women, even the prostitutes, and that some choices that women make are not choices at all:

> (Alice) "The difference is more than a hairdo."
> (Violet) "They're just women, you know. Like us."
> "No," said Alice. "No they're not. Not like me."
> "I don't mean the trade. I mean the women."
> [...]
> "Oh. The men. The nasty life. Don't they fight all the time? When you do their hair, you're not afraid they might start fighting?"
> "Only when they sober." Violet smiled.
> "Oh, well."
> "They share men, fight them and fight over them, too."
> "No woman should live like that."
> "No. No woman should have to."[83] (*J*, 84)

Secondly, the admission of "universalism" — that all women are still women no matter what their trade (and Violet has pointed out that these women had been good to her when no one else was) — *frees* Alice to acknowledge the feelings of fury toward the women who "took" her husband away from her, feelings she had repressed out of fear (of censure by a monologic discourse, or perhaps of her own capacity for violence). When Violet asks her if she would not fight for her man, "Alice heard her question like the pop of a toy gun," and, although she tells Violet truthfully that she had never picked up a knife, she is flooded with memories of her own desires for revenge. This throwing off of the repression of "unacceptable" behavior grants Alice a certain freedom which in turns intensifies the breakdown in hierarchy established between

---

[82] As Bakhtin writes, "The tendency to assimilate others' discourse takes on an even deeper and more basic significance in an individual's ideological becoming, in the most fundamental sense. Another's discourse performs here no longer as information, directions, rules, models and so forth – but strives rather to determine the very bases of our ideological interrelations with the world, the very basis of our behavior; it performs here as *authoritative discourse*, and an *internally persuasive discourse."* (Bakhtin, *Dialogic*; 342).

[83] One important task of the novel, according to Bakhtin, is precisely the "laying-bare of any sort of conventionality, the exposure of all that is vulgar and falsely stereotyped in human relationships" (*Dialogic*, 162).

herself and others. And thirdly, the "people's unofficial truth" surfaces in the finality of death, the ultimate equalizer, which meant that her prerogatives as wife were limited to choosing what clothes her husband would be buried in. Alice may be her husband's "official" woman, but a hierarchy established by societal norms means nothing in the end when death abolishes all distinctions. Both the "dialogue" initiated by the intromission of speech and literary genres into the narrative[84] as well as the mimetic dialogue between these two female characters exemplify "the weakening [of] the peripheries of the utterance" which lead to "a severe debilitation of both the authoritarian and the rationalistic dogmatism of utterance" (Voloshinov/Bakhtin, "Marxism"; in Morris, 65). Like jazz, the "carnivalesque" permeates the official discourse and undermines the strictures of a single world view.

Intertextuality:
Before leaving this chapter, it is interesting to note that apart from the numerous historical references[85] which locate *Jazz* in the milieu of the age, Morrison has included discreet calls to other literary texts, including (again) her own. Aside from a reference to Kate Chopin's well-know short-story "A Pair of Silk Stockings" (1896),[86] in this chapter the author calls to her (at the time) unwritten finale to the trilogy, both specifically — "Paradise. All for Paradise" (*J*, 63) — and much more subtly: "Later, and little by little, feelings, like sea trash expelled on a beach — strange and recognizable, stark and murky — returned" (*J*, 75).[87]

D. "The hat, pushed back on her forehead, gave Violet a scatty look."

While the first chapter focuses mainly on the narrator's voice, the second on Joe's, and the third on Alice's, the fourth chapter takes Violet as its main protagonist. Again, as in Joe's "remembering," the chapter is framed by Violet's musing as she sits at the "illegal tables" at Duggie's drugstore drinking chocolate malt to grow her hips (*J*, 89, 94 & 114). As in other chapters there are various ways of storytelling alluded to in the "teachings" and "lessons learned from the old folks," the stories of violence towards blacks implicit in references to Rocky Mount hangings or the castration of a "young tenor in the choir," the stories people relay (by word of

---

[84] "All understanding is constrained by borders: freedom consists in knowing insofar as possible – for our ability to know is controlled by contextual factors larger than mere individual intention – what those borders are, so that they may be substituted by, translated into different borders. Speech genres provide a good example of this *relative* degree of freedom: the better we know possible variants of the genres that are appropriate to a given situation, the more choice we have among them" (Emerson & Holquist, "Introduction" in Bakhtin, *Speech*; xix).

[85] Notice particularly the *S.S. Ethiopia* (the steam ship belonging to Marcus Garvey's Black Star Line, an instrumental part in his back-to-Africa movement), the East St. Louis (and other) riots of 1917, and the names of newspapers: the *Age*, the *News*, and *The Messenger* (1917-1928), which described itself as the "first publication to recognize the Negro problem as fundamentally a labor problem," and later was instrumental in publishing pieces by artists of the Harlem Renaissance (See Andrews, *et al*, 494).

[86] "And women who knew no English at all and would never own a pair of silk stockings moved away from her if she sat next to them on the trolley" (J, 54).

[87] Cf. the last lyrical interlude at the end of *Paradise*: "Around them on the beach sea trash gleams."

mouth or by letters home) about the wonders of the City which inspire Joe finally to leave the woods and emigrate north, the folk saying alluded to in "Idle hands, you know" (are the devil's work), or even the inclusion of a child's song that Violet imagines herself singing together with the daughter she never had. In fact, it is the power of imagination that conjures up yet another form of storytelling as Violet makes up scenes of herself fixing her imaginary daughter's hair or taking her shopping, or as she poses questions to her dead mother, trying to understand what it was that pushed Rose Dear to suicide. Even more interesting is the process through which another person's memories are made personal. In this case, it is True Belle's stories of Baltimore and of Golden Gray, memories Violet never had or could have had, which come to play an integral part in Violet's personality as she struggles to grow up:

> Who was he thinking of when he ran in the dark to meet me in the cane field? Somebody golden, like my own golden boy, who I never ever saw but who tore up my girlhood as surely as if we'd been the best of lovers? Help me God help me if that was it, because I knew him and loved him better than anybody except True Belle who is the one made me crazy about him in the first place. Is that what happened? Standing in the cane, he was trying to catch a girl he was yet to see, but his heart knew all about, and me, holding on to him but wishing he was the golden boy I never saw either. Which means from the very beginning I was a substitute and so was he. (*J*, 97)

This understanding of "adopted" memory is not new in Morrison, however. In *The Bluest Eye* she had already posited the fickleness of memory:

> There was a tornado that year (1929), she said, that blew away half of south Lorain. I mix up her summer with my own. Biting the strawberry, thinking of storms, I see her. [...] In the summer tornado of 1929, my mother's hand is unextinguished. She is strong, smiling, and relaxed while the world falls down about her. So much for memory. (*TBE*,147)

The innovation with respect to storytelling in this chapter of *Jazz* resides in two different strategies. The first is the almost imperceptible sliding of the narrator's voice into Violet's via free indirect discourse, then free direct discourse, then seamlessly moving from the third to the first person in Violet's voice proper (which thereby modifies the meaning of "she" from Violet to Dorcas), to later return to the narrator's third person relating of Violet's memories of her mother, of True Belle, and of meeting Joe and moving to the City. So skillfully handled is this melding that the voice itself becomes ambiguous. Is the return to the third person a way in which Violet can conceptualize and think about her past? Does the first person "I," trying to ascertain the moment at which Rose Dear decided on suicide, belong to Violet or the narrator? Who is "wondering" here (*J*, 101)?

In fact, this melding of the voices into one ambiguous character is the inverse reflection of the other main strategy in this chapter, and that is the projection of the self as "other" in an effort to acquire understanding. The importance of "alterity" for Bakhtin has already been discussed, but the self as a projected "alter ego" only makes its appearance in *Jazz* at this point.

112

A case could obviously be made for understanding Violet's thinking about "*that* Violet"[88] as an enacting of W.E.B. Du Bois signature concept of "double consciousness,"[89] which came to play such an important part in the thinking of the Harlem Renaissance and thereafter. However, the "tensions and divisions" that Violet examines as she reviews her past and tries to make sense of her actions might also be fodder for the psychological theories of the unconscious propagated by Sigmund Freud, who was also developing his theories of psychoanalysis at the time. For the present study, however, it is more interesting to look at Violet dealing with her violent split personality as an enactment of Bakhtin's refutation of Freud's theories. Bakhtin synthesizes Freud's preoccupation with the construction of the self as "the *strife*, the *chaos*, the *adversity* of our psychical life" which Freud referred to as "the dynamics of the psyche." He takes umbrage with Freud, however, on the notion that these conflicts move on the subconscious, positing instead that they are only "conflicts of motives in the individual human consciousness." Because Freud must depend on the verbalization of these conflicts by the patient him/herself (for, to the contrary, if the patient does not speak and divulge his private information to the psychiatrist there can be no understanding/interpretation) they must exist on a conscious level:

> Freud's whole psychological construct is based fundamentally on human verbal utterances; it is nothing but a special kind of interpretation of utterances. All these utterances are, of course, constructed in the *conscious sphere of the psyche*. To be sure, Freud distrusts the surface motives of consciousness; he tries instead to penetrate the deeper levels of the psychical realm. Nevertheless, Freud does not take utterances in their objective aspect, does not seek out their physiological or social roots; instead he attempts to find the true motives of behavior in the utterances themselves – the patient is himself supposed to provide him information about the depths of the "unconscious."
> (Voloshinov/Bakhtin, *Freudianism*; in Morris, 39)

Bakhtin argues that because the desires and impulses of the unconscious only take shape and find expression in a person's consciousness, "the unconscious is nothing but one of the motives of that consciousness, one of its devices for interpreting behavior ideologically" (40). But for understanding to take place, there must be alterity. "All understanding is dialogical. Understanding is opposed to utterance like one reply is opposed to another within a dialogue. Understanding is in search of a counter-discourse to the discourse of the utterer" (Voloshinov/Bakhtin, *Marxism*; in Todorov, 22). For Bakhtin, at the bottom of the "self" is not the "id" but the "other" (Todorov, 33). For Violet to come to understand her "self" and the knowledge and motivation she attributes to "that other Violet," she must describe this part of herself as "other." Bakhtin's comments on Dostoevsky are absolutely pertinent:

> This stubborn urge to see everything as coexisting, to perceive and show all

---

[88] Violet does not use the nickname "Violent," granted to her after her attempt to slash Dorcas' corpse, but refers constantly to "that other Violet" or simply "that Violet."

[89] Du Bois first advanced this term, describing tensions and divisions in an African American identity, in "The Strivings of the Negro People" (1897) and later in The Souls of Black Folk (1903) (See Andrews et al., 225).

> things side by side and simultaneous, as it they existed in space and not in time, leads
> Dostoevsky to dramatize, in space, even internal contradictions and internal stages in the
> development of a single person – forcing a character to converse with his own double,
> with the devil, with his alter ego, with his own caricature [...]
>
> (Bakhtin, *Dostoevsky*; 90-91)

> Everything that seemed simple became, in his world, complex and multi-structured. In
> every voice he could hear two contending voices, in every expression a *crack*, and the
> readiness to go over immediately to another contradictory expression; in every gesture
> he detected confidence and lack of confidence simultaneously; he perceived the
> profound ambiguity, even multiple ambiguity, of every phenomenon.
>
> (Bakhtin, *Dostoevsky*; 91; emphasis added)

This characterizes Violet exactly: The numerous references to her "cracks" in previous chapters, and the "contradictory" or meaningless fusion of expression in one sentence, specifically in the first chapter have led her into silence, believing that she cannot control her own tongue. Violet must envision her other "self" in order to establish a dialogue and strive for understanding. In doing so, she comes to recognize (through her memories of her mother's suicide and True Belle's stories of Baltimore, which become "memories she never had") the reasons for her "erratic" behavior and her own previous incapacity for verbalizing them. The parrot, which she realizes she never named and which could only repeat "I love you," symbolizes the dialogue she could never establish with Joe (which parallels those things Joe had never shared with Violet, but could with Dorcas). But once she can establish a dialogue with "that other Violet," coming to understand herself in the process, and reclaiming the strength and motivation she had as a young woman ("the powerfully strong young woman who could handle mules, bale hay and chop wood as good as any man"[90]), the cracks can begin to heal:

> [...] NO! *that* is not somebody walking round town, up and down the streets wearing my
> skin and using my eyes shit no *that* Violet is me!   (*J*, 95-96)

But the process of achieving wholeness is incomplete as long as Violet only dialogues with herself, for "we can never see ourselves as a whole; the other is necessary to accomplish [...] a perception of the self that the individual can achieve only partially with respect to himself" (Todorov, 94). According to Bakhtin,

> [...] one can speak of the absolute aesthetic need of man for the other, for the other's
> activity of seeing, holding, putting together and unifying, which alone can bring into
> being the externally finished personality; if someone else does not do it, this personality
> will have no existence.   (Bakhtin, "Author & Character"; qtd. in Todorov, 95)

Again, it is no coincidence that the last part of this chapter, dedicated to Violet's search for her self, is given precisely to dialogue with Alice. In one of her visits to see Alice, Violet arrives

---

[90] An intertextual reference to Sojourner Truth.

literally and figuratively "frayed," "holding her coat lapels closed, too embarrassed to let her hostess hang it up lest she see the lining" (*J*, 109). After an intense exchange which leads them both to silence, Alice, exasperated, says "Give me that coat. I can't look at that lining another minute" (*J*, 110). As the conversation is renewed, Alice forces Violet to examine her options; "Her stitches were invisible to the eye" (*J*, 111). Through her dialogue with Alice, Violet's consciousness is expanded and her understanding of herself more complete.[91] Alice figuratively stitches Violet back together.

It is also no coincidence that this dialogue between Violet and Alice ends with their shared laughter, and brings in reference to two extremely painful memories, one collective and one personal. The immediate prompting of the laughter is Alice's burning of the piece she is ironing: "the black and smoking ship burned clear through the yoke" calls up memories of the Middle Passage; the other is the memory of True Belle as she came into the single room of their cabin to find her grandchildren "hunched like mice near a can fire" and "laughed to beat the band." Nonetheless, Violet suddenly remembers what Bakhtin well knew, "that laughter is serious. More complicated, more serious than tears" (*J*, 113).[92] Violet, reconciled to her "self," thinks of how she must have looked to others as she tried to cut the dead girl. "She laughed until she coughed and Alice had to make them both a cup of settling tea" (*J*, 114).

E. "And when spring comes to the City people notice one another in the road; [...]"

On the face of it, chapter five begins with the narrator's voice talking once again about the City, leading into comments about Joe, but basically it is an excuse to intervene in the narrative. Once again her intrusiveness is made explicit with phrases like "My own opinion," "I know him so well," "but I was never deceived," "he thinks he is free" (*J*, 118, 119, 120), though she shows her actual hand in other statements like "I imagine him as," "Makes me wonder about Joe," and her wondering about how things might have turned out if only Joe had confided (told his story to) Stuck or Gistan (*J*, 120 & 121). And again there are incidences of pseudodiegesis such as imitation blues lyrics and intertextual allusions such as "Everybody knows your name."[93] The narrator picks up on comments made earlier about how much she knows about the characters (later belied by her own admission) and hinting that something more dramatic or scandalous will

---

[91] For Bakhtin, "Human thought becomes genuine thought, that is, an idea, only under conditions of living contact with another and alien thought, a thought embodied in someone else's voice, that is, in someone else's consciousness expressed in discourse. At that point of contact between voice-consciousnesses the idea is born and lives" (Bakhtin, *Dostoesky*; in Morris, 98).

[92] In an interview with Bessie W. Jones and Audrey Vinson, Morrison stated that "[o]ther people call it humor. It's not really that. It's not sort of laughing away one's troubles. And laughter itself for Black people has nothing to do with what's funny at all. And taking that which is peripheral, or violent or doomed or something that nobody else can see any value in and making value out of it or having a psychological attitude about duress is part of what made us stay alive and fairly coherent, and irony is a part of that — being able to see the underside of something, as well"(in Taylor-Guthrie, 175).

[93] Immediately calling to James Baldwin's *Nobody Knows My Name* (1961), though I suppose some could pick up a reference to the television series "Cheers."

take place in the Joe/Violet saga: "Meaning to or not meaning to, she got him to go through it again — at springtime when it's clearer then than as at no other time that citylife is streetlife" (*J*, 119), though just what this "it" means is left ambiguous. Perhaps most importantly the idea of inevitability is put forward in her play on the word "track," later to be picked up by Joe in his narration, both with reference to his hunting and to the "hooves" on Dorcas' face. The "track" of the City which she alleges Joe is "bound to" just like to the groove or track of a Bluebird record speak to the narrator's belief in a naturalistic agenda unaffected by human agency, and play directly to Joe's prowess on the trail that made him the admiration of even so important a tracker as Hunter's Hunter. There is a tension in these contradictory voices: for the narrator, Joe could not get off the track because "That's the way the City spins you" (*J*, 120); for Joe, he could locate Dorcas precisely because of his skills as a tracker and what happened is all his fault, "all of it's mine. All of it" (*J*, 129). It is precisely this tension that marks the development in the novel away from the monologic, authorial control of the narrative to the dialogic, multi-voiced discourse where control becomes impossible.

The rest of this chapter is related in Joe's voice but is actually divided into two clearly differentiated sections. The first of these is Joe's "metamorphosis" (already mentioned above as a major characteristic of the "everyday novel of adventure") in which Joe relates his life according to major events which "made him new," leading him to affirm that "You could say I've been a new Negro all my life" (*J*, 129).[94] On the narrative level, these stages in Joe's life give necessary background for understanding him as a character. On the conceptual level, Joe's "becoming" parallels the emphasis on "process" (rather than "product") that is a signature characteristic not only of jazz but, as we have seen, of the novel itself. On the contextual level, Joe's different "lives" are an efficient manner of commenting on the difficult social history of blacks between Reconstruction and the Harlem Renaissance. After the first episode in which Joe recounts his naming of himself and the second in which he relates his training as a tracker with Victory by Hunter's Hunter, each of the following "changes" in his life have much to do with contextual information:

3) 1893 explains the rise of the Klan and the impossibility of earning a living at tenant farming, which was just a version of uninstitutionalized slavery; in 1901 he relates the optimism over Booker T. Washington's being invited to the White House to dine with President Theodore Roosevelt, and the theft by whites of the land he had paid for;

4) 1906 comments upon the Jim Crow laws imposed during their train ride north to the City and their confined life in the Tenderloin district;

5) Joe recalls his belief that this would be his permanent self in that they had managed to leave behind "the stink of Mulberry Street and Little Africa, then the flesh-eating rats on West Fifty-third and moved uptown," but includes comments on the "colorism" of light-skinned blacks who could be just as vicious as the whites in trying to keep darker blacks out of their neighborhoods;

6) refers to the racial unrest of 1917 (already previously commented) and the brutal

---

[94] A clear reference, as Matus makes clear, to Alain Locke's concept of the New Negro of the Harlem Renaissance (129-130).

treatment by whites (one of whom , "had a heart and kept the others from finishing me right then and there") because of their anger over the waves of black people emigrating from the South to take on work during World War I; and

7) when in 1919 Joe marched with "the colored troops of the three six nine" whose men "with the cold faces" and the drums had so affected Alice.[95]

Much has been said about Joe's giving himself (in the first change) his own last name of "Trace," which through his own retelling, acquires the status of myth, as do the terms of his birth in the following chapter. In his long essay on "Forms of Time and Chronotope in the Novel" Bakhtin discusses myths and legends which "attempt, through history, to make sense out of space" :

> Local myth explains the genesis of a geographical space. Each locality must be explained, beginning with its place-name and ending up with the fine details of its topographical relief, its soil, plant life and so forth – all emerging from the human event that occurred there and that gave to the place its name and its physiognomy. A locality is the trace of an event, a trace of what had shaped it. (Bakhtin, *Dialogic*; 189)

Obviously, the "genesis" that Joe refers to is his own and not a topographical space, but it is interesting that for Bakhtin the "trace" belongs to an "event" which forms the chronotope which is the organizing center for the "fundamental narrative events of the novel." "The chronotope is the place where the knots of narrative are tied and untied" (189). This is made even more explicit in the latter of the two sections narrated by Joe in this chapter when, while trying to find Dorcas, he returns to the place where they first met clandestinely. The trace of this event, the clear beginning of the narrative that propels the whole novel, is made explicit in that Joe carved their initials onto the rock: "D. and J."[96] (*J*, 134).

Though Joe's narrative in the second chapter also discusses some of the circumstances of his past and his love affair with Dorcas, there is a fundamental difference between the second and this fifth chapter which greatly bears on the style of storytelling. Consider that the narrator's final thought (as to what might have happened if Joe had told Stuck or Gistan [*J*, 177-121]) links the introductory section with the beginning of Joe's voice and may also be a clue as to the narrator's identity in that the immediate following sentence is Joe's statement, "It's not a thing you tell to another man" (*J*, 121). This might imply that he is talking to the narrator, hence a woman because he cannot talk about Dorcas to other men, reinforced by the fact that this time Joe's narration (both sections) is included entirely in quotation marks, that is, it is entirely

---

[95] Joe does not list as independent "changes" in his metamorphosis his meeting and falling in love with Dorcas, nor his murder of her and subsequent despair, which would seemingly constitute major moments in his life making a total of "nine lives," while his later reconciliation with Violet at the end of the book would constitute yet another for a "final" total of ten lives. But in this chapter these involve less social commentary.

[96] Joe remembers the "treats" he would bring to Dorcas to make her smile, the very first one mentioned being precisely the phonograph records. The clear association with DJ makes the reader smile. It is also interesting to note that in Michael Holquist's analysis of *The Great Gatsby* to which he applies the Bakhtinian theory of "otherness", he remarks that "'Jay Gatsby' for all its author's attempts to make it so, is less a name than it is a story" ("Stereotyping," 467).

mimetic. Naming the narrator as the objective of his narrative, however, does not hold up well logically with the narrator's obsession with her "eavesdropping" and "observational tactics" which fail her by the end of the novel. Though in the first part we are not told *to whom* Joe is speaking, the almost imperceptible change in personal pronoun from "she" (*J*, 130) to "you" (*J*, 131) in the second section indicates that here his speech is a "monologue" directed toward his deceased lover.

The ambiguity of the "listener" seems to bring up yet another of Bakhtin's concerns with discourse in general and in the novel in particular, i.e., the problem of the *addressee*. "An essential (constitutive) marker of the utterance is its quality of being directed to someone, its *addressivity*" (*Speech*, 95), which will in turn determine its "double-voicedness":

> Orientation of the word toward the addressee has an extremely high significance. In point of fact, *word is a two-sided act.* It is determined equally by whose word it is and for whom it is meant. As word, it is precisely *the product of the reciprocal relationship between speaker and listener, addresser and addressee.*
>
> (Voloshinov/Bakhtin, *Marxism*; in Morris, 58; emphasis in original)

This is so even if the discourse is produced as a monologue, as in the second section, for "[e]ach person's inner world and thought has its stabilized *social audience* that comprises the environment in which reasons, motives, values, and so on are fashioned" (in Morris, 58). The fact that Joe's discourse is colloquial, as if he were speaking to someone he knew well, is also important. In *Speech Genres* Bakhtin explains that because familiar and intimate genres perceive their addressees "more or less outside the framework of the social hierarchy and social conventions" ("without rank"), the inclusion of these genres in literature became an ideological statement.[97] The importance of the addressee will take on more and more significance as the novel proceeds.

F. "Risky, I'd say, trying to figure out anybody's state of mind."

With the very first sentence of chapter six the narrator "lays bare" the impossibility of any real understanding of the desires and motivation of characters, thereby exposing the falsity behind any pretense of "realistic" narrative. But she immediately thereafter describes herself as "curious, inventive and well-informed," even after admitting that she does not "know," and cloaks herself in the manteau of omniscient storyteller to relate (because "it's not hard to imagine") the stories of True Belle and Vera Louise, Golden Gray, and the circumstances of Joe's birth. Even within the most "straight-forward" first section of this chapter, the story of True Belle and Vera Louise Gray itself emphasizes other stories: True Belle "fills Violet's head with stories about her

---

[97] In other periods as well, when the task was to destroy traditional official styles and world views that had faded and become conventional, familiar styles became very significant in literature. Moreover, familiarization of styles opened literature up to layers of language that had previously been under speech constraint (Bakhtin, *Speech*; 97).

whitelady and the light of both their lives [...] Golden Gray" (*J*, 139); "Vera Louise dressed [Golden] like the Prince of Wales and read him vivid stories" (*J*, 140); True Belle answered her daughter Rose's pleas "by coming back to Vesper with Baltimore tales for grandchildren she had never seen" (*J*, 142); although Golden Gray left at eighteen, True Belle's "memories of the boy were more than enough" (*J*, 143) and she relates them incessantly to the children; and Vera Louise consistently told Golden lies "about practically everything including the question of whether she was his owner, his mother or a kindly neighbor" (*J*, 143). While Lestory is an expert at "reading trails" (*J*, 148), in a later section Golden Gray is "shaping a story for himself to tell somebody, to tell his father, naturally" (*J*, 154), and he remembers True Belle telling him the story of the "man who saved the rattler, nursed the rattler, fed the rattler [...]" (A folk story within the memory of the protagonist of this story that the narrator is narrating). Golden is imagined as imagining himself as the protagonist of a myth scenario, a "knight errant bragging about his coolness as he unscrews the spike from the monster's heart and breathes life back into the fiery nostrils"(*J*, 154); even more interestingly, the reason given for his not leaving the naked and pregnant black woman lying in the woods is that he does not want to see himself leaving her a second time, "and does not want to spend any part of the time to come remembering having done that" (*J*, 145). The young black boy's allusion to what he thought was Golden's inebriation includes yet another story within the story:

> [...] he thought the man lurching down the steps was white and not to be spoken to without leave. Drunk, too, he thought, because his clothes were those of a gent who sleeps in his own yard after a big party rather than in his wife's bed, and wakes when his dogs come to lick his face.   (*J*, 155)

The repeated reference to "stories" of all kinds is a subtle counterpoint to the real focus of this chapter — the narrator herself as storyteller and the *process* of telling a story. As True Belle tells Golden, "Go on," she said. "I'll tell you how to find him, or what's left of him. It don't matter if you do find him or not; *it's the going that counts*"(*J*, 159; emphasis added). Though the narrator at the beginning of the chapter ostensibly says that it is "risky" to understand True Belle's "state of mind," the pitfalls of novelistic characterization are explicitly examined in her relating of Golden Gray's arrival at Henry Lestory's cabin with the pregnant Wild. Although the "same" story is told twice, we actually learn as much about the narrator as we do about Golden Gray and his quest.

The narrator clearly marks her intervention in the text on page 143, when she begins the "first version" with a reference to her own imagination — "I see him in a two-seat phaeton." — which also marks a pronounced change in style which will be characterized by straight-forward declaratory sentences reminiscent of simple oral storytelling:

> He ties his horse to a sapling and sloshes back in driving rain to the place where the woman fell. She is still sprawled there. Her mouth and legs open. A small hickey is forming on her head. Her stomach is big and tight. He leans down, holding his breath against infection or odor or something. Something that might touch or penetrate him. She looks dead or deeply unconscious. And she is young. There is nothing he can do

for her and for that he is relieved. Then he notices a rippling movement in her stomach. Something insider her is moving. (*J*, 144-145)

The "second version" resorts to sentences with more subordinate clauses and a style that is at once rhetorical (in Golden's "voice") and pastoral in the descriptions of his journey.

On the face of it the narrator simply retells the story of Golden's encounter with Wild and his arrival at Lestory's cabin by enhancing certain parts or elaborating on more details and by employing a more pastoral or "lyrical" style of narration. Closer examination, however, reveals that, apart from style, there are subtle changes in the circumstances of Golden's arrival: the "hickey" on Wild's head caused by her crashing into the tree (*J*, 146) is later "a "lip of skin" hanging from her forehead (*J*, 154); the fireplace that "has a heap of ash, but no embers" (*J*, 147) becomes "[c]lean, set for a new fire, braced with scoured stones [...]" (*J*, 152); the door to Lestory's cabin which is "closed but not latched" (*J*, 147) is "rope-locked" in the "second version"; and although Golden "pulls into the yard, finds a shed with two stalls in back, and "takes his horse into one" (*J*, 146) in the course of the "first version," later "the fence gate is wide enough for a stout woman but no more" and he must unharness the horse before walking behind the cabin (to find two stalls) and tying his horse to a stake (*J*, 151).

The most noteworthy change in the narration, however, concerns the narrator herself and how she envisions Golden Gray. The fact that this contrast takes shape around events that occurred in the past, as well as the fact that Golden Gray actually thinks of himself in mythical terms, serves to heighten the contrast that Bakhtin makes between the epic and the novel:

> The epic past is called the "absolute past" for good reason: it is both monochronic and valorized (hierarchical); it lacks any relativity, that is, any gradual, purely temporal progressions that might connect it with the present. It is walled off absolutely from all subsequent times, and above all from those times in which the singer and his listeners are located. This boundary, consequently, is immanent in the form of the epic itself and is felt and heard in its every word. (Bakhtin, *Dialogic*; 15-16)

> The present is something transitory, it is flow, it is an eternal continuation without beginning or end; it is denied an authentic conclusiveness and consequently lacks an essence as well. (Bakhtin, *Dialogic*; 20)

The "inconclusiveness" of modern narration in this chapter is made evident by the narrator's "re-writing" of the story in slightly different terms, and more importantly by her "waffling" on how she conceives her "hero" in this story. In the first version, Golden is selfish and unfeeling, worrying more about his property than the well-being of a pregnant woman; her blackness nauseates him, yet he finds it "odd" that he takes such pride in his beautiful black horse,[98] and "he is a touch ashamed" (*J*, 144). He positions her on his carriage so that she will not lean toward him or touch him, and is unhappy that her dirty bare feet are touching his "splendid but muddy boots." On arriving at the cabin, he makes sure that his horse is cared for

---

[98] A reference to the equivalency made during slavery of black people with chattel.

and carries his trunk into the cabin before he tends to this woman. For all of his short life he had always thought that "there was only one kind [of black person] — True Belle's kind. Black and nothing. Like Henry LesTroy," but now he must deal with the fact that "there was another kind — like himself" (*J*, 149).[99]

The second version of this story is a more "subjective" interpretation of Golden, who is portrayed as (or suggested to be) a young man struggling unhappily with his newly revealed identity as a mulatto. Now the pregnant woman is more than an undesireable inconvenience, a vision he hopes will somehow leave him alone and unaffected. Instead, Wild becomes the "other," at once "a proper protection against and anodyne to what he believed his father to be, and therefore (if it could just be contained, identified) — himself" (*J*, 148). Moreover, he begins to deal with the "meaning of blackness," as well as the unsettling contradiction that the repulsion Wild's blackness causes in him is mirrored by his attraction to the only real black presence in his life: "True Belle had been his first and major love, which may be why two gallops beyond that hair, that skin, their absence was unthinkable" (*J*, 150). Golden Gray's meditation on what blackness means to him and to the construction of his identity reflects Morrison's own affirmation that the "black other" was a crucial element in the formation of the "American" identity in the early nineteenth century, and that understanding the "racial" context of early American "canonical" writers is fundamental to the explication of their works.[100] By avoiding Wild, Golden can put off his own identity crisis; though he acts as if he were "always under the reviewing gaze of an impressionable but casual acquaintance" (*J*, 153), he is afraid that Wild might be awake and that he would have to look into her "deer eyes." Still, he confections a "story" abut his own courage in saving this woman-monster, and while in the first rendition he "curses himself for not having pulled [the cot's blanket] back" before laying Wild upon it (*J*, 147), now in his revised story about himself he believes that he "thought of the blood, [...] dirtying the mattress" (*J*, 154). This struggle with his identity, with who he believes he is or might be, with how others will perceive him, takes its toll, and after pulling fresh clothing out of his trunk, he sits on the bed and discovers that he is crying. In the lyrical passage that follows, molded like a prayer and written in his free direct discourse, Golden comes to terms with his loss, with the "phantom" arm and father that he never knew he had. It is significant that this young man, who has always believed himself to be white, must now pray for "wholeness" through the reclamation of his "blackness" in an unacknowledged and recently revealed black progenitor. That his own father did not know of his birth and his mother had lied to him for his eighteen years creates a crisis of identity that well reflects the national experience. "Wholeness" will only come with full recognition of both "progenitors" of the "American identity."

There are, in the two stories of Golden Gray, two intimately linked questions: the first is the acknowledgment of the other as the self, and the second is the impossibility of seeing the "self" as complete; that is, identity as well as modern narrative is inconclusive. Moreover, it is through the "other" that the "self" is substantiated:

---

[99] A reference to the idea of the "superiority" of mulattos, cultivated especially at the end of the nineteenth century and early twentieth century.

[100] Cf. *Playing in the Dark: Whiteness and the Literary Imagination* (1992).

> This other human being whom I am contemplating, I shall always see and know
> something that he, from his place outside and over against me, cannot see himself: parts
> of his body that are inaccessible to his own gaze (his head, his face and its expression),
> the world behind his back [...] are accessible to me but not to him. As we gaze at each
> other, two different worlds are reflected in the pupils of our eyes. [...] to annihilate this
> difference completely, it would be necessary to merge into one, to become one and the
> same person.   (Bakhtin, "Author"; qtd. in Morris, 6)

As Pam Morris comments, "This excess of seeing allows the other to offer me that unified bodily image of myself as a 'gift.' Similarly, only another consciousness can offer me a unified sense of my personality" (6).

But the story of Golden Gray, of self and other, is not the only one, or even the most important one being told in this chapter. As in Morrison's observation of the figures of the literary canon, "The subject of the dream is the dreamer" (*PD*, 17), the real "story" in this chapter is the story of the narrator and how her conscious re-envisioning of Golden Gray's story changes her own thinking. Having "though about him a lot, wondered whether he was what True Belled loved and Violet too," the narrator begins the story of Golden's quest with "I see him [...]" (*J*, 143), and proceeds through a fairly straightforward narrative. But because Morrison chooses her words so carefully, and because the technique of free indirect discourse is so liberally employed throughout *Jazz,* the continuous intrusion of the narrator into her story (and even her choice of the word "scene"), the ambiguity of the expression "Maybe," set off at the end of a passage that discusses precisely his "state of mind," may refer either to Golden or the narrator herself:

> Also there is something about where he has come from and why, where he is going and
> why that encourages in him an insistent, deliberate recklessness. The scene becomes an
> anecdote, an action that would unnerve Vera Louise and defend him against patricide.
> Maybe.   (*J*, 145)

The second narration of this story sees a marked rise in the number of the narrators personal comments, beginning with the inclusion of "perhaps" in the first sentence of this section, and followed immediately by rhetorical questions which again, given their ambiguity, could pertain to Golden's interior monologue or to the narrator's own indecision. When at the end of this paragraph the narrator describes him as overcoming his natural aversion to Wild, overcoming the "shudder" at "the possibility of her leaning on him," she remarks, "I like to think of him this way" (*J*, 150). But because he tends to his horse before caring for Wild, the narrator "worries" about him, though when he wipes the mud from his boots before entering the cabin with a dirt floor, she does not "hate him much anymore" (*J*, 151).

The questions posed at the end of the next paragraph on page 152 overtly reflect the narrator's musing: "Does he think she will wake up and run off, relieving him of his choice, if he leaves her alone? Or that she will be dead, which is the same thing," speaking decidedly of Golden as a "real" ethical human being, able to exercise choice and free will, rather than her own invention. Immediately thereafter she returns to the authoritative "I know," yet on the next page the ambiguity of reference is even more pronounced:

The sign he makes is deep, a hungry air-take for the strength and perseverance all life, but especially his, requires. Can you see the fields beyond, crackling and drying in the wind? The blade of blackbirds rising out of nowhere, brandishing and then gone?

(J, 153)

Because the last sentence in the same paragraph "clearly" relates to Golden ("Carry yourself the way you would if you were always under the reviewing gaze of an impressionable but casual acquaintance"), the narrator is seemingly directing her question ("Can you ...?") to Golden as he searches for strength. But the positioning of the question creates such ambiguity that we could easily interpret that this is the narrator inviting us, the readers, to imagine the scene with her.

The narrator continues to vacillate as Golden invents a story for himself that leaves him in a favorable light: "I know he is a hypocrite; that he is shaping a story for himself to tell somebody [...]" and later, "He is lying, the hypocrite," and in spite of Golden's "self-delusion," she states that "I know better" (*J*, 154). Again, immediately thereafter on the following page, she abruptly qualifies this "knowledge" ("Why doesn't he wipe her face, I wonder") and speculates on his decision. Then taking her own interpretation as valid, she takes yet another position:

Aw, but he is young, young and he is hurting, so I forgive him his self-deception and his grand, fake gestures, and when I watch him sipping too quickly the cane liquor he has found, worrying about his coat and not tending to the girl, I don't hate him at all [...] he is a boy after all [...]

(J, 155)

The section immediately following this second version is straight-forward mimetic dialogue between Golden and the young black boy, used to advance the plot line. Thereafter Golden's interior monologue in free indirect discourse melds into the narrator's diegetic interpretation of his dilemma, only to return to the evaluation of her own imaginative powers: "What was I thinking of ? How could I have imagined him so poorly? [...] I have been careless and stupid and it infuriates me to discover (again) how unreliable I am" (J, 160).

For Bakhtin the "stupidity" of the narrator is a strategy to lay bare the conventions of official discourse, which had "enormous significance" for what he calls the "Second Line" of the development of the novel :

Stupidity (incomprehension) in the novel is always polemical: it interacts dialogically with an intelligence (a lofty pseudo intelligence) with which it polemicizes and whose mask it tears away. Stupidity, like gay deception and other novelistic categories, is a dialogic category, one that follows from the specific dialogism of novelistic discourse. [...] At its heart always lies a polemical failure to understand someone else's discourse, someone else's pathos-charged lie that has appropriated the world and aspires to conceptualize it, a polemical failure to understand generally accepted, canonized, inveterately false languages with their lofty labels for things and events: poetic language, scholarly and pedantic language, religious, political, judicial language and so forth. (Bakhtin, *Dialogic*; 403)

But what discourse is Morrison's narrator trying to problematize? What mask is she trying to tear away? Certainly not Golden Gray's, whose "story" and "state of mind" she has both invented and critiqued. I would venture that the narrator's admission of "carelessness" and "stupidity" are "a deliberate (polemical) failure to understand the habitual way of conceiving the world" (402); that is, that the assumptions or "interpretations" of complex human motivation are at best superficial and that it is more than risky to assume that we "know" about someone without complete understanding of their context and history. And without that knowledge and understanding, in Bakhtin's eyes, we can never really know ourselves.

That our assumptions about the "other" (any other, but particularly the "racialized" other) are called into question can be immediately made apparent in our conception of the narrator herself. Heretofore we have accepted the general convention of the majority of the critics who have evaluated *Jazz* in conceiving of the narrator as female and black. (Though Gates insists that the narrator "remains indeterminate: it is neither male nor female; neither young nor old; neither rich nor poor. It is *both* and *neither*" [Gates, "Review"; 54], he makes no mention of race, which reveals his own automatic assumption that the narrator is black.) It is a conceptualization that can be "easily" defended based on assumptions about how black people and (gossipy) women talk, and on the "speakerly" nature of the text. And even though John Leonard asserts that the "the Voice is the book itself, this physical object, our metatext" (49), the conventions of storytelling inevitably demand our conceptualizing of the anonymous "voice" in order better "understand" the position of the narrator.

No matter how we envision the narrator, Golden Gray clearly figures as "other" in the text. But what happens when we "re-conceptualize" the narrator as, say, white and male is startling, and reveals to us the nature of our own assumptions which may, in fact, be quite precarious. Repositioning the narrator allows us to delve into not only Golden Gray's struggle with a "changed" identity but to witness the narrator's own struggle (and subsequent admission of inadequacy) with (now) his preconceptions and facile critique. The phantom with which Golden must deal is also the phantom plaguing the "racial" identity of so-called "white-Americans." Reading the narrator's final monologue in this chapter in this way takes on additional meaning:

> Now I have to think this through, carefully, even though I may be doomed to another misunderstanding. I have to do it and not break down. Not hating him is not enough; liking, loving him is not useful. I have to alter things. I have to be a shadow who wishes him well, like the smiles of the dead left over from their lives. I want to dream a nice dream for him, and another of him. Lie down next to him, a wrinkle in the sheet, and contemplate his pain and by doing so ease it, diminish it. I want to be the language that wishes him well, speaks his name, wakes him when his eyes need to be open. *(J, 161)*

The engagement of the "other" is precisely what Golden Gray's quest is all about, the location of the "severed part" of the national body, the search for "wholeness" that can only come from the mutual recognition of and by the "not-me." For both Golden and the narrator (and by extension, for us, as readers), the search for self inevitably involves the search for and the dialogue with the "other."

124

G. "A thing like that could harm you."

The opening sentence immediately indicates two focal points of the story of Wild, the first of which is the powerful influence of two different types of story: superstition and rumor: In such an "oral" novel devoted precisely to the concepts of heteroglossia and dialogics, it is noteworthy that the only character who has no voice at all is the "wild" woman who may be Joe's mother. This black woman may or may not exist, but her presence in the novel is crucial. Though she herself never utters a word, her silence leaves a void that is filled with the voice of the folk who superstitiously blame her for all sorts of calamity: "Just thinking about her, whether she was close or not, could mess up a whole morning's work" (*J*, 166). The possibility of her still being alive and somewhere near at hand, and, from Hunter's inferences, the probability that she was Joe's mother, lends a palpable presence to her continuous absence.[101] Morrison deliberately calls to the end of the former novel, *Beloved*, "This is not a story to pass on," which reappears here as "Wild was not a story of a used-to-be-long-ago-crazy girl [...] She was still out there — and real" (*J*, 167).[102] Certainly her absence and lack of acknowledgment is real enough in Joe's mind to induce him first to emigrate north and then (the narrative insinuates) to murder Dorcas. Though she is described as "powerless, invisible, wastefully daft," the power of her story is undeniable.

The second type of "powerful" story referred to here, closely related to these superstitions and folktales, is found in rumor, whose influence in the black community is so ably discussed in Patricia Turner's *I Heard it Through the Grapevine*: "One week of rumors, two days of packing, and nine hundred Negroes, encouraged by guns and hemp, left Vienna [...] *(J*, 173). Nevertheless, the innovative storytelling technique in this seventh chapter is the equally powerful influence of the past on the present, emphasized linguistically by repeated references to Victory and his memory, and structurally by the intercalation and (con)fusion of the narrated past and present.

The juxtaposition of Joe's search for Wild and his chronologically later search for Dorcas is intensified by a certain ambiguity in the use of references:

It must have been the girl who changed his mind.	
Girls can do that.	(*J*, 173)
What would she want with a rooster?	(*J*, 182)
Wild, even. But alone.	(*J*, 182)
"She don't have to explain."	(*J*, 183)
But where is she?	(*J*, 184)

---

[101] The stories the community tell about her enter into the local folklore and alter their behavior in much the same way as the community of the Bottom was consolidated around their fear and hatred of Sula in Toni Morrison's novel of the same name.

[102] While this may be more fodder for critics who want to see Wild as the reappearance of Beloved, it is also useful to note that the exchange between Lestory and Golden Gray calls directly to Jadine, another culturally "misplaced" mulatta figure in *Tar Baby*, Morrison's novel prior to *Beloved*: "Get a hold of yourself. A son ain't what a woman say. A son is what a man do"(*J*, 172).

When the narrative deals with the first search, Joe's thoughts are related either through the narrator's voice or through the free indirect discourse of interior monologue. When relating his thoughts as he searches for Dorcas, however, even his interior monologue is set off in quotation marks.

The meshing of the two searches can be read psychoanalytically as the heavy interference of Joe's unresolved "motherlessness" with his fear of losing Dorcas, or as the clear embodiment of the characteristic search of the hard-boiled private detective novel in which the past plays a crucial part in the solution of the crime. It is also a clear presentation of the mixing of chronotopes which, according to Bakhtin, "are mutually inclusive, they co-exist, they may be interwoven with, replace or oppose one another, contradict one another or find themselves in ever more complex interrelationships" (*Dialogic*, 252).

Joe's search for Wild and his search for Dorcas, though obviously pertaining to different chronotopes within the novel, are explicitly interwoven to show the relevance of the past to the present. At the same time, however, and perhaps even more importantly, the relationship of these chronotopes metaphorically manifest the relationship of the represented world of the literary text with the "real" world of the readers:

> [W]e get a mutual interaction between the world represented in the work and the world outside the work. This interaction is pinpointed very precisely in certain elementary features of composition: every work has a beginning and an end, the event represented in it likewise has a beginning and an end, but these beginnings and ends lie in different worlds, in different chronotopes that can never fuse with each other or be identical to each other but that are, at the same time, interrelated and indissolubly tied up with each other.[103]
>   (Bakhtin, *Dialogic*; 255)

By demonstrating via the explicit fusion of the two stories the interdependence of what on the surface look like independent events in different chronotopes, Morrison also illustrates Bakhtin's idea as to the relevance of literary works to the culture in which they arise. He likens this to the interdependence of the living organism to its environment:

> As long as the organism lives, it resists a fusion with the environment, but if it is torn out of its environment, it dies. The work and the world represented in it enter the real world and enrich it, and the real world enters the work and its world as part of the process of its creation, as well as part of its subsequent life, in a continual renewing of the work through the creative perception of listeners and readers.
>   (Bakhtin, *Dialogic*; 254)

---

[103] "[...T]he event that is narrated in the work and the even of narration itself (we ourselves participate in the latter, as listeners or readers); these events take place in different times (which are marked by different durations as well) and in different places, but at the same time these two events are indissolubly united in a single but complex event that we might call the work in the totality of all its events, including the external material givenness of the work, and its text, and the world represented in the texts, and the author-creator and the listener or reader; thus we perceive the fullness of the work in all its wholeness and indivisibility, but at the same time we understand the diversity of the elements that constitute it" (Bakhtin, *Dialogic*; 255).

Thus, the "author's relationship to the various phenomena of literature and culture has a dialogical character, which is analogous to the interrelationships between chronotopes within the literary work" (*Dialogic*, 256). It is noteworthy that this relationship is made explicit at this point, because its relevance to the significance of Morrison's *Jazz* becomes progressively more important, culminating in the final chapter (see below).

The last short section of this chapter returns to Joe's incursion into Wild's cave and includes a relation of the things he saw there. The description of Golden's trousers and shirt, which had obviously been mended — "Carefully folded, a silk shirt, faded pale and creamy – except at the seams. There, both thread and fabric were a fresh and sunny yellow" (*J*, 184), the clothes that he wore "for as long as anyone in Vienna knew him" (*J*, 158) — together with the reference to "that queer boy she set so much store by" (*J*, 168) have been taken by some critics as an indication that Golden Gray stayed on to live with Wild. But this story, as the many invented by the local people about Wild, may simply be another (unelaborated) story which sparks the imagination but is unsubstantiated further in the text.

H. "There she is."

The eighth chapter in *Jazz*, the shortest in the novel (pages 87-193), begins as usual with the voice of the narrator, though her choice of diegesis is the impersonal second person narration. Though its narrative purpose is to describe the *ambience* of a rent party, typical in the 1920s among the black population, the stylistic choice of the "you" form serves to heighten the participation of the reader in the development of the story, much as oral storytellers do. The ambiguous "you" of the previous chapter becomes the definite addressee located in the chronotope of the reading experience. "There she is," but there the reader is also, involved in the "dazzle and the mischief," and therefore more disposed to understand Dorcas' emotions and excitement. Toward the end of the brief introduction, the narrator slides into free indirect discourse thereby preparing the way for Dorcas interior monologue, interrupted twice by the narrator's comments.

Up until this point Dorcas has only been revealed through the comments of other characters or the narrator, so the inclusion of her voice is at once strategic and problematic. The interior monologue draws on a popular modernist technique and the mimetic form imitates the continuous flow of the present as Dorcas narrates her last thoughts before dying (which in some measure tries to explain why she did not reveal the name of the man who shot her). Since Dorcas has been dead since the very first page of the book, her "intrusion" with her own narration serves to mix up the chronotopes, especially since she prophetically "expects" Joe to find her. Whereas in the previous chapter the different chronotopes were juxtaposed, here they are collapsed altogether: "They need me to say his name so they can go after him. Take away his sample case with Rochelle and Bernadine and Faye inside. I know his name but Mama won't tell" (*J*, 193). The narrator's change in style to include the reader more directly, as well as her affirmation that "Everything is now"(*J*, 191), reinforces the immediacy of the event; so does Dorcas' short narration of her own dying, which fuses past and present, and her repetition of key phrases which emphasize cyclicity rather than progression.[104] This interruption in the flow of time recalls "folkloric time and the ancient matrices" which in the development of the novel became the "lost ideal"; these gave way to the "philosophical sublimation" of the ancient cyclical complex — nature, love, the family and childbearing, death: "Love becomes an elemental, mysterious and – more often than not– fatal force for those who love, and all this is interiorized. It comes to us associated with nature and death" (Bakhtin, *Dialogic*; 230). Thus Dorcas' final thoughts are not of Acton nor of Joe, but of oranges on a tray "full to spilling" (*J*, 193), of itself a subtle but lovely call to the paradise she had found with her first lover: "So clear the dark bowl the pile of oranges. Just oranges. Bright. Listen. I don't know who is that woman singing but I know the words by heart." Wallace Stevens, an outstanding modernist poet whose "Sunday Morning" is itself a celebration of the natural world (Parini, 12) chose the same images to reflect on the afterlife:

> The pungent oranges and bright, green wings
> Seem things in some procession of the dead,
> Winding across wide water, without sound.   (Stanza 1, v. 9-11)

> Shall she not find in comforts of the sun,
> In pungent fruit and bright, green wings, or else
> In any balm or beauty of the earth,
> Thinks to be cherished like the thought of heaven?   (Stanza 2, v. 4-7)

Equally pertinent are his references to a woman (or the sea) singing in "The Idea of Order at Key West":

> Even if what she sang was what she heard,
> Since what she sang was uttered word by word.   (Stanza 2, v. 3-4)

I. "Sweetheart. That's what that weather was called."

The introduction by the narrator to chapter nine mostly serves to set the scene for Felice's story but also marks the "beginning of the end" of the narrator's "delusion" of control — "Now she is disturbing me, making me doubt my own self just looking at her sauntering through the sunshafts like that" (*J*, 198) — which will characterize the final chapter. Certain themes are echoed, particularly in Violet's relating of her struggle with her internal other ("Violent") to find her true "self":

---

[104] "The mark of cyclicity, and the consequently of cyclical repetitiveness, is imprinted on all events occurring in this type of time. Time's forward impulse is limited by the cycle. For this reason even growth does not achieve an authentic 'becoming'" (Bakhtin, *Dialogic*; 210).

"'How did you get rid of her?'
"'Killed her. Then I killed the me that killed her.'
"'Who's left?'
"'Me.'   (*J*, 209)

The "lost ideal" and "ancient matrix" of idyllic life which arose in the previous chapter appears again here in Violet's nostalgia for another time — 'Before I came North I made sense and so did the world. We didn't have nothing but we didn't miss it' (*J*, 207) — in which memory has softened the brutality of living in the South. This relegation of "meaning" to the past is what Bakhtin refers to as "historical inversion," the essence of which is found in the fact that "mythological and artistic thinking locates such categories as purpose, ideal, justice, perfection, the harmonious condition of man and society and the like in the *past*" (Bakhtin, *Dialogic*; 147, emphasis in the original). Bakhtin later goes on to say that the significance of the idyll in the development of the novel cannot be overestimated, and that

> [o]pposed to this little world, a world fated to perish, there is a great but abstract world, where people are out of contact with each other, egoistically sealed-off from each other, greedily practical. [...] In place of the limited idyllic collective, a new collective must be established capable of embracing all humanity [...]
>
> (Bakhtin, *Dialogic*; 234)

Such is the quest for the characters in *Jazz*, and by extension, the task of contemporary society.

Most of chapter nine, however, is given to Felice's voice, recited completely in mimesis with quotations marks beginning every paragraph. As to be expected, it contains the now "obligatory" references to different ways in which stories are told: newspaper stories (*J*, 199), gossip (*J*, 199), secrets (*J*, 201), lies (*J*, 205), recounting plays from baseball games (*J*, 216), Dorcas and Felice inventing "love scenes" which were "fun and a little smutty," though the picture she had of herself when she did it was "as somebody I'd seen in a picture show or a magazine" (*J*, 209), and even real photographs which run from the absence of Dorcas' picture from the mantel (*J*, 197) to the one of Dorcas' parents "sitting under a painted palm tree" in which Dorcas thought her parents to be good looking, but Felice thought they looked sad (*J*, 200). The mention of photographs is meaningful precisely in this chapter because Felice's story of Dorcas' dying moments relates the circumstances explained to Morrison about a photo by James Van Zee she had seen in Camille Billop's *The Harlem Book of the Dead*, precisely the germ around which the author constructed this novel (Cf. Gates & McKay, 2097).

Felice's direct speech relates many stories of her own life, her parents, Dorcas, and especially the story of the ring. The innovation in this section, however, is a technique not often seen in the novel, i.e., direct speech of one character which includes the direct speech of another character which again contains reported and direct speech of yet another. While all of this section is Felice's direct speech (set off in double quotation marks), a good deal of it includes her repetition of other characters' speech (marked by single quotation marks), and fully two instances contain reports of her own conversations with others which themselves contain reported speech (marked by double, then single, then double quotation marks again):

[Felice relating the circumstances of Dorcas' death to Violet and Joe]

"I could hardly find my tongue. 'I'm not like her!'
"I didn't mean to say it so loud. They both turned to look at me. So I said it even though I didn't plan to. I told them even before I asked for the ring. 'Dorcas let herself die. The bullet went in her shoulder, this way.' I pointed. 'She wouldn't let anybody move her; said she wanted to sleep and she would be all right. Said she'd go to the hospital in the morning. "Don't let them call nobody," she said. "No ambulance; no police, no nobody." I thought she didn't want her aunt, Mrs. Manfred, to know. Where she was and all. And the woman giving the party said okay because she was afraid to call the police. They all were. People just stood around talking and waiting. Some of them wanted to carry her downstairs, put her in a car and drive to the emergency ward. Dorcas said no. She said she was all right. To please leave her alone and let her rest. But I did it. Called the ambulance, I mean; but it didn't come until morning after I had called twice. The ice, they said, but really because it was colored people calling. She bled to death all through that woman's bed sheets on into the mattress, and I can tell you that woman didn't like it one bit. That's all she talked about. Her and Dorcas' boyfriend. The blood. What a mess it made. That's all they talked about.'   (*J*, 209-210)

"He [Joe] didn't laugh at me so I said, 'I didn't tell you everything.'
"'There's more?'
"'I suppose I should. It was the last thing she said. Before she [...] went to sleep. Everybody was screaming, "Who shot you, who did it?" She said, "Leave me alone. I'll tell you tomorrow." She must have thought she was going to be around tomorrow and made me think so too. Then she called my name although I was kneeling right beside her. "Felice. Felice. Come close, closer." I put my face right there. I could smell the fruity liquor on her breath. She was sweating, and whispering to herself. Couldn't keep her eyes open. Then she opened them wide and said real loud: "There's only one apple." Sounded like "apple." "Just one. Tell Joe."[105]   (*J*, 213)

In the first of these examples, Felice repeats the explanation she gave to Joe and Violet which includes direct speech (by Dorcas), reported speech ("Dorcas said no."), and reported free direct speech (And the woman giving the party said okay [...]). In the second, Felice repeats her confession to Joe in which she includes Dorcas' last words to her in direct speech. Although the punctuation of these discourses must of necessity be elaborate, they do, in fact, give a faithful rendition of how we tell stories with great immediacy, a technique that heightens the interest of the listener in the story.

---

[105] Felice's faithful rendition of Dorcas' words and her hesitation ('Sounded like "apple"') supports Bakhtin's allegation that a "grammatically complete sentence" does not necessarily function meaningfully. "Tell Joe there is only one apple" exemplifies Bakhtin's assertion that "the single utterance [...] can in no way be regarded as a completely free combination of forms of language" and that an utterance can only signify if it is surrounded by the "entire landscape" of its context (*Speech*, 81 & 83).

The punctuation makes the discourse clear. It is, in the words of Michael Holquist, "a formal means that seeks to contain the volatility of semiotic operations" ("Stereotyping," 467), an explicit way of sorting out the voices in the narration. There is only one unresolved problem: Who is Felice speaking *to*? And the fact that Morrison goes to such elaborate pains to distinguish speakers points even more glaringly to this absence. If the utterance does not and cannot exist without the addressee, then Felice has to be speaking to someone, and the fact that her stories are recounted in direct speech highlights the fact that

> speakers always shape an utterance not only according to the object of discourse (*what* they are taking *about*) and their immediate addressee (*whom* they are speaking to), but also according to the particular image in which they model the belief they will be understood, a belief that is the *a priori* of all speech. [...They have] a *superaddressee* in mind [...]
> (Emerson & Holquist, in Bakhtin, *Speech*; xviii)

Todorov is absolutely correct when he writes that "in fact, to understand the strategy of writing it is necessary to identify this 'super-recipient' imagined by the author" (110), what Lodge, referring to Wolfgang Iser, calls the "implied reader," who is "the ideal reader of the text, the reader whom the implied author seems to invite to collaborate in the production of the text's meaning" (145). The elaborate devices of Felice's storytelling, while talking about other characters, actually focus the narrative away from the stories themselves and onto the "superaddressee," that is, onto the reader/listener. This strategy is crucial in that it clearly points the way for reading the final chapter in which the centrality of the reader to the process becomes obvious and through which the overall significance of the novel can be discerned.

J. "Pain. I seem to have an affection, a kind of sweettooth for it."

While the tenth chapter of *Jazz* acts rather as an *afterward* in that it offers some explanation as to what "happened" to the main characters who were the focus of the previous chapters, it mostly concerns the narrator's confession of inadequacy and incapability of "controlling" her own characters. Her opening statement of the novel, "I know that woman," and the authority she claims as a "private eye" ("And I the eye of the storm" [*J*, 220]) dissolves into her admission of just the inverse: "Now it's clear why they contradicted me at every turn: they knew me all along" (*J*, 220). While she "invented stories about them," she thought "I'd hidden myself so well," but finds that she was "the predictable one, confused in my solitude into arrogance, thinking my space, my view was the only one that was or that mattered" (*J*, 220). The narrator in these pages abandons all ambiguity as to the addressee. Her discourse in this chapter is unabashedly directed toward the reader, and her hedging is openly an illustration of Bakhtin's hidden polemic. Her "embarrassment" over "misreading" (or rather "miswriting") Joe and Violet is short-lived, however, as at the end of the third page she returns to her conceit: "Now I know." And she returns to her omniscient haughtiness in speaking of Felice: "She thinks she can trick me again — moving so slow people nearby seem to be running. Can't fool me [...]" (J, 222). But she is ultimately "defeated" in her attempt at control because she "cannot bring to bear against their subjective position a more authoritative and objective world" (Voloshinov/Bakhtin, *Marxism*; in Morris, 66).

In good Morrison technique, the circularity of the novel, the closing of the circle as it were, is achieved through repetition of phrases and major metaphors which have been strewn through the novel: the Okeh records, the unbelievable sky, the young ghost, the men with the long-distance eyes, the references to the well and the redwings and, of course, the ineluctable music. What is more difficult and infinitely more interesting is the discourse of the narrator herself, full of double-entendre and apparent contradictions, puzzling statements. But as in all good detective novels, she leaves clues for interpretation.

The narrator's final lament over not being able to speak out loud and share a love that Violet and Joe demonstrate publically once again recalls the origin of the eavesdropping narrator which was crucial for the beginnings of the novel form (e.g., *The Golden Ass*). Perhaps the most important clue, however, is the metaphor of the bird that Violet bought "cheap because it wasn't well" (*J*, 223-224), so isolated within itself that it responds neither to food or to Violet's affection. It is crucial that the first reference to this new bird appears in the same sentence as Violet and Joe's "little personal stories" and that the remedy for its isolation is precisely the music: "They took the cage to the roof one Saturday, where the wind blew and so did the musicians in shirts billowing out behind them. From then on the bird was a pleasure to itself and to them" (*J*, 224). As Richard Hardack has so astutely pointed out, the "bird" here is an intertextual reference to Charlie Parker, the Bird or Yardbird, the highly innovative jazz musician who is a myth in his own right (457). The self-absorption and isolation of Violet's bird is remedied by its contact with the special powers of jazz, just as the arrogance of the narrator ("[...] thinking my space, my view was the only one that was or that mattered") is mediated by the understanding that popular discourse(s), the "carnivalesque" voice of the market place, will not allow the imposition of one monologic, authoritarian view. Even in their "undercover whispers" Violet and Joe remember "the carnival dolls they won and the Baltimore boats they never sailed on," intentionally repeated in "[...] bound and joined by carnival dolls and the steamers that sailed from ports they never saw" (*J*, 228).

Taking Bakhtin's heteroglossia or doublevoicedness as cue (or clue) will also clarify the narrator's longing for "Wild's chamber of gold" and her conspiracy of complicity: "She has seen me and is not afraid of me. She hugs me. Understand me. Has given me her hand. I am touched by her. Released in secret" (*J*, 221). Not only in secret, but in silence, for we remember that Wild is the only character in the novel without a voice. Her "meaning" lies precisely in this silence. In his essay "The Storyteller," Walter Benjamin extolls the role of the storyteller for providing "counsel and wisdom" in his stories and attributes the demise of storytelling to the rise of the novel at the beginning of modern times. The problem as he sees it is that the novel "neither comes from oral tradition nor goes into it."

> The novelist has isolated himself. The birthplace of the novel is the solitary individual, who is no longer able to express himself by giving examples of his most important concerns, is himself uncounseled, and cannot counsel others.   (Benjamin, 87)

For Bakhtin, however, it is precisely the "silencing" of the novel that makes it the genre *par excellence* for conserving the multiplicity of meaning, the continuous irruptions of popular voices into monologic discourse. "The book, i.e., a *verbal performance in print*, is also an element of verbal communication" (Voloshinov/Bakhtin, *Marxism*; 58; emphasis in original) and "the meaning we identify in a text is never final [...] interpretation is infinite" (Todorov, 110), precisely because the text is silent: "Such discourse is not only double-voiced but also double-accented; it is difficult to speak it aloud, for loud and living intonation excessively monologizes discourse and cannot do justice to the other person's voice present in it" (Bakhtin, *Dostoevsky*; in Morris, 109).[106] Hence parody, irony, satire, and all other forms of hybridization containing a multitude of references to and about other types of discourse make their presence more effectively felt in the novel than in any other form of linguistic communication. The last fragment Bakhtin wrote in 1975 concerns this quality of "limitlessness" of dialogical discourse:

> There is no first or last discourse, and dialogical context knows no limits (it disappears into an unlimited past and in our unlimited future). Even past meanings, that is, those that have arisen in the dialogue of past centuries, can never be stable (completed once and for all, finished), they will always change (renewing themselves) in the course of the dialogue's subsequent development, and yet to come. At every moment of the dialogue, there are immense and unlimited masses of forgotten meanings, but, in some subsequent moments, as the dialogue moves forward, they will return to memory and live in renewed form (in a new context). Nothing is absolutely dead: every meaning will celebrate its rebirth. (Bakhtin, "Aesthetics," 373; qtd. in Todorov, 110)

Let us suppose, then, that the narrator is not a person, nor the book, nor the text, but the discourse (of the novel) itself. Wild (as silence) "understands me. Has given me her hand. I am touched by her. *Released in secret*" (emphasis added).

The memory section concerning an evening in 1906 serves to focus on dreams — yet another form of storytelling — leading to the lyrical musing of the narrator set up as a dream-like sequence, though for her, "they are real." The shade[107] at once enacts the shadow-world of dreams and calls to the ambivalent meaning of blackness to white people —

> Pushed away into certain streets, restricted from others, making it possible for the inhabitants to sigh and sleep in relief, the shade stretches — just there — at the edge of the dream, or slips into the crevices of a chuckle [...] Shade. Protective, available. Or sometimes not; sometimes it seems to lurk rather than hover kindly, and its stretch is not a yawn but an increase to be beaten back with a stick. (*J*, 227)

---

[106] "Only this "silencing" of prose could have made possible the multileveledness and voice-defying complexity of intonational structures that are so characteristic for modern literature" (Morris, 70). Contrast this opinion with Seymour Chatman's affirmation that "All written texts are realizable orally; they are not being performed but could be at any moment. That is, they are innately susceptible of performance" (28).

[107] According to Clarence Major, "Shade" was in use from the 1850s to the 1900s and meant "a Negro, picked up from derogatory white use" (406).

—a "blackness" that is socially constructed as "other," and therefore as threat, and whose power is perpetuated in the monologic discourse that surrounds it.

If discourse and storytelling are the underlying yet overriding themes of *Jazz* and the narrator is the embodiment of the techniques and strategies we use to tell stories, the "laying bare of the device," as the Formalists would say, the final paragraph of the novel, which has bedeviled so many critics, realizes another crucial aspect of Bakhtinian theory: the issue of "response-ibility." Bakhtin believes that the orientation of the utterance is not only toward its "meaning" but toward its addressee or recipient, and that to some degree discourse anticipates a response: "The fact is that when the listener perceives and understands the meaning (the language meaning) of speech, he simultaneously takes an active, responsive attitude toward it" (Bakhtin, *Speech*; 68). This is true of spoken as well as written discourse for "[t]he work, like the rejoinder in dialogue, is oriented toward the response of the other (others), toward his active responsive understanding [...] The first and foremost criterion for the finalization of the utterance is the possibility of responding to it [...] of assuming a responsive attitude toward it" (75-76 & 76). Morrison herself speaks of the capacity of the reader and the writer to become aware of "the serene achievement of, or sweaty fight for, meaning and response-ability (*sic*)" (*PD*, xi).

Both Bakhtin and Morrison emphasize both the *ability* to respond to the utterance (taken here as the whole novel) and the *obligation* to do so; the responsibility for meaning and, in the specific case of *Jazz*, for language. In the fable that Morrison tells in "The Dancing Mind" (her lecture on receiving the Nobel Prize for literature) of the old blind woman whom the children try to trick, she interprets the bird that the children hold as language and the old woman as a writer. The old woman's rejoinder ("I do not know if the bird is alive or dead; I do know that it is in your hands.") Morrison hears as the woman's admonition to her young listeners to take responsibility precisely for language. For Bakhtin, the speaker (or writer) ends his utterance "in order to relinquish the floor to the other or to make room for the other's active responsive understanding" (*Speech*, 69), precisely the situation that Morrison makes explicit through the voice of her narrator in the very last lines of the novel: "If I were able I'd say it. Say make me, remake me. You are free to do it and I am free to let you because look, look. Look where your hands are. Now" (*J*, 229).

The progression of procedures for telling stories (different strategies and techniques for each subsequent chapter) points decidedly to Morrison's experimentation with language and with its innate heteroglossia. The dialogical nature of the word, particularly in the novel, consistently refuses the authoritarianism of monologic discourse; language, it seems, is the ultimate manifestation of the democratic impulse, and as such it cannot, will not, be silenced. Moreover, just as Bakhtin locates the perception of the "self" in discourse with the other and affirms that this "self" through dialogue is always in the process of becoming, never finished, Morrison finds the imaginative skills employed in the creative work are not themselves aimed at the production of a "text," but instead are part and parcel of the process of "*becoming*" (*PD*, 4). Hence, the metaphor of jazz as a music that emphasizes process over product, a music that Morrison says is never "finalized" although it may have a final chord, and is itself very bound up with notions of "response-ability" as well as the dialogic, takes on an enriched meaning when viewed as representation of the popular voice of the market-place, and of the carnivalesque.

The Conclusion

VIII. THE WINDING UP OF THE MATTER

In his "Response to a Question from the *Novy Mir* Editorial Staff" (*Speech*, 1-7) Mikhail Bakhtin speaks of the ineluctable relationship of literature and culture: "Literature is an inseparable part of culture and it cannot be understood outside the total context of the entire culture of a given epoch" (2). That this is so could never be more clearly demonstrated than in an analysis of Toni Morrison's *Jazz*, a work that arises during the last decades of the twentieth century in which the voices of multiculturalism and the critical inquiry into the "other" have repeatedly fired national debate. Her concerns with the importance of language and narrative in both her social criticism (on the Thomas-Hill Hearings and on the O.J. Simpson Trial) and her acceptance speech for the Nobel Prize in 1993 are foregrounded in this second novel of her trilogy, which taken as a whole deals with the intricate relationship of history, memory and story. To this social criticism we must add her revolutionary critique of the canonical works of the early nineteenth century, the "founding fathers" of our national literature, so to speak, in which she alleges that the one most important "ingredient" for the recipe of a new "American" identity was the presence of a large ("silent") black population which came to signify the "ultimate other."

That Morrison should take as her *sujet* the centrality of language and storytelling to the development of ethics and, indeed, to the human experience (*homo narrans*) concurs perfectly with the attention given to narration by critics in a wide range of fields over the past two decades.[108] That this author should take the novel as the most outstanding medium for her participation in the current cultural debates is not surprising, for literature refracts the "generating socioeconomic reality" just as it "reflects and refracts the reflections and refractions of other ideological spheres." But in addition to the fact that Morrison's most important contribution to the contemporary cultural environment is as a novelist, the novel itself is the art form *par excellance* for embodying the *heteroglossia* inherent in this culture, in which the centrifugal and centripetal forces are constantly at play. For Bakhtin, and obviously for Morrison,

---

[108] "The enormous significance of the motif of the speaking person is obvious in the realm of ethical and legal thought and discourse. The speaking person and his discourse is, in these areas, the major topic of thought and speech" (Bakhtin, *Dialogic*; 349).

> The novel is the expression of a Galilean perception of language, one that denies the absolutism of a single and unitary language – that is, that refuses to acknowledge its own language as the sole verbal and semantic center of the ideological world.
>
> (Bakhtin, *Dialogic*; 366)

Bakhtin noted that the "special historical conditions" of Dostoevsky's time[109] provided him with highly creative perceptions, a "dialogic moment" which was "charged with the potential of creative change" (Morris 18) which he recorded in his writing. The novel presumes a "verbal and semantic decentering of the ideological world" in that the languages that it contains demand equality and refuse "the hegemony of a single and unitary language [...] as an absolute form of thought" (367). Morrison has also been able to recognize another very important "dialogic moment." At a time of increasing acrimony over the "national identity, language and culture" confronted with the "divisiveness" of competing "minority" cultures in the U.S., the importance of Bakhtin's premise cannot be overestimated. In order to reduce the tensions created by the "threat" of a loss of "national identity" by "ethnic minorities," Bakhtin's counsel should be taken as word to the wise: "It is necessary that heteroglossia wash over a culture's awareness of itself and its language, penetrate to its core, relativize the primary language system underlying its ideology and literature and deprive it of its naive absence of conflict" (Bakhtin, *Dialogic*; 368). However, this "verbal-ideological decentering" will not occur until "a national culture loses its sealed-off and self-sufficient character, when it becomes conscious of itself as only one among *other* cultures and languages" (370; emphasis in original).

It is therefore easy to see the attraction a thinker such as Bakhtin would have for Morrison; the dialogical nature of the word and the "decentering" of language and culture to make room for a "Babel" of discourses competing on a "level playing field" definitively makes the "other" an integral part of society. "Languages do not *exclude* each other, but rather intersect with each other in many different ways" (291). To this we must add, perhaps most importantly, that for Bakhtin there is no "self" without the "other," in that the *self* becomes aware of its individuality *only* through discourse with the other. The "other" becomes not only admissible, s/he is an absolute *necessity* for the construction of our identity. Reading Bakhtinian theory as a backdrop to *Jazz*, then, is illuminating in that it provides a thorough theoretical support for the explication of the text and explains contradictions and paradoxes not readily resolved with other approaches. What is fascinating to observe, however, is just how skillfully Morrison uses *Jazz* to enact Bakhtin's theories of language as applied to the novel.

For almost every critic, the identity of the narrator of *Jazz* has presented a challenge; even given the postmodern intrusiveness, her contradictions and paradoxes tend to confuse more that clarify the story. The "story" of *Jazz*, however, is not the *histoire* but the *discours* itself, the manifold ways in which stories can be related, the "double-voicedness" of the word, so that as the prominent voice in the novel the narrator is not so much an identifiable storyteller as a strategy through which the devices of storytelling are "laid bare." While Bakhtinian theory makes room for multiple meanings and readings, in order to "make sense" of the novel as a whole, it is

---

[109] "The impact of capitalism upon Russian ways of life maximized social and ideological contradictions so that the epoch itself became a creative borderzone between opposing historical consciousnesses" (Morris, 18).

necessary to understand the author's "control and design" (Lodge, 158) in its development. Writes Bakhtin,

> Behind the narrator's story we read a second story, the author's story; he is the one who tells us how the narrator tells stories, and also tells us about the narrator himself. [...] We puzzle out the author's emphases that overlie the subject of the story, while we puzzle out the story itself and the figure of the narrator as he is revealed in the process of telling his tale. If one fails to sense this second level, the intentions and accents of the author himself, then one has failed to understand the work.　　(Bakhtin, *Dialogic*, 314)

As James Guetti (153) points out, the "puzzling out of the story" using the cues and clues provided by the text makes the work of the literary critic similar to that of the private eye of the detective novel, the popular genre which Morrison's has chosen as her "ghost text," on which she hangs the expectations of her readers only to subvert them. On the "macro-level" of the novel's structure, this is itself a supreme form of Bakhtin's concept of "hybridization," the literary reference behind the reading of *Jazz*, a reinvention of the detective genre in which the search for the criminal becomes the search for the self, and the "self" is found in the discourse with the "other."

Apart from the fact that the opening phrase of *Jazz* immediately indicates that the narrator is going to tell us a "secretive" story about a "criminal act," the solution to the paradox of the novel's epigraph from "Thunder Perfect Mind," which Benton Layton understands as a "riddle text," also provides a clue to the focus of the text. Understanding this enigmatic beginning ("I am the name of the sound and the sound of the name. I am the sign of the letter and the designation of the division.") as language, the vehicle for all forms of storytelling, prepares us for the virtuosity of Morrison's art, as strikingly beautiful and intricate as a virtuoso jazz performance.

It is important, however, to remember that jazz, contrary to many critics' appreciation, is *not* the basis for the structure or even the aesthetics of the text, but rather a brilliant metaphor for the focal point of the novel, i.e., popular language, specifically in this case, the black vernacular. The hybridization of western and African music forms and the pervasive insinuation of jazz music first into the popular culture (both black and white) and then progressively into its present status as a high art form, closely parallel Bakhtin's assertion that, contrary to the Russian Formalists' insistence that literature is "violence done to language"(which presupposes that the forms must exist in literature before they can be modified by new creative art), the formation and renovation of "high" literary forms come from the popular expression, and that hybridization and double-voicedness are essential characteristics of the highest artistic expression. The story of jazz becomes a perfect metaphor for the story of *Jazz* with its emphasis on the versatility of black language and its multiple inflections and fascination with word play. Just as jazz music has become the "American" contribution to the world of "classical" music, so the black vernacular has served to enrich the literary expression of the New World to such a degree that a black female writer could be acclaimed the most outstanding author in the contemporary United States with the awarding of the 1993 Nobel Prize for Literature.

Once we recognize the clues that Morrison has set out in her text, the trail she leaves becomes quite clear. In spite of the "distractions" provided by the narrator's voice, and indeed, beginning with the same "distraction," the author experiments with the multiple ways and means of telling stories, either via the narrator's and other characters' voices, via the inflection of words and phrases that call to intertextual references, or via the techniques of hybridization which include other types of discourse within the surface narration. Beginning with the first chapter and with each successive chapter, in addition to extensive use of "free direct and indirect discourse" to incorporate other voices directly into the narrator's story, Morrison both makes references to the means by which stories can be told and introduces new and various ways in which her narrator and characters tell the stories themselves. The delaying of critical information, the extensive use of repetition, the intrusiveness of the narrator, and free association and circularity, all techniques employed by expert storytellers, are all introduced in the first chapter and sprinkled throughout the remaining nine chapters. Immediately thereafter, however, subtle variations are also introduced.

Chapter two of *Jazz* employs hearsay, gossip, letters, telephone conversations and even papers left in the trash as conveyers of stories, while hybridization is apparent in the adopting of the "street cries" or advertising into the narrator's style. The narrator's opening section frames Joe's reveries in interior monologue which themselves frame Dorcas' voice in free indirect speech. Winsome Clark's letter poses the question of polyglossia (coexisting languages) and the incorporation of "social ideologemes" (the ideologies contained in different languages), as well as the illustration of the difference in the chronotopes that can coexist in the novel and between the real and represented world.

The undermining of "monologic discourse" by the dialogic nature of "the sign" is the crux of the third chapter in which the unofficial discourse of the "public market place" continually disrupts the "official" discourse of texts such as the Declaration of Independence or the Holy Bible and including sermons, editorials and other forms of the voice of authority. The semiotics of the drums and of jazz music is a consciously wrought theme, but perhaps the most striking example here is the discourse of public signs which the author explicitly calls attention to. Silence which is imposed by monologic discourse is contrasted by the "abuse" of the teasing women, the lyrics of the "blues," the hybrid incorporation of the radio series, folk sayings, the black sermon, the church litany, and the messages conveyed by newspaper headlines. The incorporation of the "carnivalesque" popular voices all contribute to a breakdown in the hierarchy sustained by a monologic view of the world and to an expression of freedom by the people constrained by that authority.

Stories in chapter four are found in the "teachings" of the old folks, the relay of information about the possibilities of immigrating north, folk sayings, children's songs, imagination, and the appropriation of others' stories to become part of the personal repertoire. There are two innovations in technique: the smooth gliding of the narrator's voice into Violet's in order to create ambiguity, and the inverse projection of Violet's "self" onto her alter ego, which she calls "that Violet" but which popular voices refer to as "Violent." Both of these techniques reinforce the search for the self; Violet's "split personality" will become whole through dialogue, first with her own "other" and then with Alice.

The narrator's own contradictions surface explicitly in chapter five; her control of the narrative begins to waver. Joe's "metamorphosis" at once calls to the "everyday novel of adventure," allows for extensive social commentary, and emphasizes the importance of "process," a key theme in the novel. In addition, the indeterminacy of the recipient of Joe's discourse, which is encased in quotation marks, brings up the question of addressivity. Yet in chapter six, in spite of her admission that describing what goes on in her characters' minds is "risky," she explicitly "lays bare" the fact that she is going to imagine her narration, but once again pretends to be omniscient. The stories that characters have heard from others and which have proved to be highly influential in their lives are specifically highlighted here, but the most demonstrative manifestation of the narrative process is the narrator's telling the story of Golden Gray in two distinct versions in which her own attitudes toward her character change. Questions about the identity of both the narrator and the addressee are again raised.

The story of "Wild" in the seventh chapter is notable on first sight in that she is the only character in this highly "vocal" novel that has no voice. But it is precisely her silence that lends itself to other stories which wield powerful influence: superstitions and rumors. The strategy of intermingling Joe's search for Wild and his search for Dorcas demonstrates the juxtaposition of different chronotopes of which the former plays an important role in the denouement of the latter. The short eighth chapter plays with the actual *fusion* of the chronotopes, experiments with the "voice" of Dorcas in her final moments of life and emphasizes the "now" of the narrative as she lies dying.

Chapter nine marks the beginning of the end of the narrator's pretense of omniscience and control in that she is made to doubt. Moreover, Violet's romanticizing of life in the South demonstrates the idea of "historical inversion," to which all ideals and noble thoughts and harmony are relegated. The most interesting innovation is found in the reproduction of Felice's narration, which contains within it other voices with yet again other mimetic voices; the use of punctuation is unusual and again brings up the question of the addressee, or even more, the "superaddressee" or "superrecipient" of the discourse. This dilemma feeds directly into the major concern of the tenth and last chapter, in which the narrator admits "defeat" and drops any pretense of being a traditional "realistic" narrator and, in the final passage, directs her remarks directly to the reader.

The narrator's dramatic and explicit turn to address the reader directly once again "lays bare" the devices of the text, for as Bakhtin understood, "every literary work *faces outward away from itself*, toward the listener-reader, and to a certain extent thus anticipates possible reactions to itself" (*Dialogic*, 257; emphasis in original). That any utterance is oriented toward the other in expectation of a response that to a certain degree conditions it is part and parcel of Bakhtin's theory of language, specifically his emphasis on "response-ibility." Morrison's subtle change to "response-*ability*" signals the reader's capacity to respond and make ethical decisions based on enriched understanding. The narrator at the end of *Jazz* literally "hands over" the responsibility for language and for telling stories to the reader ("Say make me, remake me. You are free to do it and I am free to let you because look, look. Look where your hands are. Now."), but accepting this responsibility entails making ethical choices in the language that we use and the stories that we tell.

For Michael Holquist the philosophical suggestion of Bakhtin's entire *oeuvre* as a whole is that "our ultimate act of authorship results in the text which we call our self":

> Bakhtin, then, reminds us that literature is important not merely because it gives pleasure
> or leads us to a kind of arcane knowledge we might otherwise lack. No, literature is
> important because it gives the most rigorous on-the-job training for a work we must all
> as men [*sic*] do, the work of answering and authoring the text of our social and physical
> universe. (Holquist, "Answering"; 315 & 318)

The search latent in the second novel of the trilogy turns out to be much more involved, much more difficult and ultimately much more rewarding than in any other Morrison novel. The intricate weaving of the stories through which we understand our lives are shown to be the process (rather than a product) flowing from myriad sources whose influence can scarcely be discerned. The importance of the dialogic nature of language and its consequent shaping of our perception is, in this novel, second only to understanding that the "self" can only be formed and perceived through the "other." The story of *Jazz* is ultimately the story of the relationship of language to the conceptualization of the self. For Morrison as for Bakhtin, "[a]n independent, responsible and active discourse is *the* fundamental indicator of an ethical, legal and political human being" (*Dialogic*, 349-350). The response she expects from her readers speaks to a high standard indeed.

140

BIBLIOGRAPHY

Abrams, M.J. *A Glossary of Literary Terms* (Seventh Edition). Fort Worth, et al.: Harcourt Brace College Publishers, 1999.

Aguiar, Sarah Appleton. "'Everywhere and Nowhere': Beloved's 'Wild' Legacy in Toni Morrison's *Jazz* "in *Notes on Contemporary Literature*, Vol. XXV:4 (September 1995):11-12.

Andrews, William L., Frances Smith Foster, & Trudier Harris, eds. *The Oxford Companion to African American Literature.* New York & Oxford: Oxford UP, 1997.

Alwes, Derek. "The Burden of Liberty: Choice in Toni Morrison's *Jazz* and Toni Cade Bambara's *The Salt Eaters* in *African American Review*, Vol. 30:3 (1996):353-365.

Badt, Karin Luisa. "The Roots of the Body in Toni Morrison: A *Mater* of 'Ancient Properties'" in African American Review, 29:4 (1995): 567-577.

Bakerman, Jane. "The Seams Can't Show: An Interview with Toni Morrison" in *Black American Literature Forum* 12.2 (Summer 1978): 56-60. Reprinted in *Conversations with Toni Morrison*. Danille Taylor-Guthrie, ed. Jackson: UP of Mississippi, 1994. Pp. 30-42

Bakhtin, M.M. "Author and Hero in Aesthetic Activity" in *Art and Answerability*. M. Holquist and V. Liapunov, eds. Austin, Texas: University of Texas Press, 1990.

——. *The Dialogic Imagination*. Michael Holquist, ed. Caryl Emerson & Michael Holquist, trans. Austin & London: University of Texas Press, 1981.

——. *Estetika slovesnogo tvorchestva [The Aesthetics of Verbal Creation]*. Moscow: S.G. Bocharov, 1979. In Todorov.

——. and P.N. Medvedev, *The Fomal Method in Literary Scholarship* (1928). Trans. A.J. Wehrle. Baltimore, Maryland: Johns Hopkins UP, 1978. In Pam Morris. *The Bakhtin Reader: Selected Writings of Bakhtin, Medvedev, Voloshinov*. London, New York, Sydney & Auckland: Edward Arnold, 1994, 1997. Pp. 124-160.

——. "K metodologii gumanitarnyk mauk" [Concerning methodology in the human sciences] in Estetika slovesnogo tvorchestva. Pp 361-373. In Tzvetan Todorov. *Mikhail Bakhtin: The Dialogical Principle*. Wlad Godzich, trans. Minneapolis & London. University of Minnesota Press, 1984.

——. *Problems of Dostoevsky's Poetics* (1963). Trans. C. Emerson. Minneapolis, Minn.: University of Minnesota Press, 1984. In Pam Morris. *The Bakhtin Reader: Selected Writings of Bakhtin, Medvedev, Voloshinov*. London, New York, Sydney & Auckland: Edward Arnold, 1994, 1997. Pp. 89-112.

——. *Rabelais and His World* (1965). Transl H. Iswolsky Bloomington, Ind.: Indiana UP, 1984. In Pam Morris. *The Bakhtin Reader: Selected Writings of Bakhtin, Medvedev, Voloshinov.* London, New York, etc.: Edward Arnold, 1994, 1997. Pp. 195-244.

——. *Speech Genres and Other Late Essays*. Caryl Emerson and Michael Holquist, eds. Vern W. McGee, trans. Austin: University of Texas Press, 1986.

——. Tworchestvo Frasua Rable i narodnaya kul´tura srednevekovýa i Renessa (1965). Moscow, 1990 .

Barnes, Deborah H. "Movin' on up: The Madness of Migration in Toni Morrison's Jazz" in *Toni Morrison's Fiction: Contemporary Criticism*. David L. Middleton, ed. New York and London: Garland Publishing, Inc., 1997. Pp. 283-295.

Baron, Jane B. "Storytelling and Legal Legitimacy" in *College Literature*, Vol. 25:1 (Winter 1998): 63-76.

Beekman, E.M. "Raymond Chandler & An American Genre" in *The Massachusetts Review: A Quarterly of Literature, the Arts and Public Affairs*, vol. 4 (1973):149-73.

Benjamin, Walter. "The Storyteller" in *Illuminations*.Hannah Arendt, ed. Harry Zohn, trans. New York, 1969. Pp. 83-109.

Bennett, W. Lance and Murray Edelman. "Toward a New Political Narrative" in *Journal of Communications* 35:4 (Autumn 1985):154-171.

Belsey, Catherine. *Critical Practice*. New York: Methuen, 1980. Qtd. in Vincent A. O'Keefe. "From 'Other' Sides of the Realist Tracks: (A)Gnostic Narratives in Toni Morrison's *Jazz*" in *The Centennial Review*, Vol 41:2 (Spring 1997):331-349.

Birch, Eva. *Black American Women's Writing: A Quilt of Many Colours*. New York, London, Sidney: Harvester Wheatsheaf,1994.

Bluestein, Gene. *The Voice of the Folk: Folklore and American Literary Theory*. University of Massachusetts Press, 1972.

Bormann, Ernest G. "Symbolic Convergence Theory: A Communication Formulation" in *Journal of Communications* 35:4 (Autumn 1985):128-138.

Briggs, Charles L. and Richard Bauman. "Genre, Intertextuality, and Social Power" in *Journal of Linguistic Anthropology* 2:2 (1992):131-172.

Burton, Angela. "Signifyin(g) Abjection: Narrative Strategies in Toni Morrison's *Jazz*" in *Toni Morrison*. Linden Peach, ed. New York: St. Martin's Press, 1998. Pp. 170-193.

Calvo, Clara. "Telephone Conversation in the Fiction of Raymond Chandler: Opening up Openings and Closings" in *Estudios Ingleses de la Unviersidad Complutense,* 3 (1995): 69-85.

Cannon, Elizabeth M. "Following the Traces of Female Desire in Toni Morrison's *Jazz*" in *African American Review*, Vol. 31:2 (1997):235-247.

Carby, Hazel V. "The Canon: Civil War and Reconstruction"in *Michigan Quarterly Review* 28:1(Winter 1989):35-43.

Carmean , Karen. "Trilogy in Progress: *Beloved* and *Jazz* " in *Toni Morrison's World of Fiction*. Troy, New York: Whitston Publishing Company, 1993.

Carribí, Angeles. "Interview with Toni Morrison" in *Belle Lettres*, 10:2 (1995):42.

Chandler, Raymond. *Farewell, My Lovely* (1940). New York: Vintage Books, 1992.

——. *The High Window*. New York: Ballantine, 1971.

——. *The Lady in the Lake*. New York & London: Garland, 1976.

Chatman, Seymour. *Story and Discourse: Narrative Structure in Fiction and Film*. Ithaca & London: Cornell UP, 1978.

Christian, Barbara. "Community and Nature: The Novels of Toni Morrison" in *The Journal of Ethnic Studies* 7:4 (Winter 1980): 65-78.

Clark, Katerina and Michael Holquist. *Mikhail Bakhtin*. Cambridge, Massachusetts: Harvard UP, 1984. Reviewed in Michael Sprinkler. "Boundless Context: Problems in Bakhtin's Linguistics" in *Poetics Today*, Vol. 7:1 (1986):117-128.

Collier, James Lincoln. "Black Consciousness and the White Jazz Fan" in James Campbell, ed. *The Picador Book of Blues and Jazz*. London, 1995. Pp. 332-336.

Crombie, Winifred. "Raymond Chandler: Burlesque, Parody, Paradox" in *Language and Style*, 16:2 (Spring 1983):151-167.

Culler, Jonathan. *Literary Theory: A Very Short Introduction*. Oxford & New York: Oxford UP, 1997.

Davis, Christina. "An Interview with Toni Morrison" in *Presence Africaine: Revue Culturelle Du Monde /Cultural Review of the Negro World* 1145 (1988): 141-50. Reprinted in *Conversations with Toni Morrison*. Danille Taylor-Guthrie, ed. Jackson: UP of Mississippi, 1994. Pp. 223- 233.

Dreifus, Claudia. "Going Ape" in *Ms.* IX:5 (1999): 48-54.

Dubey, Madhu. "Narration and Migration: *Jazz* and Vernacular Theories of Black Women's Fiction" in *American Literary History*, Vol. 10:2 (Summer 1998):291-316.

Durham, Philip. *Down These Mean Streets a Man Must Go: Raymond Chandler's Knight*. Chapel Hill: University of North Carolina Press, 1963.

Eckard, Paula Gallant. "The Interplay of Music, Language, and Narrative in Toni Morrison's *Jazz*" in *CLA Journal*, Vol. XXXVIII:1 (September 1994):11-19.

Falconer, Rachel. "Bakhtin's Chronotope and the Contemporary Short Story" in *South Atlantic Quarterly*, Vol. 97:3/4 (Summer/Fall, 1998):699-732.

Farrell, Thomas B. "Narrative in Natural Discourse: On Conversation and Rhetoric" in *Journal of Communications* 35:4 (Autumn 1985):109-127.

Fisher, Walter R. "Narration as a Human Communiation Paradigm: The Case of Public Moral Argument" in Communication Monographs 51 (March 1984).

Fisher, Walter R. "The Narrative Paradigm: In the Beginning" in *Journal of Communications* 35:4 (Autumn 1985):74-89.

Forner, Eric. "The Canon and American History" in *Michigan Quarterly Review* 28:1 (Winter 1989): 44-49.

Gates, Henry Louis, Jr. "Preface" in *Toni Morrison: Critical Perspectives Past and Present*. Henry Louis Gates, Jr., and K.A. Appiah, eds. New York: Amistad, 1993. Pp. ix-xiii.

——. "Jazz" in *Toni Morrison: Critical Perspectives Past and Present*. Henry Louis Gates, Jr., and K.A. Appiah, eds. New York, New York: Amistad, 1993. Pp 52-53.

——., and K.A. Appiah, eds. *Toni Morrison: Critical Perspectives Past and Present*. New York, New York: Amistad, 1993.

——. and Nellie Y. McKay, Gen. Eds. *The Norton Anthology of African American Literature*. New York & London: W.W. Norton & Company, 1997.

——. *The Signifying Monkey: A Theory of African-American Literary Criticism*. New York and Oxford: Oxford UP, 1988.

Gregory, Sinda. *Private Investigations: The Novels of Dashiell Hammett*. Carbondale and Edwardsville: Southern Illinois UP, 1985.

Grewal, Gurleen. *Circles of Sorrow, Lines of Struggle: The Novels of Toni Morrison*. Baton Rouge: Louisiana State UP, 1998.

Guetti, James. "Aggressive Reading: Detective Fiction and Realistic Narrative" in *Raritan* 2:1 (Summer, 1982):133-154.

Hagemann, E.R., ed. *A Comprehensive Index to* Black Mask, *1920-1951*. Bowling Green, Ohio: Bowling Green State Popular Press, 1982.

Hardack, Richard. "'A Music Seeking Its Words': Double-Timing and Double-Consciousness in Toni Morrison's *Jazz*"in *Callaloo* 18:2 (1995):451-471.

Harris, Trudier. *Fiction and Folklore: The Novels of Toni Morrison*. Knoxville: The University of Tennessee Press, 1991.

——. "Toni Morrison" in *The Heath Anthology of American Literature*, Vol.2. Paul Latuer, General Editor. Lexington, Massachusetts &Toronto: D.C. Heath and Company, 1994. Pp. 2872-2876.

——. "The Worlds That Toni Morrison Made" in *The Georgia Review* 3 Vol. XLIX:1 (Spring 1995): 324-330.

Haycraft, Howard, ed. *The Art of the Mystery Story*. New York: Simon and Schuster, 1946.

Hedrick, Charles W. and Robert Hodgson, Jr., eds. *Nag Hammadi, Gnosticism and Early Christianity*. Peabody, Massachusetts: Hendrickson Publishers, 1986.

Hedrick, Charles W. "Introduction: Nag Hammadi, Gnosticism, and Early Christianity -- A Beginner's Guide" in *Nag Hammadi, Gnosticism and Early Christianity,* Hedrick, Charles W. and Robert Hodgson, Jr., eds. Peabody, Massachusetts: Hendrickson Publishers, 1986. Pp. 1-11.

Himes, Chester. *If He Hollers Let Him Go* (1945). New York: Thunder's Mouth Press, 1986.

——. *Run Man Run* (1966). New York: Carroll & Graf Publishers, Inc., 1995.

——. *Blind Man with a Pistol* (1969). New York: Vintage Books, 1989.

Hirschkop, Ken. "Bakhtin Myths, or, Why We All Need Alibis" in The *South Atlantic Quarterly*, Vol 97:3/4 (Summer/Fall 1998):579-598.

Hodges, Graham. "Foreward" in Chester Himes. *If He Hollers Let Him Go*. New York: Thunder's Mouth Press, 1945, 1986. Pp. vii-ix.

Holloway, Karla F.C., and Stephanie A. Demetrakopoulos. *New Dimensions of Spirituality: A Biracial and Bicultural Reading of the Novels of Toni Morrison*. Westport, Connecticut & London: Greenwood Press, 1987.

Holquist, Michael. "Answering as Authoring: Mikhail Bakhtin's Trans-Linguistics" in *Critical Inquiry*, Vol. 10 (December 1983):307-319.

——. "Bakhtin and Beautiful Science" in *Dialogue and Critical Discourse*. Michael Macovski, ed. New York & Oxford: Oxford UP, 1997. Pp. 215-236.

——. "Bakhtin and the Formalists: History as Dialogue" in *Russian Formalism: A Retrospective Glance*. Robert Louis Jackson and Stephen Rudy, eds. New Haven: Yale Center for International and Area Studies, 1985. Pp. 82-85.

——. "Bakhtin and Rabelais: Theory as Praxis" in *Boundary 2: A Journal of Postmodern Literature and Culture* (Fall Winter, II 1982-1983):5-19.

——. "The Carnival of Discourse: Baxtin and Simultaneity" in *Canadian Review of Comparative Literature* (June 1985):220-234.

——. "From Body-Talk to Biography: The Chronobiological Bases of Narrative" in *Yale Journal of Criticism*, Vol. 3:1 (1989):1-35.

——. "Inner Speech as Social Rhetoric" in *Dieciocho*, Vol. 10:1 (1987):41-52.

——. "Introduction" in *Studies in 20th Century Literature*, Vol. 9:1 (Fall 1984):7-12.

——. "The Irrepressible I: The Role of Linguistic Subjectivity in Dissidence" in *Yearbook of Comparative and General Literature*, Vol. 31 (1982):30-35.

——. "The Politics of Representation" in *Allegory and Representation*. Stephen J. Greenblatt, ed. Baltimore and London: The Johns Hopkins UP, 1981. Pp. 163-183.

——. "Stereotyping in Autobiography and Historiography: Colonialism in *The Great Gatsby*" in *Poetics Today* Vol. 9:2 (1988):453-472.

House, Elizabeth B. "Toni Morrison's Ghost: The Beloved Who Is Not Beloved," in *Studies in American Fiction* 18 (Spring 1990): 17-26.

Howard, Camille. "Blues for Toni Morrison" in *Express Books* (June 1992):1, 8-9.

Jameson, Fredric. "On Raymond Chandler" in *The Southern Review*, Vol. VI New Series:3 (Summer 1970):24-650.

Janet, Pierre. *Psychological Healing: A Historical and clinical Study* (New York, 1919), vol. 1, pp. 661-2; cited in Ruth Leys's "Traumatic Cures: Shell-shock, Janet and the Question of Memory" in Paul Antze and Michael Lambek, eds., *Tense Past: Cultural Essays in Trauma and Memory* (New York: Routledge, 1992), p. 123-4. Qtd. in Jill Matus. *Toni Morrison. Contemporary World Writers.* Manchester & New York: Manchester UP, 1998.

Johnson, David E. "Voice, the New Historicism, and the Americas" in *Arizona Quarterly* 482 (Summer 1992):81-116.

Jones, Bessie W. and Audrey Vinson. "An Interview with Toni Morrison" in *The World of Toni Morrison: Explorations in Literary Criticism.* Bessie W. Jones and Audrey Vinson, eds. Dubuque, Iowa: Kendall Hunt, 1985. Pp. 127-51. Reprinted in *Conversations with Toni Morrison.* Danille Taylor-Guthrie, ed. Jackson: UP of Mississippi, 1994. Pp. 171-187.

Jones, Carolyn M. "Traces and Cracks: Identity and Narrative in Toni Morrison's *Jazz*" in *African American Review*; Vol. 31:3 (1997):481-495.

Lambek, Michael. "The Past Imperfect: Remembering as Moral Practice" in *Tense Past*. Antzy and Lambek, eds. Qtd. in Gurleen Grewal. *Circles of Sorrow, Lines of Struggle: The Novels of Toni Morrison.* Baton Rouge: Louisiana State UP, 1998.

Lanser, Susan S. "Toward a Feminist Narratology" in *Style*, Vol. 20:3 (Fall 1986): 341-363.

Lawrence, D.H. *Mr Noon.* Cambridge: Lindeth Vasey, 1984.

Layton, Bentley. "The Riddle of The Thunder (NHC VI,2): The Function of Paradox in a Gnostic Text from Nag Hammadi" in *Nag Hammadi, Gnosticism and Early Christianity,* Hedrick, Charles W. and Robert Hodgson, Jr., eds. Peabody, Massachusetts: Hendrickson Publishers, 1986. Pp. 37-54.

LeClair, Thomas. "The Language Must Not Sweat: A Conversation with Toni Morrison" in *New Republic* 184 (21 March 1981): 25-29. Reprinted in *Conversations with Toni Morrison.* Danille Taylor-Guthrie, ed. Jackson: UP of Mississippi, 1994. Pp. 119-128.

Leonard, John. "Jazz (1992)" in *Toni Morrison: Critical Perspectives Past and Present.* Henry Louis Gates, Jr., and K.A. Appiah, eds. New York, New York: Amistad, 1993. Pp. 36-49. Originally published in *The Nation* (May 25, 1992).

Lewis, Barbara Williams. "The Function of Jazz in Toni Morrison´s *Jazz*" in *Toni Morrison´s Fiction: Contemporary Criticism.* David L. Middleton, ed. New York and London: Garland Publishing, Inc., 1997. Pp. 271-281.

Lodge, David. *After Bakhtin: Essays on Fiction and Criticism.* London & New York: Routledge, 1990.

Lucaites, John Louis and Celeste Michelle Condit. "Re-constructing Narrative Theory: A Functional Perspective" in *Journal of Communications* 35:4 (Autumn 1985):90-107.

MacRae, George. "Gnosticism and The Church of John's Gospel" in *Nag Hammadi, Gnosticism and Early Christianity,* Hedrick, Charles W. and Robert Hodgson, Jr., eds. Peabody, Massachusetts: Hendrickson Publishers, 1986. Pp. 89-96.

Major, Clarence. *Juba to Jive: A Dictionary of African-American Slang.* New York: Penguin Books, 1994.

Manzanas, Ana Maria. "What is Jazz in Toni Morrison's Jazz?" in *Revista de Estudios Nortreamericanos*, n° 2 (1993):97-104.

Matus, Jill. *Toni Morrison. Contemporary World Writers.* Manchester & New York: Manchester UP, 1998.

Mawer, Randall R. "Raymond Chandler´s Self-Parody" in *The Armchair Detective* vol. 14:4 (1981):355-58.

Mayberry, Katherine J. "The Problem of Narrative in Toni Morrison´s *Jazz*" in *Toni Morrison´s Fiction: Contemporary Criticism.* David L. Middleton, ed. New York and London: Garland Publishing, Inc., 1997. Pp. 297-309.

McGee, Vern W. "Introduction" in *Speech Genres and Other Late Essays.* Caryl Emerson and Michael Holquist, eds. Vern W. McGee, trans. Austin: University of Texas Press, 1986. Pp. ix-xxiii.

McGee, Michael Calvin and John S. Nelson. "Narrative Reason in Public Argument" in *Journal of Communications* 35:4 (Autumn 1985):139-155.

McKay, Nellie. "An Interview with Toni Morrison" in *Toni Morrison: Critical Perspectives Past and Present.* Henry Louis Gates, Jr., and K.A. Appiah, eds. New York, New York: Amistad, 1993. Pp. 396-411.

Middleton, David L. *Toni Morrison´s Fiction: Contemporary Criticism.* New York and London: Garland Publishing, Inc., 1997.

Morris, Pam. *The Bakhtin Reader: Selected Writings of Bakhtin, Medvedev, Voloshinov.* London, New York, Sydney & Auckland: Edward Arnold, 1994, 1997.

Morrison, Toni. "City Limits, Village Values: Concepts of the Neighborhood in Black Fiction" in *Literature and the Urban Experience: Essays on the City and Literature.* Michael C. Jaye and Ann Chalmers Watts, eds. New Brunswick, New Jersey: Rutgers UP, 1981. Pp. 35-43.

——. *Playing in the Dark: Whiteness and the Literary Imagination.* Cambridge, Massachusetts, & London: Harvard UP, 1992.

——. *Nobel Lecture* (December 7, 1993) in *The Georgia Review* XLIX:1 (Spring 1995): 318-323.

——. "The Art of Fiction CXXXIV." *Paris Review* 128 (1993):83-125.

——. "Rootedness: The Ancestor as Foundation" in Mari Evans, ed. *Black Women Writers.* London & Sidney: Pluto Press, 1983. Pp. 339-345.

——. "The Site of Memory" in *Inventing the Truth: The Art and Craft of Memoir.* William Zinsser, ed. Boston & New York: Houghton Mifflin Company, 1988. Pp. 183-200.

——. "Inteview with A. S. Byatt". Northbrook Roland Films and Video, 1989.

——. "Interview with Salman Rushdie" on BBC2 "The Late Show," (Summer) 1992.

——. *Jazz.* London: Chatto & Windus, 1992.

——. "Unspeakable Things Unspoken: The Afro-American Presence in American Literature" in *Michigan Quarterly Review* 28:1 (Winter, 1989): 1-34.

——, and Claudia Brodsky Lacour, eds. *Birth of a Nation'hood.* New York: Pantheon Books, 1997.

——, ed. *Race-ing Justice, En-Gendering Power.* London: Chatto & Windus, 1993.

Morson, Gary Saul with Caryl Emerson. "Extracts from a *Heteroglossary*" in *Dialogue and Critical Discourse.* Michael Macovski, ed. New York: Oxford UP, 1997. Pp. 256-272.

Munton, Alan. "Misreading Morrison, Mishearing Jazz: A Response to Toni Morrison's Jazz Critics" in *Journal of American Studies*, Vol. 31:2 (1997):235-251.

Nickerson, Edward A. "'Realistic' Crime Fiction: An Anatomy of Evil People" in *The Centennial Review* Vol. XXV:2 (Spring, 1981):101-132.

Nolan, William F. "The Black Mask Boys in the '20s and '30s" in *The Armchair Detective* vol. 27:4 (fall, 1994):408-416.

Nowlin, Michael. "Toni Morrison's *Jazz* and the Racial Dreams of the American Writer" in *American Literature*, Vol. 71:1 (March 1999):151-174.

O'Brien, Edna. "Review of Jazz" in *Toni Morrison: Critical Perspectives Past and Present.* Henry Louis Gates, Jr., and K.A. Appiah, eds. . New York, New York: Amistad, 1993. Pp. 49-55. Originally published in *The New York Times Book Review* (April 5, 1992).

Ogre, Kathy J. *The Jazz Revolution: Twenties America and the Meaning of Jazz.* New York: Oxford UP, 1989.

O'Keefe, Vincent A. "From 'Other' Sides of the Realist Tracks: (A)Gnostic Narratives in Toni Morrison's *Jazz*" in *The Centennial Review*, Vol 41:2 (Spring 1997):331-349.

O'Reilly, Andrea. "In Search of My Mother's Garden, I Found My own: Mother-Love, Healing and Identity in Toni Morrison's *Jazz*" in *African American Review*, Vol. 30:3 (1996):367-379.

Page, Philip. "Traces of Derrida in Toni Morrison's *Jazz*" in *African American Review*, Vol. 29:1 (1995):55-66.

Parini, Jay, ed. *The Columbia Anthology of American Poetry.* New York & Chichester, West Sussex: Columbia UP, 1995.

Peretti, Burton W. *The Creation of Jazz: Music, Race, and Culture in Urban America.* Urbana: Univ. of Illinois Press, 1992.

Peterson, Dale E. "Response and Call: The African American Dialogue With Bakhtin" in American Literature, 65:4 (December 1993):761-775.

Ponder, Anne. "The Big Sleep" in *The Armchair Detective* vo. 17:2 (Spring, 1984):171-174.

Puckett, Newbell Niles. *Folk Beliefs of the Southern Negro*. Chapel Hill: The University of North Carolina Press, 1926.

Reilly, John M. "The Politics of Tough Guy Mysteries" in *University of Dayton Review* vol. 10:1 (1973):25-31.

Rice, Alan. "Jazzing It Up A Storm: The Execution and Meaning of Toni Morrison's Jazzy Prose Style" in *Journal of American Studies*, 28 (1994), 423-32.

Rice, Herbert William. *Toni Morrison and the American Tradition: A Rhetorical Reading*. New York: Peter Lang, 1996.

Richter, David H. "Bakhtin in Life and in Art" in *Style*, Vol 20:3 (Fall 1986):411-419.

Rodell, Marie. *Mystery Fiction*. New York: Duell, Slaon, and Pearce, 1943.

Rodrigues, Eusebio L. "Experiencing Jazz" in *Toni Morrison: Critical and Theoretical Approaches*. Nancy J. Peterson, ed. Baltimore & London: The Johns Hopkins UP, 1997. Pp. 245-266. Also published in *Toni Morrison*. Linden Peach, ed. New York: St. Martin's Press, 1998. Pp. 154-169.

Rose, Carol M. "Property as Storytelling: Perspectives from Game Theory, Narrative Theory, Feminist Theory" in *Yale Journal of Law and the Humanities*, Vol. 2:1 (Winter 1990):37-57.

Ruas, Charles. "Toni Morrison" in Conversations with American Writers. New York: McGraw Hill, 1984. Pp. 215-243. Reprinted in Danille Taylor-Guthrie, ed. *Conversations with Toni Morrison*. Jackson: UP of Mississippi, 1994. Pp. 93-118.

Sabatini, Arthur. "Perfomance Novels: Notes Toward an Extension of Bakhtin's Theories of Genre and the Novel" in Discours social - Social Discourse, Vol. 3:1-2 (1990):135-145.

Sigelman, Lee & William Jocoby. "The Not-So-Simple Art of Imitation: pastiche, Literary Style, and Raymond Chandler" in *Computers and the Humanities*, vol. 30 (1996):11-28.

Silet, Charles L.P. "Past Crimes" in *The Armchair Detective* vol. 29:1 (Winter, 1996):101.

Smith, David. "The Public Eye of Raymond Chandler" in *Journal of American Studies*, vol. 14:3 (1980):423-42.

Spanos, William. *Repetitions: The Postmodern Occasion in Literature and Culture*. Baton Rouge, Louisiana State UP, 1987. Qtd. in Vincent A. O'Keefe. "From 'Other' Sides of the Realist Tracks: (A)Gnostic Narratives in Toni Morrison's *Jazz*" in *The Centennial Review*, Vol 41:2 (Spring 1997):331-349.

Sprinkler, Michael. "Boundless Context: Problems in Bakhtin's Linguistics" in *Poetics Today*, Vol. 7:1 (1986):117-128.

Steele, Timothy. "The Structure of the Detective Story: Classical or Modern?" in *Modern Fiction Studies*, Vol. 27:4 (Winter, 1981-1982):555-570.

Stepto, Robert. "Intimate Things in Place: A Conversation with Toni Morrison" in the *Massachusetts Review* 18 (1977): 473-89. Reprinted in Danille Taylor-Guthrie, ed. *Conversations with Toni Morrison*. Jackson: UP of Mississippi, 1994. Pp. 10-29

Tannen, Deborah. "Involvement as Dialogue: Linguistic Theory and the Relation between Conversation and Literary Discourse" in *Dialogue and Critical Discourse*. Michale Macovski, ed. New York & Oxford: Oxford UP, 1997. Pp. 136-157.

Tally, Justine. "Literary Theory and All that Jazz: Critical Approaches to Toni Morrison's Latest Novel" in *Odense American Studies International Series (OAISIS)*, 18 (October 1995): 1-10.

——. *Paradise Reconsidered: Toni Morrison's (Hi)Stories and Truths*. (FORECAAST, Vol. 3) Hamburg: Lit Verlag, 1999.

——. "'A Specter I Have to Behold and Be Held B'": The Southern Legacy in Toni Morrison's *Jazz*" in *Remembering the Individual/Regional/National Past. (Transatlantic Perspectives Series;* Tuebingen, Germany: Stauffenberg Publishers, 1999). Pp. 215-228.

——. "Reality and Discourse in Toni Morrison's Trilogy: Testing the Limits" in *Literature and Ethnicity in the Cultural Borderlands* (Amsterdam: Rodpoi, 2001).

Tate, Claudia. *Black Women Writers at Work*. New York: Continuum, 1983.

Taylor-Guthrie, Danille, ed. *Conversations with Toni Morrison*. Jackson: UP of Mississippi, 1994.

Thibault, Parl. "Narrative Discourse as a Multi-Level System of Communication: Some Theoretical Proposals concerning Bakhtin's Dialogic Principle" in *Studies in 20th Century Literature*, Vo. 9:1 (Fall 1984):89-117.

The Thunder, Perfect Mind (VI,2). Introduced and translated by George W. MacRae. Edited by Doublas M. Parrot, in *The Nag Hammadi Library in English*. San Francisco: Harper & Row, Publishers, 1977. 270-277.

The Nag Hammadi Library in English. Trans. by members of the Coptic Gnostic Library Project of the Institute for Antiquity and Christianity. James M. Robinson, Director. San Francisco: Harper & Row, Publishers, 1977.

Thomson, Clive. "Bakhtin's 'Theory' of Genre" in *Studies in 20th Century Literature*, Vol. 9:1 (Fall, 1984):29-40.

Thompson, George J. "The Problem of Moral Vision in Dashiell Hammett's Detective Novels" in *The Armchair Detective* Vol. 8:2 (1975):124-130.

Todorov, Tzvetan. *Mikhail Bakhtin: The Dialogical Principle*. Wlad Godzich, trans. Minneapolis & London. University of Minnesota Press, 1984.

Turner, John D. *Sethian Gnosticism: A Literary History*, qtd. in Website 14 (below).

Turner, Patricia A. *I Heard It Through the Grapevine: Rumor in African -American Culture*. Berkeley, Los Angeles & London: University of California Press, 1993.

Voloshinov, V.N. *Freudianism: A Critical Sketch*, 1927. Trans. I.R.Titurin. Indianapolis, Indiana: Indiana U.P., 1987. In Pam Morris. *The Bakhtin Reader: Selected Writings of Bakhtin, Medvedev, Voloshinov*. London, New York, Sydney & Auckland: Edward Arnold, 1994, 1997. Pp. 161-174.

——. *Marxism and the Philosophy of Language* (1929). Trans. L. Matejka and I.R. Titunik Cambridge, Mass.: Harvard UP, 1973. In Pam Morris. *The Bakhtin Reader: Selected Writings of Bakhtin, Medvedev, Voloshinov*. London, New York, Sydney & Auckland: Edward Arnold, 1994, 1997. Pp. 50-73.

Walter, Roland. "The Dialectics Between the Act of Writing and the Act of Reading in Alice Walker's *The Temple of My Familiar*, Gloria Naylor's Mama Day and Toni Morrison's *Jazz*" in *The Southern Quarterly*, Vol. 35:3 (Spring 1997):55-66.

Wellek, René. "Bakhtin's View of Dostoevsky: 'Polyphony' and 'Carnivalisque' in Russian *Formalism: A Retrospective Glance*. Robert Louis Jackson and Stephen Rudy, eds. New Haven: Yale Center for International and Area Studies, 1985. Pp. 231-241.

White, Hayden. "Storytelling: Historical and Ideological" in *Centuries' Ends, Narrative Means*. Robert Newman, ed. Stanford, California: Stanford UP, 1996. Pp. 58-78.

Wilkerson, Margaret B. "The Dramatic Voice in Toni Morrison's Novels" in *Critical Essays on Toni Morrison*. Nellie Y. McKay, ed. Boston, Massachusetts: G.K. Hall & Co., 1988. Pp. 179-190.

Willis, Susan. "Eruptions of Funk: Historicizing Toni Morrison" in *Black American Literature Forum* 16:1 (Spring 1982): 34-42.

WEBLIOGRAPHY

On Gnosticism

1) wysiwyg://69/file:/Cl/01/Nag Hammadi/ApocryphonJohn.html
2) wysiwyg://71/file:/Cl/01/Nag Hammadi/archetypal_man.html
3) wysiwyg://73/file:/Cl/01Nag Hammadi/Cyclic_Historical_and_Dramaturgic.html
4) wysiwyg://75/file:/Cl/91/Nag Hammadi/dualism.html
5) file:///Cl/01/Nag Hammadi/Gnosticism.html
6) file:///Cl/01Nag Hammadi/fall.html
7) file:///Cl/01/Nag Hammadi/Gnosticism_and_Apocalyptic.htm
8) file:///Cl/Nag Hammadi/Gnosticism_as_anti-religion.html
9) file:///Cl/01/Nag Hammadi/Gnosticism_Neoplatonism_and_psychology.html
10) file:///Cl/01/Nag Hammadi/Gnosticism-dramaturgy.html
11) file:///Cl/01/Nag Hammadi/Gnosticism-sources.html
12) file:///Cl/01/Nag Hammadi/intro.html
13) file:///Cl/01/Nag Hammadi/nagham.htm
14) file:///Cl/01/Nag Hammadi/Sethian.html
15) file:///Cl/01/Nag Hammadi/supreme_principle.html
16) file:///Cl/01/Nag Hammadi/Valentianian.html

FORECAAST
(Forum for European Contributions
to African American Studies)

Maria Diedrich; Carl Pedersen;
Justine Tally (eds.)
Mapping African America
History, Narrative Formation, and the Production of Knowledge
The world of African America extends throughout
the northern, central, southern and insular parts
of the American continent. The essays included
in this volume take the creation of that world
as a single object of study, tracing significant
routes and contacts, building comparisons and
contrasts. They thus participate in the reworking
of traditional approaches to the study of history,
the critique of literature and culture, and the
production of knowledge. All are engaged in an
effort to locate the African American experience
within a wider pan-African vision that links the
colonial with the postcolonial, the past with the
present, the African with the Western.
Mapping African America sketches lines that,
far from limiting our geography, extend our
knowledge of the Africanist influence on and their
participation in what is generally called "Western"
culture. This creative challenge to traditional
disciplines will not only enhance the reader's
understanding of African American Studies but
will also help forge links with other academic
fields of inquiry.
Bd. 1, 1999, 256 S., 59,80 DM, pb., ISBN 3-8258-3328-3

Stefanie Sievers
Liberating Narratives
The Authorization of Black Female Voices in
African American Women Writers' Novels of
Slavery
Three contemporary novels of slavery – Margaret
Walker's *Jubilee* (1966), Sherley Anne Williams's
Dessa Rose (1986) and Toni Morrison's *Beloved*
(1987) – are the central focus of *Liberating
Narratives*. In significantly different ways that
reflect their individual and socio-political contexts
of origin, these three novels can all be read as
critiques of historical representation and as
alternative spaces for remembrance – 'sites of
memory' – that attempt to shift the conceptual
ground on which our knowledge of the past is
based.
Within a theoretical framework informed by recent
black feminist and narratological discussions,
the study analyses in particular the textual
strategies that Walker, Williams and Morrison
use to conceptualize and authorize these liberatory
imaginative spaces – spaces in which African

American women become central historical
agents. It shows how revisionary shifts in thematic
emphasis require careful reconsiderations of a
literary text's formal organization to allow for
the representation of a 'free' black and female
subject.
Bd. 2, 1999, 232 S., 49,80 DM, pb., ISBN 3-8258-3919-2

Justine Tally
Toni Morrison's (Hi)stories and Truths
Toni Morison's *Paradise* (1998) arrived on
the scene amid vociferous acclaim and much
consternation. Third in the trilogy begun with
Beloved and *Jazz*, this fascinating yet complicated
the novel has sown as much confusion as
admiration. How does it work? How does the
novel close the trilogy? Indeed, a major complaint
amog reviewers, why does Morrison overload us
with so many characters and stories?
In this first book-length study of *Paradise,* Justin
Tally securely links the work to Morrison's entire
oeuvre and effectively argues that while all of
the novels of the trilogy are deeply analytical of
the relationship of memory, story and history,
the historical narrative: memory is fickle, story is
unreliable, and history is subject to manipulation.
A master narrative of the past is again dictated by
the dominant discourse, but this time the control
exerted is black und male, not white and male.
Though this stranglehold threatens to deaden life
and put the future on hold, Morrison's narrative
disruptions challenge the very nature of this
"paradise" on earth.
With these considerations, *"Paradise"
Reconsidered* locates the author at the center
of the on-going literary and cultural debates of
the late 20th century: the postmodern discussion
of history, particularly Afro-centrist history, the
production of knowledge, the class divisions that
are shattering the black community, and questions
of "race" and essentialism. What does ist mean to
be "black"? And who is the white girl anyway?
*A learned and at the same time accessible early
reading of a highly complex novel. Further
Morrison scholarship will need to return to Tally's
sophisticated and courageous explorations of
this text.* Professor Maria Diedrich, University of
Muenster
Bd. 3, 1999, 112 S., 34,80 DM, pb., ISBN 3-8258-4204-5

Dorothea Fischer-Hornung; Alison
D. Goeller (eds.)
EmBODYing Liberation
The Black Body in American Dance
A collection of essays concerning the black body
in American dance, EmBODYing Liberation
serves as an important contribution to the growing
field of scholarship in African American dance,

LIT Verlag Münster – Hamburg – London
Bestellungen über:
Grevener Str. 179 48159 Münster
Tel.: 0251 – 23 50 91 – Fax: 0251 – 23 19 72
e-Mail: lit@lit-verlag.de – http://www.lit-verlag.de
Preise: unv. PE

in particular the strategies used by individual artists to contest and liberate racialized stagings of the black body. The collection features special essays by Thomas DeFrantz and Brenda Dixon Gottschild, as well as an interview with Isaac Julien.
Bd. 4, Herbst 2001, ca. 152 S., ca. 39,80 DM, pb., ISBN 3-8258-4473-0

Patrick B. Miller; Therese Frey Steffen; Elisabeth Schäfer-Wünsche (eds.)
The Civil Rights Movement Revisited
Critical Perspectives on the Struggle for Racial Equality in the United States
The crusade for civil rights was a defining episode of 20th century U.S. history, reshaping the constitutional, political, social, and economic life of the nation. This collection of original essays by both European and American scholars includes close analyses of literature and film, historical studies of significant themes and events from the turn-of-the century to the movement years, and assessments of the movement's legacies. Ultimately, the articles help examine the ways civil rights activism, often grounded in the political work of women, has shaped American consciousness and culture until the outset of the 21st century.
Bd. 5, Herbst 2001, ca. 224 S., ca. 48,80 DM, pb., ISBN 3-8258-4486-2

Fritz Gysin; Christopher Mulvey (Hrsg.)
Black Liberation in the Americas
Black Liberation in the Americas: The recognition that Africans in the Americas have also been subjects of their destiny rather than merely passive objects of European oppression represents one of the major shifts in twentieth-century mainstream historiography. Yet even in the eighteenth and nineteenth centuries, slave narratives and abolitionist tracts offered testimony to various ways in which Africans struggled against slavery, from outright revolt to day-to-day resistance. In the first decades of the twentieth century, African American historians like Carter G. Woodson and W. E. B. Du Bois started to articulate a vision of African American history that emphasized survival and resistance rather than victimization and oppression. This volume seeks to address these and other issues in black liberation from interdisciplinary and comparative perspectives, focusing on such issues as slave revolts, day-to-day resistance, abolitionist movements, maroon societies, the historiography of resistance, the literature of resistance, black liberation movements in the twentieth century, and black liberation and post colonial theory. The chapters span the disciplines of history, literature, anthropology, folklore, film, music, architecture, and art, drawing on the black experience of liberation in the United States, the Caribbean, and Latin America.
Bd. 6, Herbst 2001, ca. 208 S., ca. 48,80 DM, br., ISBN 3-8258-5137-0

Anglophone Literaturen
Anglophone Literatures
Hamburger Beiträge zur Erforschung neuerer englischsprachiger Literaturen
Hamburg Studies in the New Literatures in English
Herausgeber/General Editor: Gerd Dose

Gerd Dose; Bettina Keil (Eds.)
Writing in Australia
Perceptions of Australian Literature in Its Historical and Cultural Context
A Series of Lectures Given at Hamburg University on the Occasion of the 1st Festival of Australian Literature in Hamburg 1995
This volume is concerned with the fascinating process of deconstructing self-sufficient "Anglo-Australian" national identity, and sheds light on the intense and sustained efforts of Australian writers to contribute to the country's self-definition as a post-colonial and multi-cultural society against the traditional predominance of a "White" British culture that aims at cultural homogeneity. Another focus of the book is on the unique experience of Australian landscape and nature, which has been a major subject of Australian writing since the 19th century and as a theme has never lost its topicality and irresistible appeal. WRITING IN AUSTRALIA is a must for everyone who wants to embark on the study of this new terrain of literary study which is growing in importance so rapidly.
Bd. 1, 2000, 232 S., 38,80 DM, br., ISBN 3-8258-2796-8

Susanne Braun-Bau
Natur und Psyche
Landschafts- und Bewußtseinsdarstellung in australischen Romanen des 20. Jahrhunderts
Die Untersuchung australischer Romane lädt zu einer Reise durch literarische Landschaften ein. Sie beginnt zur Jahrhundertwende mit Joseph Furphy als frühem Vertreter des modernen Romans und zeigt eine Entwicklung auf, die schließlich in der Auflösung realer Landschaften in eine *Psychogeographie* bei Gerald Murnane gipfelt. Mentale Prozesse sind Filterinstanzen, die zwischen die Landschaft und ihre literarische Umsetzung treten. Die literarische Umsetzung dieser 'Filter' wird analysiert, um ein umfassendes

LIT Verlag Münster – Hamburg – London
Bestellungen über:
Grevener Str. 179 48159 Münster
Tel.: 0251 – 23 50 91 – Fax: 0251 – 23 19 72
e-Mail: lit@lit-verlag.de – http://www.lit-verlag.de
Preise: unv. PE

Erklärungsmodell für die kominierende Busch-bildlichkeit in der Literatur Australiens, die bis heute fortwirkt, zu entwerfen. Das Stereotyp des menschenfeindlichen *Outback* erweist sich als Frustration der perzipierenden Figur, die eine an britische Konventionen geprägte Bewußtseins-haltung auf die Natur projiziert. Diese mentale Haltung ist den Naturgegebenheiten Australiens unangemessen.

Dabei ermöglicht die breite Auswahl von Roma-nen die Ableitung einer historische Stufenfolge, bei der sich im Verhältnis von Protagonist und Landschaft eine zunehmende Bewußtseinsdomi-nanz herauskristalliert. Die Untersuchung liefert daher einen wichtigen Beitrag zur australischen Literaturgeschichte und stellt ein Stufenmodell als Analyserahmen für die (post-)moderne Romanent-wicklung vor.
Bd. 2, 1996, 264 S., 58,80 DM, br., ISBN 3-8258-2824-7

Horst Prießnitz; Marion Spies (Hrsg.)
Neuere Informationsmittel zur Literatur Australiens
Ein bibliographischer Essay
Der bibliographische Essay richtet sich an litera-turwissenschaftliche Intersssenten auf der Suche nach Basisinformationen zur Literatur- und Kul-turgeschichte des 5. Kontinents. Gleichzeitig ist er als Hilfe beim Aufbau einer Spezialabteilung mit forschungsrelevanten Informationsmitteln in Bibliotheken konzipiert.
Bd. 3, 1996, 72 S., 19,80 DM, br., ISBN 3-8258-3169-8

Hallenser Studien zur Anglistik und Amerikanistik
herausgegeben am Institut für Anglistik und Amerikanistik (Martin-Luther-Universität Halle-Wittenberg)

Martin Meyer; Gabriele Spengemann; Wolf Kindermann (Hrsg.)
Tangenten: Literatur & Geschichte
Die Hallenser Studien zur Anglistik und Ameri-kanistik wollen an die Tradition des Dialogs unter den inzwischen vielfältig verzweigten Teilgebieten eines einstmals einheitlichen Faches anknüpfen, wie sie durch den Hallenser Anglisten Hans Wey-he und seine Kollegen gepflegt wurde.
Der vorliegende erste Band der Reihe ist dem Weyhe-Schüler Martin Schulze gewidmet, dessen Werdegang und Tätigkeit als Hochschullehrer die vielschichtigen Entwicklungen des Faches im Schatten des Ost-West-Konfliktes spiegelt, und dessen Initiative die Hallenser Anglistik die Chan-ce eines Neubeginns verdankt.
Die hier versammelten Beiträge zur englischen

und amerikanischen Literatur, zu Geschichte, Sprachwissenschaft und Bildungspolitik eint trotz aller Vielfalt der Blick auf die Wechselbeziehun-gen zwischen europäischer und amerikanischer Kulturtradition sowie das Bemühen um den Dialog zwischen den philologischen und den historisch-sozialwissenschaftlichen Disziplinen.
Bd. 1, 1996, 278 S., 48,80 DM, br., ISBN 3-8258-2907-3

Wolf Kindermann (Hrsg.)
Entwicklungslinien: 120 Jahre Anglistik in Halle
Das Institut für Anglistik und Amerikanistik an der Martin-Luther-Universität in Halle und Wit-tenberg feierte im Jahr 1996 sein 120jähriges Bestehen. Als erstes rein englisches Seminar in deutschen Landen kann es auf eine lange Tradi-tion der anglistischen Forschung und Lehre, vor allem auf dem Gebiet von Sprachwissenschaft und Sprachgeschichte, zurückblicken. Namhaf-te Fachgelehrte, unter ihnen Friedrich E. Elze, Max Förster, Max Deutschbein, Hans Weyhe und Otto Ritter, haben die Geschichte der Hallenser Anglistik mit geprägt. Heute steht das Institut vor einem Neubeginn, der sich aber auch den Entwicklungslinien der Hallenser Anglistik ver-pflichtet fühlen muß.
Der vorliegende Band soll durch Forschungs-ergebnisse und Arbeitsproben von Mitarbeitern und Gästen des Instituts die thematische Viel-falt des Neubeginns dokumentieren. Er umfaßt neben einem kurzen Überblick zur Institutsge-schichte Beiträge zur Realismusproblematik in der englischen Literatur des 18. Jahrhunderts, zu H.G. Wells, zur anglo-irischen (Yeats, Joyce, Hea-ney und Friel) und zur amerikanischen Literatur (Poe, Hemingway und Heller, Zora Neale Hurston und Alice Walker). Ferner finden sich sprach-wissenschaftliche Beiträge zu den "Anglo-Saxon Wills", zum Verhältnis von Sprache und Ideologie bei Burke und Paine, zu "Intertextuality in Press Correspondence", zum "Pendel des sprachlichen Handelns" sowie ein Beitrag zum Stellenwert von Einstellungen im Fremdsprachenunterricht.
Bd. 2, 1997, 240 S., 49,80 DM, br., ISBN 3-8258-3304-6

Pamela Winchester
Indian Myth and White History
Bd. 3, 1997, 240 S., 48,80 DM, br., ISBN 3-8258-3446-8

Gisela Hermann-Brennecke; Wilhelm Geisler (Hrsg.)
Zur Theorie der Praxis & Praxis der Theorie des Fremdsprachenerwerbs
Der Band thematisiert die reziproke Einheit em-pirisch orientierter Theorie und theoriegeleiteter Praxis fremdsprachendidaktischer Fragestellungen. Während sich Theorie als Ergebnis und Prozeß

LIT Verlag Münster – Hamburg – London
Bestellungen über:
Grevener Str. 179 48159 Münster
Tel.: 0251 – 23 50 91 – Fax: 0251 – 23 19 72
e-Mail: lit@lit-verlag.de – http://www.lit-verlag.de
Preise: unv. PE

der Fremdsprachenforschung im Wechselspiel mit und an der fremdsprachlichen Unterrichtspraxis als ihrem Gegenstand ausrichtet, liefert die Praxis die Basis, von der Forschung überhaupt erst ihre Impulse empfängt. Beides geschieht immer unter der Prämisse, die eigenen Voraussetzungen, Bedingungen und Grenzen unter Einbeziehung des Verhältnisses zu anderen Bezugswissenschaften kritisch zu hinterfragen.

Die hier vorgelegten Beiträge behandeln verschiedene Aspekte des Theorie-Praxis-Bezugs, eine Thematik, die die Forschung und Lehre von Wolfgang Butzkamm, dem zu Ehren dieser Sammelband erscheint, wie ein roter Faden durchzieht. So stehen neben wissenschaftstheoretischen, paralinguistischen, quantenphysikalischen, empirischen und mentalistischen Reflexionen auch solche zum Umgang mit Literatur, Bilingualismus, Mehrsprachigkeit, gesprochener Sprache und ihrer Kontextualisierung aus suggestopädischer Sicht. Gleichwertig und reziprok.

Bd. 4, 1998, 224 S., 49,80 DM, br., ISBN 3-8258-3840-4

Gisela Hermann-Brennecke (Hrsg.)
Frühes schulisches Fremdsprachenlernen zwischen Empirie & Theorie
Die hier versammelten Beiträge behandeln Zugriffe auf frühes schulisches Fremdsprachenlernen in verschiedenen europäischen Ländern, in der russischen Föderation sowie in den USA und berichten von den dabei gesammelten Erfahrungen. Sie wollen zu weiteren Forschungsaktivitäten anregen und dadurch zu bildungspolitischen Entscheidungsprozessen beitragen.

The present collection of articles deals with various approaches to foreign language learning at primary school in different European countries, in the Russian Federation and in the USA. The results presented want to stimulate further research activities and to contribute to processes of educational decision making.

Bd. 5, 1999, 216 S., 49,80 DM, br., ISBN 3-8258-4351-3

Martina Ghosh-Schellhorn (ed.)
Writing Women Across Borders and Categories
Generally held to be rigid, borders and categories are nonetheless expanded when those bounded by the demarcations of hegemony, challenge its strictures. Significant instances of this constructive transgression can be found in the women's writing with which this collection of essays by international critics engages. Whereas in travel writing by women (Sarah Hobson, Dervla Murphy, Jan Morris) 'transgression' is seen to have settled into a familiar strategy, in autobiography (Ann Fanshawe. Margaret Cavendish, Christine Brooke-Rose), cultural

analysis (Virginia Woolf, Marianna Torgovnick, Donna Haraway), and fiction (Michelle Cliff, Jeanette Winterson, Ellen Galford, Fiona Cooper), women have succeeded in creating an innovative space for themselves.

Bd. 6, 2000, 176 S., 39,80 DM, pb., ISBN 3-8258-4639-3

Claudia Franken
Gertrude Stein, Writer and Thinker
Gertrude Stein, Writer and Thinker, "presents the first sensible overview which includes a demonstration of the 'content' which may be found in each of Stein's presumably 'abstract' key works" (Robert Bartlett Haas, Foreword).
This study offers a guided commentary on the *about* and the "literariness" of her works which helps the reader to understand and appreciate her writing and thinking. Exploring Stein's figures of thought within the context of the philosophies of William James and A. N. Whitehead and considering the aesthetic and ethical significance of texts of all phases and genres of her writing, this commentary convinces us that Stein was indeed one of the 20th century's most original and complex authors.

Bd. 7, 2000, 400 S., 49,80 DM, pb., ISBN 3-8258-4761-6

Angela Kuhk
Vielstimmige Welt
Die Werke St. John de Crèvecœurs in deutscher Sprache
"Das Werk hat unter den Händen des Teutschen Übersetzers noch gewonnen." Die europaweite Begeisterung für die Werke Crèvecœurs äußerte sich auch in einer Flut an deutschen Übersetzungen: Zwischen 1782 und 1802 entstanden mehr als 30 Schriften, die auf die Zeilen des berühmten "Amerikanischen Landmanns" zurückgingen. Erstmals erfolgt hier eine bibliographische Erfassung und eine chronologische Vorstellung dieser Texte wie auch der Rezeptionsdokumente.

Ausführliche Übersetzungsanalysen zu den Themen Indianer, Quäker, Sklaverei, deutsche Einwanderer, Walfang, Flora und Fauna liefern neue Beiträge zum deutschen Amerikabild im ausgehenden 18. Jahrhundert und erlauben einen detaillierten Einblick in die vielstimmige Welt Crèvecœurs.

Bd. 8, Herbst 2001, 480 S., 49,80 DM, br., ISBN 3-8258-4882-5

LIT Verlag Münster – Hamburg – London
Bestellungen über:
Grevener Str. 179 48159 Münster
Tel.: 0251 – 23 50 91 – Fax: 0251 – 23 19 72
e-Mail: lit@lit-verlag.de – http://www.lit-verlag.de
Preise: unv. PE

Erlanger Studien zur Anglistik und Amerikanistik

herausgegeben von
Rudolf Freiburg und Dieter Meindl

Rudolf Freiburg; Jan Schnitker (Hrsg.)
"Do you consider yourself a postmodern author?"
Interviews with Contemporary English Writers

This book presents a collection of twelve interviews with eminent English contemporary writers held during a period of four years. The book allows an illuminating insight into a very lively and thought-provoking literary culture, stirred not only by recent ideas of postmodernism but also by the manifold issues of nationality, culture, and gender subjected to permanent redefinitions towards the end of the twentieth century. The interviews with Peter Ackroyd, John Banville, Julian Barnes, Alain de Botton, Maureen Duffy, Tibor Fischer, John Fowles, Romesh Gunesekera, Tim Parks, Terry Pratchett, Jane Rogers, and Adam Thorpe cover topics such as the relationship between writer and public, the role of the literary tradition, the relevance of contemporary literary theory for the production of literature, images of nationality, intertextuality, changes in the attitude towards language and meaning, and the reception of literary texts by critical reviewers and literary critics.
All the interviewers have worked for the *ECCEL* (*Erlangen Centre for Contemporary English Literature*).

Bd. 1, 1999, 248 S., 39,80 DM, br., ISBN 3-8258-4395-5

Hannah Jacobmeyer
Märchen und Romanzen in der zeitgenössischen englischen Literatur
Im Zentrum einer vielfach konstatierten Renaissance des "Wunderbaren" in der Kultur des ausgehenden 20. Jahrhunderts stehen die Formen und Strukturen von Märchen und Romanze. Gelten sie uns einerseits als Merkmale einer prämodernen Narrativik, so sind sie andererseits zu Konstanten von Literatur geworden, die sich durch die Jahrhunderte bis in die sogenannte postmoderne Literatur hinein nachweisen lassen. Anhand ausgewählter zeitgenössischer Texte der englischen Literatur zeigt die Autorin, wie Märchen und Romanzen fortleben - aber auch, wo sie sich überschneiden und auf welche Weise sie in eine endlose, intertextuelle "Echokammer" eingebunden werden. Romanzenmuster erlauben zudem, Einsicht in die Gemeinsamkeiten hoher und "trivialer" Literatur zu nehmen. Autoren der detailliert analysierten Märchen und Romanzen

sind u. a. Salman Rushdie, A. S. Byatt, Graham Swift, Angela Carter und Barbara Cartland.
Bd. 2, 2000, 224 S., 68,80 DM, br., ISBN 3-8258-4686-5

Populäre Musik und Jazz in der Forschung
Interdisziplinäre Studien

herausgegeben von Rainer Dollase (Universität Bielefeld), Hans-Jürgen Feurich (Universität Cottbus), Thomas Münch (Universität Oldenburg), Albrecht Schneider (Universität Hamburg), Ilse Storb (Universität Duisburg) und Peter Wicke (Humboldt Universität Berlin)

Fritz Schmücker
Das Jazzkonzertpublikum
Das Profil einer kulturellen Minderheit im Zeitvergleich
Bd. 1, 1993, 264 S., 34,80 DM, br., ISBN 3-89473-565-1

Johannes Feldmann Bürgers
Tango und Jazz
Kulturelle Wechselbeziehungen?
Tango - das ist mehr als nur der in Europa bekannte Gesellschaftstanz. Tango ist eine Musik, die vor etwas mehr als einem Jahrhundert, zeitgleich mit dem Jazz in den USA, in Argentinien entstanden ist. Interessanterweise findet man gewisse Parallelen in der Entstehungsgeschichte beider Musikformen, und gerade in seiner Anfangsphase wurde der Jazz vom Tango und seinen Vorläufern wie der Habanera beeinflußt.
Diese Parallelen und "Berührungspunkte" untersucht der Autor in diesem Buch; darüber hinaus beschäftigt er sich intensiv mit zwei Vertretern des "Tango Nuevo', nämlich *Astor Piazzolla* und *Juan José Mosalini*. Neben Notenbeispielen und musikalischen Analysen dürfte für die Tangointeressierten wohl das ausführliche Interview von Interesse sein, welches der Autor mit dem Bandoneonisten *Mosalini*, dem Pianisten *Beytelmann* und dem korsischen Bassisten *Caratini* geführt hat.
Bd. 2, 1996, 148 S., 29,80 DM, br., ISBN 3-8258-2416-0

Jens Fliege
Von der Aufklärung zur Subversion
Sprechweisen deutschsprachiger Popmusik
Aufklärung und Subversion - mit diesen zwei Ausdrücken versucht der Autor dieses Buches die Entwicklung deutschsprachiger Popmusik von den späten 60er Jahren bis in die frühen 80er Jahre zu charakterisieren. Warum der Pop-Song hierzulande erst nach der "New Wave" über die Ausdrucksmöglichkeiten verfügte, die in der anglo-amerikanischen Popmusik schon seit den späten 60er Jahren vorhanden waren und warum sich aus der "Agitationswut" der frühen 70er Jahre

LIT Verlag Münster – Hamburg – London
Bestellungen über:
Grevener Str. 179 48159 Münster
Tel.: 0251 – 23 50 91 – Fax: 0251 – 23 19 72
e-Mail: lit@lit-verlag.de – http://www.lit-verlag.de
Preise: unv. PE

nur Ton Steine Scherben in das nächste Jahrzehnt retten konnten – davon handelt diese 1997 in Oldenburg verfaßte Magisterarbeit.

Bd. 3, 1997, 120 S., 24,80 DM, br., ISBN 3-8258-3388-7

Ilse Storb

Jazz meets the world – the world meets Jazz

Jazz ist vital, kreativ und demokratisch, offen für Musiksprachen aller Zeiten und Räume. Jazz wird die erste wirkliche Weltmusik sein. Die Musiker der Zukunft werden global und total sein. – "Jazz meets the world" ist ein Kompendium zum Jazz, mit ethno-soziologischen Aufsätzen zu "Schwarzafrika", zum "Rassismus" und zum "Eurozentrismus," mit Einsichten zur Stellung der Frau im Jazz und mit historischen Abschnitten zur Entwicklung des Jazz und zum ökonomischen Spannungsverhältnis von Markt und Musik. – Die Hinweise auf Musikbeispiele innerhalb der Texte sind zur praktischen Hörerfahrung gedacht.

Bd. 4, 2000, 240 S., 39,80 DM, br., ISBN 3-8258-3748-3

Horst Herold

Symphonic Jazz – Blues – Rock

Zum Problem der Synthese von Kunst- und Unterhaltungsmusik in symphonischen Werken des 20. Jahrhunderts

Die gegenseitige Beeinflußung verschiedenster musikalischer Stile und Stilrichtungen ist kein spezifisches Phänomen des 20. Jahrhunderts. Sie reicht nachweislich bis ins Hochmittelalter zurück und stellt damit die zeitgenössischen Stile unseres Jahrhunderts in eine bewußte Tradition.

Anhand der drei großen Musikbereiche Jazz, Blues und Rock wird eine Präzisierung solcher Synthesen an ausgewählten und prägnanten Beispielen bis in die jüngste Gegenwart hinein versucht. Der Jazz war der erste Stil aus dem Bereich der später sogenannten Unterhaltungsmusik, dessen Musiker nach neuen Möglichkeiten suchten, ihre Kompositionen ebenfalls gesellschaftlich aufzuwerten. Ihm ist es bereits gelungen, als Kunst- und Kultmusik anerkannt zu werden. In Bezug auf den Blues und die Rockmusik wurde dieser Schritt noch nicht oder nur zu einem geringen Teil vollzogen.

Im Mittelpunkt der Untersuchungen zum Symphonic Rock stehen die Werke des britischen Rockmusikers Jon Lord, der parallel zu seinen Aktivitäten im Metier der reinen Rockmusik immer wieder nach neuen klanglichen Facetten suchte und dabei zwangsläufig auf die Symphonische Musik stieß.

Bd. 5, 1999, 320 S., 59,80 DM, br., ISBN 3-8258-4296-7

Susanne Schedtler

"Das Eigene in der Fremde"

Einwanderer-Musikkulturen in Hamburg

Was bedeutet "kulturelle Identität", musikalisch gesprochen? Wie verändern sich die Musik und das musikalische Selbstverständnis von Migranten in der Fremde? Ist das Exil "die Brutstätte für schöpferische Taten" (Vilém Flusser), oder bedeutet es einen unaufhaltsamen Verfall der "importierten" Musikkultur? Und, nicht zu vergessen: Welche Faktoren bestimmen (und belasten) die Zusammenarbeit von eingewanderten und einheimischen Musikern? Welches Licht wirft der Kontakt mit Vertretern weitgehend "intakter" traditioneller Musikkulturen auf das Verhältnis deutscher Musiker zu ihrer eigenen Tradition? Die Befragung von 32 Musikerinnen und Musikern, die Susanne Schedtler in Hamburg unter dem Blickwinkel einer "urban ethnomusicology" durchführte, liefern erhellende Aufschlüsse über solche Kernfragen soziomusikalischer Dynamik in den multikulturellen Metropolen der Gegenwart. Ausführliche Portraits von vier Musikern aus Kolumbien, Brasilien, dem Iran und der Türkei (samt Beispiel-CD) vertiefen und konkretisieren die Ergebnisse.

Bd. 6, 1999, 240 S., 39,80 DM, br., ISBN 3-8258-4256-8

Ilse Storb

Dave Brubeck – Improvisationen und Kompositionen

Die Idee der kulturellen Wechselbeziehungen

Der Pianist und Komponist Dave Brubeck vertritt die Idee des "cultural exchange" als Grundlage für musikalische Völkerverständigung. Er verbindet mit dem akkulturierten Musik Jazz europäische Konzertmusik und sogenannte außereuropäische Musik. Sein besonderes Anliegen gilt auch der Integration von Improvisation und Komposition. In Brubecks Klangharmonik nehmen Blockakkorde, im metrisch-rhythmischen Bereich die "Time Experiments" mit asymmetrischen Rhythmen, einen großen innovativen Raum ein. Vielfach wird Dave Brubeck mit dem Standard "Take Five" identifiziert: "Essentially I'm a composer, who plays the piano." Das vorliegende Buch über Dave Brubeck gibt einen detaillierten Überblick über seine Improvisationen und Kompositionen.

Bd. 7, 2. Aufl. 2000, 174 S., 29,80 DM, br., ISBN 3-8258 4763-2

LIT Verlag Münster – Hamburg – London

Bestellungen über:
Grevener Str. 179 48159 Münster
Tel.: 0251 – 23 50 91 – Fax: 0251 – 23 19 72
e-Mail: lit@lit-verlag.de – http://www.lit-verlag.de

Preise: unv. PE